Puzzles
of the Past

Puzzles
of the Past

AN INTRODUCTION
TO THINKING ABOUT HISTORY

Michael T. Isenberg

TEXAS A & M UNIVERSITY PRESS
 COLLEGE STATION

Library of Congress Cataloging in Publication Data

Isenberg, Michael T.
    Puzzles of the past.

    Includes index.
    1. Historiography.   I. Title.
D13.I745   1984   907'.2   84-40131
ISBN 0-89096-208-1
ISBN 0-89096-216-2 (pbk.)

Manufactured in the United States of America
FIRST EDITION

For the finest relatives anyone could ever enjoy:
    Carl Krimbill
    Glen Meihak
    Margaret Sturtevant Meihak
    Wanda and Fred Morgen

And, in loving memory, for:
    Helen Krimbill
    Margaret Vander Vorste Meihak
    Ronald Meihak

"To think is to differ"

 —Clarence Darrow, for the defense, in the case of *Tennessee* v. *John Thomas Scopes*, Dayton, Tennessee (1925)

Contents

Introduction

This little book had its genesis in the classroom. It is the product of the frustration of a generation of college and university students with their assigned history reading and with my teaching, compounded by my own frustration in trying to transmit what are, for me, the very real pleasures of examining and reflecting upon the past.

If I have heard the phrases once, I have heard them hundreds of times: "What do you want us to know?" "Are you going to emphasize names and dates on the exam?" "How should we study for this test?" And the old standbys: "There's too much reading!" and "I can't get anything out of this textbook!" In the age of "M.A.S.H." and *Penthouse*, teaching history is no cinch.

As a persevering but not overly skilled golfer, I fully endorse the old saw that the sport the Scots call "the humblin' game" is at least 90 percent mental; even more so is the study and perception of the past. But mental work can be tough, and other attractions compete for our attention. Most of us begin to erect our defenses against history as early as grade school and junior high. By the time we matriculate, or are off on our own making a living, we have become stolidly resistant to "more of the same." History at these elementary levels is usually taught as revealed wisdom. The subject comes glossily packaged in outrageously priced textbooks and is often visited upon us in most punishing fashion (one of my high school teachers tortured his reluctant pupils by having us outline chapters of the text as a daily assignment).

The basic reason for this common mode of cultural transmission is that, as young people, we simply lack wide experience in living. Our memory banks are expanding, right enough, but we often do not bother to connect our unique lives with what has generally gone before. History is, for a goodly share of our population, undeservedly dysfunctional. And this is too bad, for if we are anything, as individuals and in groups, we are a rich and infinitely complex compound of our history.

But history is "hard," you say, when it is not simply tedious. This protest has the ring of truth to it, and for two reasons. First, there is so much of the past, even of that portion we know something about; who can swallow all or even a significant part of this indigestible lump? The answer is a somewhat cheeky "no one"— so do not worry about it. Second, there seems to be no single or unique history, except perhaps in textbooks, and when one masters the subject there, between those elegant covers, along comes experience to upset the applecart. Most frustrating. As a result, only a relative few of us ever, in our adult lives, read and reflect upon history for pure pleasure.

Certainly no claim is made here for history as some kind of marvelous panacea, or even as a constant guide to useful knowledge. Some of the most dreadful acts ever visited by human beings upon each other have been committed "in the name of history." But, in addition to having the capacity to soothe, entrance, and inform (as well as infuriate), the study of history has a further bonus: it may keep the mind alive—thinking, pondering, questioning—and this is no small reward.

Because of our need for experience before we can ask sound historical questions, many of us begin to think about history relatively late, compared, say, to thinking about biology or mathematics in their purer forms. We become impatient with the never-ending avalanche of more and more facts, names, and dates tumbling down upon us. As a result, almost everyone parts company with the subject as soon as history courses become elective or that final diploma is awarded. The last time I looked, our biggest professional historical group, the American Historical Association (which is open to all comers), had a membership equivalent to about .05 percent of our population. In our classrooms we are trained to assimilate before we think, and since there is so much assimilating to do, that much and no more is generally what we do. Naturally, we are eager to drop this particular anvil as quickly as we can.

Therefore, I have designed this material to be open-ended. Many of the questions asked herein, as well as some of the topics discussed, are considered ancient news by many professionals, and many others as well will long ago have made up their minds concerning some of the subject matter. Yet individual thought and discovery remain ever fresh—never mind that some German guy said the same thing two centuries ago, or that the Romans knew all about it. These questions, and many others concerning history that could as justly have been asked, are perhaps forever moot. They constitute "puzzles," or points to ponder, if you will. There are no right answers, and no wrong ones, either. Thinking about history, therefore, partakes of the indeterminate; let us dare to greet the subject and call it fun.

I am grateful for the patience of my family, particularly that of Spuddy and Seri, as I labored away on the manuscript. My thanks to the many students, graduate and undergraduate, who have unwittingly aided me in sharpening my focus on historical study through their questions and responses to my questions, both formal and informal. The manuscript has passed through many hands and received a wide range of commentary, as might be expected. I am particularly grateful to the following friends and colleagues for sharing their wisdom with me: Richard Abels, Albin Anderson, Ted Bogacz, Thomas Brennan, Parks Coble, William Cogar, Nancy Ellenberger, Brison Gooch, Edward Homze, James Jankowski, Hans Kellner, Daniel Masterson, Charles Middleton, Anne Quartararo, Benjamin Rader, Craig Symonds, Larry Thompson, John Turner, and Roger Zeimet.

Many more professionals have contributed piecemeal by sharing with me the skills of their craft over the years. My apologies to all for the havoc undoubtedly wrought herein with some fairly complex ideas and trends of thought. It goes almost without saying that every reader has differing notions not only as to how this material should be presented but also as to its general worth. With these differences, I am well pleased.

I. Order

CHAPTER ONE

Some Mundane Considerations

A Nondefinition

We shall cheerfully avoid our first problem, which is one of definition. "History" is a concept capable of infinite variety, made so by the endless twists of vocabulary used in its description. Language may insulate and obscure as well as inform. Consider the following: "historical positivism," "determinism," "skeptical relativism," "antiformalism," and "technocratic rationalism." This barrage of *isms* is one way to mount an attack on history,[1] although one's own troops may surrender from sheer exhaustion before the fort is conquered. What might be effective communication to the initiated is usually a rough rite of passage for the novice.

The concept is fogged not only by our words but by the way we think about it. The metaphor of the mirror has been used to describe the thing. If we are only honest enough, some say, history will show us ourselves, warts and all. A broader approach asserts that history is very simply the memory of things said and done.[2]

---

[1] The examples are drawn from Cushing Strout, *The Pragmatic Revolt in American History: Carl Becker and Charles Beard* (Ithaca, N.Y.: Cornell University Press, 1966 [1958]), pp. 8–9, where the author helpfully gives concise definitions.

[2] William Appleman Williams, *The Tragedy of American Diplomacy*, rev. ed. (New York: Delta Books, 1962), p. 13; Carl Becker, *Everyman His Own Historian: Essays on History and Politics* (Chicago: Quadrangle Books, 1966 [1935]), p. 235. Many definitions are relentlessly circular, such as "History is what the historian does." Norman F. Cantor and Richard I. Schneider, *How to Study History* (Arlington Heights, Ill.: AHM Corporation, 1967), p. 19.

Memory is a tricky business, though. Is it individual or collective memory we speak of? Is memory the same as the anonymous written records upon which historians have partially relied for centuries to fashion their histories?[3] The question of the reliability of memory takes many diverse and conflicting shapes.

More caution intrudes when we realize that the plastic qualities of history make it the perfect plaything for intellectual gamesmanship on an extremely sophisticated scale. Sigmund Freud, one of the founding fathers of modern psychoanalysis, once wrote that the events of human history were no more than a reflection of the dynamic conflicts among the ego, the id, and the superego. Another exceptional mind, Karl Marx, declared that history was nothing but "the activity of man in pursuit of his own ends," i.e., selfishness displayed primarily in the economic sphere of our existence.[4] Vocabulary again blocks us. If we would follow Freud or Marx, we must first be armed with the knowledge of what Freud meant by "ego," "id," and "superego" and what Marx meant by "alienation," "proletariat," and "communism." We might then sally forth, only to find that specialists have inconclusively debated these and like terms for decades.

The shifty ambiguities of historical study are for many a form of mental quicksand. No formula seems to work for all seasons. History has yet to produce a Newton, although, as we shall see, there has been no dearth of candidates for this role. Memory is not enough, some argue; facts by themselves are barren of knowledge. We want explanation as well as recapitulation.[5]

Others are upset that the "lessons of history"—the trite aphorism—appear to be learned by no one. People, it seems, keep making the same mistakes. If history were worth anything, it would supply a suitable corrective to the endless procession of wars, economic crises, and other disasters of our own making. Beyond the question of utilitarianism, the discussion of whether his-

[3] This confusion is apparent even in basic primers. See, for example, Robert V. Daniels, *Studying History: How and Why*, 2nd ed. (Englewood Cliffs, N.J.: Prentice-Hall, 1972), p. 6, where history is defined as the "memory of human group experience' and, two paragraphs later, as the "record of all experience."

[4] Bruce Mazlish, *The Riddle of History: The Great Speculators from Vico to Freud* (New York: Minerva Press, 1968), pp. 393, 285.

[5] This position is that of the English philosopher Thomas Hobbes; see Mazlish, *The Riddle of History*, pp. 25–26, and 139, for the equally glum position of the German thinker Georg Wilhelm Friedrich Hegel. See also Murray G. Murphey, *Our Knowledge of the Historical Past* (Indianapolis: Bobbs-Merrill, 1973), p. 92.

tory is useful, there are those who see history simply as a pack of lies, and historians as liars of the highest order. Walt Whitman, America's nineteenth-century poet of the democratic possible, once declared he was afraid of historians—if they did not lie themselves, they were the victims of liars.[6]

Let us descend to the bottom rung with a great cynic, H. L. Mencken. As a journalist he often wrote for shock value, but his distaste for historians was beyond measure. In one breath he was capable of calling the subject "encrusted misunderstanding," "sentimental lies," and "hogwash."[7] History could be trusted only to lie, and no further. Here was meat for fools but starvation for the intellect.

Freud and Marx must be conceded their vocabulary, Whitman his fear, and Mencken his billingsgate. They each, in their way, thought about history—what it meant to them personally and what they thought it should mean to people around them. No definition could satisfy these disparate minds and the thousands more who have puzzled over the questions of history for millennia. And this is our contention: the fun of history is in the puzzle.

The Senses of History

We may not be able to define history, but we may perceive that whatever it is, there is more than one of it. History's focus is on the past, but we are not in the past; we are here and now. None of us has marched with Napoleon, heard Cicero orate, or seen what the headsman's ax did to Charles I, King of England. Yet, we have a sense of Napoleonic campaigns, the Ciceronian sway over the Roman crowds, and how it was on the scaffold of the Banqueting House in 1649.

This sense comes to us through interpreters—call them historians if you will. Civilizations and cultures, unlike television networks, have no instant (or delayed) replay device to give us historical exactitude. If such a device existed, it still could not encompass our subject. But yet we "know," as surely as we have knowledge, that such things happened; that once a Napoleon, a Cicero, an English king named Charles all walked the earth and

[6] Daniel Aaron, *The Unwritten War: American Writers and the Civil War* (New York: Oxford University Press, 1975), p. 70.

[7] Charles Angoff, *H. L. Mencken: A Portrait from Memory* (New York: A. S. Barnes, 1961), p. 12.

shared our humanity. By themselves, they are clearly history, both in and of the past. Yet they and the lives they led, the things they did, and the people they knew are meaningless unless retrieved for us.

Retrieved how? Some historians, such as Carl Becker, have implied that virtually anyone may be his own historian. Becker's is a distinctly minority view within the modern profession, a profession that has developed in the last century or so. We instead rely on specialists (Mencken might call them shamans), not all of whom are anointed with doctoral degrees, to sort out the past and present it to us.

These presentations may differ with the culture. They might be given orally, as among American Indian tribes or African societies,[8] or in pictorial form, such as cave drawings or modern murals. But written materials have most fully sustained our concern for history, and it is writing that has conveyed history most successfully for over two thousand years. Perhaps humans need to remember the past, and written materials seem most satisfactory in answering the need. This does not imply, of course, that only the literate may be history-minded—only that literacy has been the most satisfactory mode found to date for historical discourse.

Looking at the written word, or the printed word in its commercial form, we may also receive a sense of history. These words are someone's reflection on what has happened. Although we might not wish to nail history to the wall with a hard-and-fast definition, we may well ponder what it is: *that which has been, or the reflection of what has been, or both?*

On the Writing of History

Everyone has read history that has been forgotten the minute it entered the mind. "Dull and dry" is the alliterative phrase commonly attached to historical writing, although one person's nectar in this regard is often another's poison. Journalist Frederick Lewis Allen, for example, declared himself bored by the reform struggles of American Progressivism, but he summoned up enough interest

[8] For a concise comparison of the oral culture of the American Indian with the written culture of the white man, see Wilcomb E. Washburn, *The Indian in America* (New York: Harper and Row, 1975), pp. 33–35. See also Basil Davidson, *A History of East and Central Africa to the Late Nineteenth Century* (Garden City, N.Y.: Anchor Books, 1969 [1967]), p. 32.

to speak of the significance of the graduated income tax. History's reputation of exceptional aridity is well captured by the Mouse in *Alice in Wonderland*. Soaked from her immersion in her own tears, Alice sits while the Mouse launches into "the driest thing I know," which turns out to be a tedious disquisition on medieval England.[9]

The strongest criticism comes from literary aesthetes. Only the poet can bring back and display the past before our eyes, wrote Kalhana, author of the Indian *Kashmir Chronicle*. In the mind's eye, the poet sees by divine intuition and passes the vision on. But the writing of history, in the words of the seventeenth-century Englishman Sir William Davenant, takes away the liberty of a poet and fetters one in the "shackles of an historian."[10] Indeed, the shackles are there; no historian should be without imagination in practicing the craft, but source material anchors him to a degree unknown to the poet. And the anchor becomes weightier the more historical material our modern cultures produce.

The textbook is our ultimate surrender to this mass. Rather than interpret to any great degree, authors at times are reduced to making lists or compilations. The problem of historical synthesis, which is the difficult one of being meaningful and coherent at the same time, is pushed to one side by the cookbook approach. Historians often despair over the problem, and in their despair many take refuge in narrow corners of historical study where they and a few other assiduous souls may be acknowledged as masters. Space (the generalization of a cross-section of history during a given time period) and time (the chronological march of events) wage continuous war for the synthesizer's attention.[11] The successful synthesis is thus most often a product of compromises, and these also are part of Sir William's shackles.

The modern historian also keeps the audience in mind. At the broadest scope, perhaps, one writes for a national audience; although there are international markets for historians, these tend to

[9] Frederick Lewis Allen, *The Big Change: America Transforms Itself, 1900–1950* (New York: Harper and Row, 1969 [1952]), p. 95; Lewis Carroll, *Alice in Wonderland* (New York: Everyman's Library, 1929), pp. 18–19.

[10] A. L. Basham, "The Kashmir Chronicle," in C. H. Philips, ed., *Historians of India, Pakistan, and Ceylon* (London: Oxford University Press, 1961), p. 61; Samuel T. Coleridge, *Biographia Literaria*, II, ed. J. Shawcross (Oxford: Clarendon Press, 1907), p. 101.

[11] For comment on this point, see Becker, *Everyman His Own Historian*, pp. 229–30.

be restricted to communities of scholars. Sometimes paydirt is struck, and the author's reputation, the advertising of the work, the real need for such a book, or the mysterious chemistry of audience receptivity make a work popular. With luck, the historian also turns a buck. This is not to imply that historical research is some sort of divining rod by which historians seek to maximize profit by catering to popular interests or courting the textbook market. There are those, however, who approach historical writing in an aggressively entrepreneurial manner—but the type is to be found in all branches of scholarship.

Beyond a doubt, the widest audiences are those accustomed to narrative history. Narrative has a beginning and end, and in between it manages to tell a story. It has been called the basic form of historical explanation. Narrative storytelling cannot be freed from interpretation; this is what separates it from mere chronology. The problem is the endless ambiguous one of where fact leaves off and interpretation begins. Carl Becker, who is admittedly an extremist on the question, calls this a "convenient blend of truth and fancy."[12] Sometimes fancy gets the upper hand. Have you ever heard anyone praise an historical work because "it flows just like a novel"?

Regardless of the quality of the work and of the skepticism we bring to it, one basic assumption exists: that the work is the product of a human mind, and that the mind is in the work. The imperfect blending of minds often makes multi-author books a complete hash—the problems of conceptualization clash with the pressures of thematic integration. Single authors unveil their thinking for us, and this is for most writers an adventurous, even frightening, thing to do.

It does no good to be hesitant; pride in authorship implies publication, the reclusive poet Emily Dickinson notwithstanding. The father of William H. Prescott robustly declared that "the man who writes a book which he is afraid to publish is a coward."[13] Such advice must have sustained his son; the younger Prescott became one of the great gentleman amateurs of the nineteenth century, authoring the classic studies *Conquest of Mexico* and *Conquest of Peru*.

[12] W. B. Gallie, *Philosophy and the Historical Understanding*, 2nd ed. (New York: Schocken Books, 1968), pp. 1–2; Becker, *Everyman His Own Historian*, p. 242.

[13] C. Harvey Gardiner, *William Hickling Prescott: A Biography* (Austin: University of Texas Press, 1969), p. 132.

Pride in authorship exists on many levels; it may be shared by the cultured and refined Prescott and the freshman who has just painfully completed that first term paper. A term paper will not find print, but historical research seeks print as lemmings seek the sea. History as a professional discipline has insisted upon the publishing process both as a barometer of historical opinion and (less fortunately) as a mode of professional advancement. "Publish or perish" sustains the smug achievers and haunts many of the less fortunate, even though few actually perish. These are pressures that should be realized but ideally should not dominate the excitement of writing. Pride in the well-turned sentence or the tight, strong paragraph, one hopes, is infectious, in the direction of the reader. John Hicks, author of a textbook on American history that had almost as long a run on campuses as *East Lynne* did in the theater, asserted that "publish or perish" held no terrors for him. "An artist can get no more satisfaction out of a well-executed painting than a writer of a carefully wrought book."[14]

Good writing is a matter of opinion. But many opinions are made for us—this is what the worst kind of teaching does. Some people like the phraseology that reduces history to metaphor, likens it to a dramatic play with curtains raising and lowering, actors entering and leaving, and the "stage manager of history" emceeing the entire show. Others prefer the blade unsheathed, the words wearing the armor of zealotry, skepticism, or satire. Thus we remember H. L. Mencken's description of the Ozarks as "one of the great moron reservoirs of the United States." Then there are the homely comparisons, the phrases that link great events to mundane concerns, as when Edmund Burke, gloomily staring across the Channel from England, compared the French Revolution to a neighbor's blazing house. "Better to be despised by too anxious apprehensions, than ruined by too confident a security."[15]

Some phrases stick like ticks on a hound. They often carry a heavy freight in imagery but are lightly loaded in "truth." What counts is what gets across, like economist John R. Commons's de-

[14] John D. Hicks, *My Life with History: An Autobiography* (Lincoln: University of Nebraska Press, 1968), pp. 356–57.

[15] The quotes are taken in order from Frederick Lewis Allen, *Since Yesterday: The 1930's in America, September 3, 1929–September 3, 1939* (New York: Harper and Row, 1972 [1939]), p. 81; William Manchester, *H. L. Mencken: Disturber of the Peace* (New York: Collier Books, 1962 [1950]), p. 267; Edmund Burke, *Reflections on the Revolution in France* (New York: Everyman's Library, 1910), p. 8.

scription of Communists: "The Presbyterians of foreordained materialism." The beauty of balanced word play is likewise evident in Frederick Lewis Allen's description of the official greeter of New York City, Grover Whalen, as one who reduced welcoming to a science and raised it to an art.[16]

The lines with the most polish glow more often with sweat than inspiration. Even some of the more famous repay close scrutiny. Randolph Bourne was one of the rare individuals raising his voice against American involvement in World War I. His most-remembered line of criticism is "War is the health of the state." Yet in the same piece he had earlier written "War is essentially the health of the state." A small difference, but one that loops the blow enough to take steam out of the punch.[17]

Many people never get to the stage where they could appear before Prescott's father, manuscript in hand, to receive an exhortation to publish. The jump from mind to pen is a long one; that from pen to print is even longer and, once made, is at times not worth the leap. Midnight's inspirations often make hideous rereading at dawn. The topic may just be overwhelming, as for the young Confederate artillery officer who wrote, "Why is it that I can never let myself loose and write on without feeling somehow ashamed? There must be some taste of the ludicrous in high degree of emotion of whatever kind the instant we cease to sympathize with it."[18]

Others may scheme for years to construct the magnum opus. The English historian Lord Acton announced in 1875 his intentions to write a History of Liberty. If anyone could have addressed successfully such a sprawling topic, it was Acton, of whom the trite phrase "encyclopedic mind" is an apt description. As the years passed, the piles of notes grew—but nothing got written, and the great history became the "Madonna of the Future." Acton himself called it his "tiresome book." It remains one of the great unwritten achievements of the English language.[19]

[16] John R. Commons, *Myself: The Autobiography of John R. Commons* (Madison: University of Wisconsin Press, 1964 [1934]), p. 10; Frederick Lewis Allen, *Only Yesterday: An Informal History of the 1920's* (New York: Harper and Row, 1964 [1931]), p. 8.

[17] Randolph S. Bourne, *War and the Intellectuals: Collected Essays, 1915–1919*, ed. Carl Resek (New York: Harper and Row, 1964), pp. 71, 69.

[18] Aaron, *The Unwritten War*, p. 230.

[19] Gertrude Himmelfarb, *Victorian Minds: A Study of Intellectuals in Crisis and of Ideologies in Transition* (New York: Harper and Row, 1970 [1952]), pp. 167–69.

Most of the time, for better or worse, something gets written. If fortune smiles, it gets published. Even then, how refreshing it is to hear an author explain that the book was written simply because its author wanted to read it. Some authors never get over their shock of appearing in print; this is a healthy condition and is to be encouraged. Leslie Stephen, a countryman of Acton's and a somewhat younger historian, was convinced before each of his publication dates that he was an impostor and would be found out in due course.[20] Such humility is surely preferable to the conviction of some writers that they and only they have custody of the keys.

Success is humility's archfoe. Publishers dearly love a consistent seller, particularly a text. The author may be, in John Hicks's words, "tied to a juggernaut" for a lifetime. Hicks was as kind and gentle as an historian could be, yet he freely admitted to using his own textbooks in his classes, not being "man enough" to chuck them and assign other authors.[21]

Publishing is also rationalized by the author as "contributing" to our body of knowledge. Sometimes, often accidentally, this happens: our opinion of the author diminishes. Graduate students are encouraged to toil industriously to make their "original contribution" and thus their mark. Professor Hicks was typical of the contribution ideal, bemoaning only half seriously the fact that his number of author cards in the Library of Congress was far outweighed by those of a friend who was an expert in soil chemistry. This misapplied emphasis may result in the graduate student's quarrying a dry vein, of no interest to any but the persevering laborer and the thesis advisor. The more admirable side of this process is professionalization, which is necessary up to the point where it inhibits imagination. The eccentric narratives, wrote the humane Albert Schweitzer, are the ones that advance history, for they are the ones that radiate imagination.[22]

The writing of history, however achieved, is something few do for a living and even fewer for fun. Most of us so infected formed our primary love of history by reading rather than writing. Reading gives us vocabulary, which is really the only basic tool the his-

[20]John Malcolm Brinnin, *The Sway of the Grand Saloon: A Social History of the North Atlantic* (New York: Delacorte Press, 1971), p. xiii; Himmelfarb, *Victorian Minds*, p. 200.

[21]Hicks, *My Life with History*, pp. 196, 220.

[22]Ibid., p. 25; Albert Schweitzer, *The Quest of the Historical Jesus: A Critical Study of Its Progress from Reimarus to Wrede* (New York: Macmillan, 1961 [1906]), p. 9.

torian possesses. It is the vocabulary that distinguishes our best historians—not their use of big words, but the way they fit words together. In fact, the greater part of historical study is the study of vocabulary, of finding out what the words mean. The more we read, the more we attach "Napoleon" to a man and "Napoleonic" to a series of concepts.

Reading becomes the best experience for the historian, for here one's own experience in being human fuses with that of others to form opinion. Unless one is versed in the writings of the ancients, commented the suave Castiglione in his advice to Renaissance courtiers, it is difficult to write well. Moreover, experience in the world is needed to match the experience of the book, else the author is doing the thinking for the reader. If one is lucky, this reading experience is never ending and continuously fresh; even the bad book instructs. Carl Becker put it best:

> The writer will read for information, but also with an ear always open to catch the meaning and overtones of words and the peculiar pitch and cadence of their arrangement. There will thus be deposited in the mind, in the subconscious if you prefer, an adequate vocabulary, and a sure feeling for the idioms, rhythms, and grammatical forms that are natural to the language. In time these become so much a part of the writer's mentality that he thinks in terms of them, and writes properly by ear, so to speak, rather than by rule. Thinking too precisely on the rule is apt to give one's writing a certain correct rigidity, even a slightly archaic quality, often found in the writing of professors.[23]

On the Reading of History

There is little doubt that the proliferation of the visual media has seriously eroded contemporary reading habits. Yet reading will remain the basis for education, one hopes, until the day we all become simply nodes in a computer network. The printed page is a pathway to imagination, and reading in history requires imagination. This observation may seem paradoxical if the plug-and-chug type of historical writing has dominated our experience. Yet good

[23] Castiglione, *The Book of the Courtier*, trans. Charles S. Singleton (Garden City, N.Y.: Anchor Books, 1959), p. 70; Louis Gottschalk, *Understanding History: A Primer of Historical Method*, 2nd ed. (New York: Alfred A. Knopf, 1969), p. 15; Charlotte Watkins Smith, *Carl Becker: On History and the Climate of Opinion* (Carbondale: Southern Illinois University Press, 1973 [1956]), p. 138.

historians, like good novelists, often use their imagination to strike responses in our own. The visual media strip our imaginations from us. As in most technological change, something is given up in return for "progress."

But is not history "fact" rather than imagination? We leave the business of historical fact for later discussion. Here we only note that facts are useless without sustaining opinion, analysis, or criticism.[24] All of these, on the printed page, separate history from mere *chronicle*, which is the cataloging of events. Imagination may lie or distort, to be sure, but it is also indispensable, not only to the historian but to readers as well.

To most people meaningful history is storytelling, what we call narrative history. Recent stress of scientific approaches to historical research does not detract from the necessity for data to be put into a form understandable to the mind. The most common form is still narrative of some type. A recent work on the life of a southern black sharecropper has lamented "the unfortunate popular assumption that history is something that takes place in books and books are to be read in school."[25] Much history does take place in books. What is unfortunate is the connection between books and school, for without the book, the marvelous storytelling of "Nate Shaw" would not be ours today.

"The history that lies inert in unread books does no work in the world," Carl Becker once asserted.[26] There has been plenty of this inert matter, and more is produced every day. The unread book, however, may have potential—if only it can find its reader (or, given today's library systems, if its reader can find it). Here is one reason college professors ideally are adept at torturing students with lengthy reading assignments. The most common student complaint in my own courses has concerned the great weight of reading—five or six books a semester for undergraduates. I thought I had this problem licked when I assigned the shortest book I could find (87 pages). The course evaluations returned from the students: the length was all right, but the words were too long.

[24] There is of course another viewpoint: That facts in and of themselves have their own character. See in particular Gallie, *Philosophy and the Historical Understanding*, p. 104. Leonard Krieger has called history "A logic of the actual." *Ranke: The Meaning of History* (Chicago: University of Chicago Press, 1977), p. 356.

[25] Theodore Rosengarten, *All God's Dangers: The Life of Nate Shaw* (New York: Avon Books, 1974), p. xxiii.

[26] Becker, *Everyman His Own Historian*, p. 252.

The progressive Kansas newspaperman William Allen White once remarked that about all anyone could get out of a college education was a capacity for trained attention to the printed page.[27] White's is a pessimistic view. Any dullard may apply rote memory to history; the results will be transitory and ineffectual. There is a great gulf between mere reading and reading that charges intellectual batteries and enables us to analyze critically and compare; to use our own judgment, no matter how faulty, based on our own experience, no matter how limited; in short—to think.

No one would claim that reading is thus the Holy Grail. "Book learning" is always inadequate. Socrates, in Plato's *Phaedrus*, even bemoaned the spread of reading and writing. Too much reading weakened memory and thus sapped critical abilities. On the other hand, observed the twelfth-century monk John of Salisbury, the more the young scholar learns the less he will read. The law of diminishing returns would seem to operate in literature as well as economics. Yen Yuan, a Chinese master of the seventeenth century, emphasized "practical learning" in all walks of life. Yen gave as his example the study of music, which is pointless unless voice, body, or instrument is utilized in a practical way.[28]

Such caution is praiseworthy, since it is possible for books to wall out the world as well as introduce the world to us. "His library is very large and numerous," publisher John Dunton wearily wrote of Yen's contemporary, the Puritan divine Cotton Mather; "But, had his books been fewer when he wrote his 'History,' it would have pleased us better." The English philosopher Thomas Hobbes is supposed to have said that if he had read as much as his contemporaries, he would have been as stupid as they.[29]

A time-honored shibboleth is at stake here: that reading brings knowledge; knowledge, power; and so on. It is nonsense to claim, as did an historian of America's role in World War I, that

[27] William Allen White, *The Autobiography of William Allen White* (New York: Macmillan, 1946), p. 145.

[28] Stephen Toulmin and June Goodfield, *The Discovery of Time* (Chicago: University of Chicago Press, 1977 [1965]), p. 25; A. L. Poole, *From Domesday Book to Magna Carta, 1087–1216*, 2nd ed. (Oxford: Oxford University Press, 1955), p. 236; Frederic Wakeman, Jr., *History and Will: Philosophical Perspectives of Mao Tse-Tung's Thought* (Berkeley: University of California Press, 1973), p. 238.

[29] Larzer Ziff, *Puritanism in America: New Culture in a New World*, 2nd ed. (New York: Viking Press, 1973), p. 217; David Ogg, *England in the Reign of Charles II* (New York: Oxford University Press, 1967), p. 741.

"in the nature of things there must be several thousand who listen to each prophet who speaks." [30] No one may be listening. Reading may or may not bring knowledge, and as for power (in any meaningful sense), tell it to the next professor you see. Some people simply "collect" books, like butterflies or stamps. Author Sherwood Anderson acutely observed that Americans possess rather than read books; owning books in most families seemed a "kind of moral necessity." [31]

Yet it was not always so. Before *Dragnet*, before *Amos 'n' Andy*, even before *The Great Train Robbery*, there is evidence that many Americans read habitually, and that this habit encompassed historical topics naturally. Nineteenth-century visitors to the United States were usually moved to comment on the compulsive reading habits of their hosts. The white population was already 90 percent literate; by 1825 the lending libraries of America's five largest cities offered twenty times the books the entire country possessed when George Washington was a young man. [32] This reading habit, which was certainly more than Anderson's "moral necessity" of the 1920s, fostered a world of print that was alive, energetic, and—with the proliferation of the dime-novel industry in the middle of the century—open to all ages and social groups.

The twentieth century has not brought the death of reading, by any means, but habitual reading is an increasing rarity. Although it is an exaggeration to say, with William Leuchtenburg, that "the history of the quarter-century after World War II could readily be told in kinescopes of TV programs," the visual media have seriously weakened our reading habits. [33] Some scholars, such as Marshall McLuhan, have gloried in this change. Most, however, have uttered soft cries of despair, arguing that the mind fed by visuals alone readily turns to mush. My impression of students as they cycle through my classes is one of spotty intellectual enthusiasm (which is a changeless condition) coupled with a lessened familiarity with books and with the habit of reading.

[30] Preston W. Slosson, *The Great Crusade and After, 1914–1928*, XII of *A History of American Life*, ed. Arthur Schlesinger and Dixon Ryan Fox (Chicago: Quadrangle Books, 1971), p. 422.

[31] Sherwood Anderson, *A Story Teller's Story* (New York: Viking Press, 1969), p. 156.

[32] Russel Blaine Nye, *Society and Culture in America, 1830–1860* (New York: Harper and Row, 1974), p. 366.

[33] William E. Leuchtenburg, *A Troubled Feast: American Society since 1945* (Boston: Little, Brown, 1973), p. 67.

Lessened familiarity means missed opportunity. If knowledge may not mean power, one still lives by what one learns. H. L. Mencken, an iconoclast among iconoclasts, nevertheless enjoyed all books and written material because everything written was the attempt of some human being to express himself.[34] And so with Walt Whitman:

> Comrade, this is no book
> Who touches this touches a man.[35]

There is no magic wand that bestows upon us the love of reading. People addicted to the literary life, of which history is a part, show surprising similarities in their first relationship to the world of books. Many reading theorists consider a person's reading habits to be formed, for better or worse, prior to the teenage period. The patterns of the earliest exposure to printed material, the life-blood of history, are thus significant.

Some individuals are compulsive readers from their earliest years. Bernard DeVoto's father taught him to read at three. At a very early age, the boy who would write his own popular epics of America's westward advance was wrestling with Greek, Latin, and Italian epics in remote Ogden, Utah. Randolph Bourne at two years of age was observed by a housemaid to be reading labels on groceries.[36] Other compulsives may be spotted perusing cereal boxes at breakfast or intensely digesting the latest in subway advertising. Nothing really explains such activity; the eye and the mind simply covet print. More prosaic are those led to reading by a literary family, a more common institution a century ago than now. George Bancroft grew up in a household of books and had the run of his father's copious library. William H. Prescott was unsatisfied by his family's library and at an early age became a browser in the Boston Athenaeum.[37] Bancroft, like Prescott, became one of the most noteworthy gentleman amateurs in nineteenth-century American historiography.

Even families without the means of the Bancrofts or the Prescotts could encourage reading. James T. Shotwell's father, a school-

[34] Manchester, *H. L. Mencken: Disturber of the Peace*, p. 68.
[35] Nye, *Society and Culture in America*, p. 73.
[36] Wallace Stegner, *The Uneasy Chair: A Biography of Bernard DeVoto* (Garden City, N.Y.: Doubleday, 1974), p. 6; Bourne, *War and the Intellectuals*, p. ix.
[37] Russel B. Nye, *George Bancroft* (New York: Washington Square Press, 1964), p. 2; Gardiner, *William Hickling Prescott*, p. 16.

teacher in Strathroy, Ontario, introduced his son to an early regimen of the Bible, Shakespeare, and Milton—useful training for the future historian and advocate of world peace. Roy F. Nichols, analyst of nineteenth-century American political practice, recalled his mother reading to him from such titles as *The History of the United States Told in One Syllable Words*. William Allen White happily remembered the nights his mother read to him: Dickens, James Fenimore Cooper, Mother Goose. (The father constantly claimed the boy was being spoiled.) Another and unrelated White, Andrew Dickson, the future founder of Cornell University and an historian of repute, grew up in a home where a businessman father encouraged reading. Andrew could not recall a time when he could not read easily. (A claim, incidentally, that also had been made by Benjamin Franklin.) Even Lincoln Steffens, growing up half-wild in California in the 1870s, channeled his dreamy nature into books—a case of benign parental neglect. This sort of neglect had the happiest consequences for twelve-year-old Edward Gibbon, whose grandfather absconded after a commercial failure. The boy thus gained the free run of a "tolerable library." "Where a title attracted my eye," later wrote the author of *The Decline and Fall of the Roman Empire*, "without fear or awe I snatched the volume from the shelf."[38]

The more authoritarian family structure of the nineteenth century sometimes encouraged direct reading. John Addams, father of the future social settlement pioneer, was not above bribing his daughter to read. Jane received five cents for each one of *Plutarch's Lives* completed and a whole quarter for each volume of Irving's *Life of Washington*. She did not wither but rather bloomed under such largesse, although she dutifully noted, through an agreement with her father, that "I am to read a certain amount of history first."[39]

[38] Harold Josephson, *James T. Shotwell and the Rise of Internationalism in America* (Rutherford, N.J.: Fairleigh Dickinson University Press, 1974), pp. 20–21; Roy F. Nichols, *A Historian's Progress* (New York: Alfred A. Knopf, 1968), p. 6; William Allen White, *Autobiography*, pp. 44–45; Andrew Dickson White, *Autobiography of Andrew Dickson White* I (New York: Century, 1905), pp. 6–7; *The Autobiography of Benjamin Franklin and Selections from His Other Writings* (New York: Modern Library, 1944), pp. 12, 16; Lincoln Steffens, *The Autobiography of Lincoln Steffens* I (New York: Harcourt, Brace and World, 1931), p. 28; George Bonnard, ed., *Edward Gibbon: Memoirs of My Life* (New York: Funk and Wagnalls, 1969), p. 37.

[39] Allen F. Davis, *American Heroine: The Life and Legend of Jane Addams* (New York: Oxford University Press, 1975), pp. 8–9. The Addams experience

But dutiful children were scarce then as now. Many more young people probably read in bits and pieces, picking up occasional scraps to feed their curiosity. Andrew Dickson White remembered digesting a hash that included *Robinson Crusoe*, Lauder's *Travels in Africa*, and Rollin's *Ancient History*, wishing he had had more beneficent guidance as a youngster. Mark Sullivan, journalist and historian, also read in eclectic fashion as a boy, limited by toilsome hours on the family farm in Pennsylvania. Yet Sullivan built these shards into an enduring edifice, and in time he and his wife read aloud to their children in the evenings. Young Omar Bradley, raised hardscrabble poor in rural Missouri, was fascinated by lurid tales of America's wars; propelled by reading time stolen from school and work, the boy who would later command the largest American army in history acted out many of his battles on the living room rug, using dominoes for fortifications and .22 shells for soldiers.[40]

It is rare that children strike first upon history as a consuming interest. Almost always the habit of reading, encouraged or not, is nurtured first. Young Walter Prescott Webb, whose family lived on the Clear Fork of the Brazos River in Texas, patiently saved premiums from Arbuckle's Four X Coffee and was thrilled by his reward: *Jack the Giant Killer*. The dreariness of farm life on the Great Plains, a region Webb would one day analyze, was made more palatable by books and periodicals such as *The Tip-Top Weekly* and *The Youth's Companion*.[41]

Key books that combine religion, literature, or adventure with history often plant lasting seeds. John Hicks, whose father owned a reasonable library, became attached to biblical history on his own, making childish tables of the kings of Israel and Judah. Growing up in Norway, far from the history department and the University of Wisconsin where he eventually settled, young Paul

might be contrasted with that of Liu Chih-chi, an historian of classical China. Liu was beaten frequently when he failed to master his early reading yet survived to become a comprehensive reader. See E. G. Pulleyblank, "Chinese Historical Criticism: Liu Chih-chi and Ssu-ma Kuang," in W. G. Beasley and E. G. Pulleyblank, eds., *Historians of China and Japan* (London: Oxford University Press, 1961), p. 137.

[40] Andrew Dickson White, *Autobiography*, I, 15; Mark Sullivan, *The Education of an American* (New York: Doubleday, Doran, 1938), pp. 35, 66–75; Omar N. Bradley and Clay Blair, *A General's Life: An Autobiography* (New York: Simon and Schuster, 1983).

[41] Necah Stewart Furman, *Walter Prescott Webb: His Life and Impact* (Albuquerque: University of New Mexico Press, 1976), pp. 21–22, 25.

Knaplund felt the same influence. His mother urged him to read the Bible aloud to visitors, and its tales of Old Testament heroes provoked him to read more.

Heroes, of course, spring not only from religious history but from the secular world as well. Andrew Dickson White began his deeper study of American life through an admiration for the life and writings of Thomas Jefferson.[42] And who could count the children brought to history by the half-mythic tales of Davey Crockett, George Washington, or Daniel Webster?

Outside the home, the forces of institutionalized education have made their mark. It must be confessed that the "subject" of history has killed more interest than it has ever fostered in this regard, yet there is sometimes a teacher, a certain type of material, one special book—and even in school, the spark may take light. Paul Knaplund dwelt on history as a favorite subject from the moment he entered school. He was allowed to work independently of his class and submerged himself in the history of Greece and Rome. Northern Norway could never be described as the most salubrious climate for learning; of Paul's five brothers, one became a businessman, and four braved the North Atlantic as fishermen. Paul remained with his books.[43]

History taught in the classroom likewise did not deter James Truslow Adams, a popular historian and a critic of American civilization in the 1920s. Adams remembered himself as a "naturally bookish and studious boy" and an "eager student."[44] He began to collect volumes assiduously at the age of twelve and garnered most of his history outside of school.

Most readers, like Adams, seem to learn more away from the school environment, devouring generalized literature to feed their habit. Adams invaded libraries early, avidly consuming Jules Verne, G. A. Henty (a popular boys' author), and Sir Walter Scott. As he grew into his teenage years, Andrew Dickson White stretched his span to encompass Emerson, Ruskin, and Carlyle—not the best of historians, perhaps, but always rewarding companions. White's deep love for Sir Walter Scott, who likewise played fast and loose with the Muse, stayed with him into his maturity. In

[42] Hicks, *My Life with History*, p. 35; Paul Knaplund, *Moorings Old and New: Entries in an Immigrant's Log* (Madison: State Historical Society of Wisconsin, 1963), pp. 57–58; Andrew Dickson White, *Autobiography*, I, 38–39.

[43] Knaplund, *Moorings Old and New*, pp. 71, 22.

[44] James Truslow Adams, *Our Business Civilization: Some Aspects of American Culture* (New York: AMS Press, 1969), pp. 147–48.

Xenia, Ohio, at the dawn of the twentieth century, a young lad named Arthur Schlesinger listed no less than 598 books he had read by the age of fourteen. Setting aside the question of compulsiveness (which is almost a necessary affliction for historians), young Arthur's compilation is impressive by its range. G. A. Henty led the list with forty-nine titles. Then in profusion came the likes of Mark Twain, Horatio Alger, James Fenimore Cooper, Louisa May Alcott, and a host of others impossible to catalog under any meaningful heading except Schlesinger's description of himself: "voracious reader."[45] Through Henty, whose boy heroes ranged from ancient Egypt to the American West, the future Harvard historian took in history with his adventure, and vice versa.

Some tastes have been more mundane. Carl Becker was a late bloomer; he discovered reading for pleasure only at the age of eleven. He had never had a book read to him or read for himself before that time. Was young Carl an autodidact on the scale of a Knaplund or a Jane Addams? His first fare encompassed *Saturday Night*, a serialized weekly of westerns, adventure, and mystery stories of the type ground out relentlessly by hacks then and now. Becker loved these tales, or, more accurately, he fell in love with reading.[46]

Malcolm X, the black radical, bloomed even later than Becker. Malcolm's world as a youngster was one of family strife, poverty, the dreary round of welfare. No book could penetrate those walls, and "Detroit Red" was soon outside the law. In prison, lonely and frustrated, he began to copy the dictionary. Then on to the prison library, where for the first time he began to understand what he read, rather than simply going through the motions. Before long, Malcolm was an omnivore, reading in his cell by the dim glow of a light in the corridor. He was light-years removed from the middle-class security of Arthur Schlesinger and the reading circles of the Knaplund and Hicks families, yet given the opportunity—he read.[47]

With all this grinding away with books, our examples (barring Malcolm, who pimped at an exceptionally young age) must seem like dull individuals indeed. A slight balancing is in order.

[45] Allan Nevins, *James Truslow Adams: Historian of the American Dream* (Urbana: University of Illinois Press, 1968), p. 13; Andrew Dickson White, *Autobiography*, I, 24; Arthur M. Schlesinger, *In Retrospect: The History of a Historian* (New York: Harcourt, Brace and World, 1963), pp. 13–14.

[46] Smith, *Carl Becker*, pp. 132–33, 136.

[47] Malcolm X, *The Autobiography of Malcolm X* (New York: Grove Press, 1966), pp. 171–85.

Not all children squirrel away their books and count them in their hundreds. Once in Missouri a young man with bad eyesight was subjected to glasses at the age of eight. His doctor warned him against rough-and-tumble sports, so the boy haunted his public library and read and reread the family Bible. Because he could not see well enough to wield a bat, his eyesight was considered perfect for umpiring neighborhood ball games. From this enforced athletic abstinence, Harry Truman drank deeply from the well of history. "I made it my business to look up the background of . . . events and to find out who brought them about."[48]

The unanticipated vector toward books did not deter Truman from a long and active career in public life. Of the young people discussed here, many went on to distinguished public careers: Bancroft as Secretary of the Navy, Jane Addams as the symbol of the social settlement movement, and Andrew Dickson White as university administrator and diplomat, to name just a few. We would be remiss if we did not include T. E. Lawrence, who "took the Oxford History School because it came in his way, and because it was a hurdle to be jumped on the road that led to action."[49] Yet even for Lawrence of Arabia, history proved a useful background for the later understanding of his desert environment.

Reading is thus at least as much an avenue into the world as a fence walling the world out. Indeed, the habit of reading is a precondition for the creation of historical order on an individual scale. It is not necessary to read history to make it: the kings of ancient Persia were illiterate, and no one will ever accuse Attila the Hun of being bookish. But to write history in a cogent manner, one must read history.

It is no longer possible to read everything, if indeed it ever was. But certainly we expect our historians to be masters of their subjects. Such mastery may be bought at the price of exasperation. It is difficult not to sympathize with the English diarist, naval administrator, and clandestine fornicator Samuel Pepys in this regard. Two centuries before Lord Acton, Pepys also planned a great history, a *Navalia*, or history of the sea. Assiduously he read, catalogued, and assembled materials for the great project. Soon he found himself oppressed and confounded, rather than enlightened, by the growing mass. Finally he exploded: "It is not imaginable to such as have not tried, what labor an historian (that would be ex-

[48] Harry S. Truman, *Memoirs*, I: *Year of Decisions* (New York: Signet Books, 1965), pp. 135, 137–41.
[49] Desmond Stewart, *T. E. Lawrence; A New Biography* (New York: Harper and Row, 1977), p. 20.

act) is condemned to. He must read all, good and bad, and remove a world of rubbish before he can lay the foundation."[50] It
would be pleasant to report that this tantrum cooled into pen and
ink, but the *Navalia*, like Acton's *History of Liberty*, remains a
great nonbook. In exculpation, Pepys speaks to us through his di-
ary more pungently and meaningfully than any grandiose project
ever could. Was Pepys, then, simply wasting his time preparing?
Only he could judge that question adequately.

To be interested in history, like Pepys, need not imply a
"project." We are under no imperative to write once we have read.
But: an interest in history implies reading in history. Further, it implies a broad range and an open mind.[51] Not every little tyke who
reads the fine print on grocery labels is on a one-way track to historical study. Yet functioning historians without the reading habit
are handicapped in several ways. First, they have made their profession a torture, for its information is communicated mostly in
print. Secondly, they have shortchanged both themselves and their
students, should they have any. Many minds slowly close with age;
some snap shut, given an intensely personal or controversial subject. Others never develop but are content to plod listlessly for
years down one early-marked path. Finally, the age of the specialist has called forth the "directed reader": one who reads inten-
sively, but only in one area because "there is not time for anything
else." This is a recipe for a certain type of expertise; it also holds
the potential for intellectual rigidity.

It is usually through reading that we gain our first perceptions
of historical order. As we read and as we pass through life,
we gather experiences through which our historical judgment is
sifted. Our impressions of historical personages, such as Napoleon,
will most likely differ when we are ten, thirty, fifty. Experience
forms in memory a marvelous blend, often delusive but seldom
valueless. This experience compounded will make the nature of
our relationship with Napoleon change through time. Since such a
relationship is part of historical order, the formulation of this order is our next concern.

[50] Richard Ollard, *Pepys: A Biography* (New York: Holt, Rinehart and
Winston, 1974), pp. 266–67.
[51] See Jacques Barzun, *Clio and the Doctors: Psycho-History, Quanto-
History, and History* (Chicago: University of Chicago Press, 1974), p. 144, for
comment on this point.

CHAPTER TWO

The "I" in History

Perhaps the human mind does not covet knowledge, but it does tend to demand certainty. Certainty in its turn may rest upon faith, science, or strange combinations thereof; in our time it is the scientific approach to human affairs that has gained the upper hand. For over a century a rather sterile debate has been conducted over the nature of history in this regard—whether it be an art or a science.

The claims for history as a science interest us first, for the scientific approach implies structure and categorical order, plus a method of analyzing the world that admits of few if any alternatives. If the practice of history is a science, then empiricism in historical research is all that is admissible, and historical evidence becomes analogous to the contents of a test tube. That is, it will be open to a set of devices ("hypotheses") that will, when properly applied, unlock its secrets.

History and Science

Mathematics is the most precise and exact of the sciences and is thus aesthetically the most beautiful. It also provides us with a convenient basis for discussion. In most mathematics there is no room for error; one is either right or wrong. Limit theory, for example, has tolerance built into it, but the nature of this tolerance is in itself mathematically precise. There is, in fine, no place for judgment. One is reminded of Voltaire's uncharitable assessment of Descartes: "He was the greatest geometrician of his age; but geometry leaves the mind where it finds it." Yet the most enlightened man, claimed the mathematician De Bonald, would be the least in-different and intolerant concerning opinion.[1]

All this is very well in the realm of numbers. But what of his-torical facts? Beyond the adding and subtracting of historical dates, there is very little in our infinitely rich past that responds to mathematical logic. Virtually everyone who writes history must come to grips with the problem of what constitutes historical fact. We may agree on the nature of what "two," "2," or "1 + 1" sig-nifies, but will a fact from the past that does not respond to such logic elicit the same agreement?

A recent definition of historical fact argues that there are two requirements: first, that the fact be particular, that is, capable of separation from its surroundings; and second, that the fact be "so-cially significant."[2] With the first requirement, there is generally no margin for disagreement, although certainly not in all cases, particularly those dealing with the sparse records of the more re-mote past. Napoleon was born in 1769, not in 1768 or 1770; he was born in Corsica, not anywhere else. But as to the second re-quirement, the significance of an historical fact is a matter that eludes lasting definition. *How should the social significance of an historical fact be ascertained?*

Accreted facts may be made to describe historical events. We do not say, "Napoleon, in spite of advancing senility brought on by old age, was nevertheless able to lead an expedition to Egypt in 1798"—we know better. The outlines of Napoleon's Egyptian Ex-pedition, to which we shall have occasion to return, are as follows: Bonaparte, with the approval of the French Directory, departed Toulon in May, 1798. He commanded an army of 38,000 troops and about 150 assorted scholars, aboard 400 transports. The des-tination of the young general was Egypt, which in its strategic posi-tion in the Middle East had interested French policymakers since the Crusades.

Along the way, the expedition narrowly and unknowingly

[1] Peter Gay and Victor G. Wexler, eds., *Historians at Work*, II: *Valla to Gib-bon* (New York: Harper and Row, 1972), p. 326; Bruce Mazlish, *The Riddle of History: The Great Speculators from Vico to Freud* (New York: Minerva Press, 1968), p. 200, n.22. One of the major intellectual earthquakes of the twentieth century, of course, has concerned the discovery of the necessary imprecision of mathematical measurement. The scientific mode of thought, however, still con-tains considerable rationale for separating it from the artistic mind.

[2] Robert V. Daniels, *Studying History: How and Why*, 2nd ed. (Englewood Cliffs, N.J.: Prentice-Hall, 1972), pp. 36–37.

avoided a collision with Lord Nelson's English fleet. The French occupied the island of Malta and then pressed on to land at Alexandria, about 150 miles from the pyramids. After moving his force inland, Napoleon won the ensuing Battle of the Pyramids against native forces, but disaster followed when Nelson demolished the French fleet at Abukir Bay in August. There followed a period when the Napoleonic army marched into Syria before logistics, typhus, and European politics forced a retreat. Napoleon left his army, made a dramatic return to France, and the expedition eventually returned, much the worse for wear, from Egyptian soil.

The results were far-reaching. Napoleon profited by the fact that news of his victories had reached France ahead of him, while his large casualty figures had not. Posing as a man of destiny, he soon forged the consulate. Beyond lay the Empire, glory, and defeat. In quite another way, the expedition succeeded, for the antiquarians eventually discovered the meaning of Egyptian hieroglyphics. For a while, Egyptian decor was the rage—what had begun as a dream of intercontinental empire ended in the drawing room.[3]

What is the nature of the facts surrounding our example as an historical event? The claim made in this regard, particularly by historians a century ago, was that scientifically determined facts made the events of which they were a part scientifically determined. Let us consider the components of such a determination.[4]

There are at least three perspectives from which we may view an historical event. First, how the main participants viewed it— the perspective, for example, of Napoleon, his soldiers, and the train of scientists who accompanied him. Second, how others affected by the event viewed it. There were, after all, Egyptians in Egypt in 1798, some of them very upset at the sight of a flock of Frenchmen in the shadows of the pyramids. Others also had opinions on the expedition, not the least of whom were Napoleon's political rivals at home. Their thoughts and actions must be considered.

With the first two perspectives we are already out of our scien-

---

[3] For details on the Egyptian Expedition, see J. Christopher Herold, *Bonaparte in Egypt* (London: Hamish Hamilton, 1963), and David G. Chandler, *The Campaigns of Napoleon: The Mind and Method of History's Greatest Soldier* (New York: Macmillan, 1966), pp. 203–49.

[4] I follow here the views of Wilhelm Dilthey; see in particular Dilthey, *Pattern and Meaning in History: Thoughts on History and Society*, ed. H. P. Rickman (New York: Harper and Row, 1962), p. 50.

tific test tube, because it is extremely unlikely that Napoleon's generous opinion of himself would be matched by that of the Egyptians or their Turkish masters. But the third perspective dashes the test tube to smithereens, because it is the perspective of posterity, which has the task of assessing the consequences of the historical event. Posterity, of course, is time-bound in its own age, just as were Napoleon, his army, the sultan, and all the rest in theirs.

In spite of these impediments, a strong argument may be made that the third perspective, which encompasses the dimension of time, is the strongest ally of the historian. The passage of time allows detachment from the event, which in turn promotes objectivity. In this sense, the logic runs, history holds the promise of science. The evidence is there, hypotheses may be formed from it, and by applying the canons of historical research, *voila!*—Truth. "To understand history," one recent historian has written, "one must stand outside history, not just to avoid bias, but to be able to perceive distinctness and relations."[5]

The argument concerning the possibility of scientific detachment was the pole-star of historians educated in the new professionalism of the later nineteenth century, particularly of the disciples of the great German historian Leopold Von Ranke. Ranke considered historical scholarship to be tantamount to a priestly calling. "The historian exists to understand and to teach others to understand the meaning of each epoch in and for itself," he wrote. "He must have in mind, with complete impartiality, only the object itself and nothing else."[6]

Detachment would enable historical observers to rise to Olympian heights, from which lofty perch they could survey all sides of an historical event, understand its causes, actuality, and results, and render impartial judgment. This is an ideal and in itself is worthy of the highest praise and emulation. The flaw was not in the ideal but in the accompanying assumption that scientific de-

[5] William Irwin Thompson, *On the Edge of History: Speculations on the Transformation of Culture* (New York: Harper and Row, 1972), p. 104. But see 109–10, where Thompson says, "We are in nature, so there is no reason that subjectivity and objectivity should be so dissonantly arranged; it is more than likely that the key in which the nerves and the stars are strung is the same." We conclude that "standing outside history" is not in itself dissonance—but this is semantic confusion at its worst.

[6] Leonard Krieger, *Ranke: The Meaning of History* (Chicago: University of Chicago Press, 1977), pp. 314–15.

tachment was possible, regardless of the nature of the historical event being discussed and regardless of the relationship of the event to the historian.

A corollary argument was that such detachment would lead to historical certainty: that history, once written, would stay written. Later historians could get on to other persons, other events, other results. This belief finds few takers today; most would agree with John Lukacs that the purpose of historical knowledge is understanding, not certainty.[7] By accepting this, however, we beg the question of how one understands without being certain. We do not wish to venture into these quicksands too soon; for the time being, the substitution of "critical thinking" for understanding and "knowing" for certainty would seem a more reasonable choice, relieving the ambiguity inherent in the word "understanding."

Minds differ, skeptics have argued, and the exceptionally capable mind may not only make of history a science but contain in itself all the necessary information. This wonderful condition apparently suffused Benjamin Jowett, the eminent Master of Balliol in England, who was victimized by the following undergraduate doggerel:

> I go first; my name is Jowett;
> I am the Master of Balliol College;
> Whatever's worth knowing, be sure that I know it;
> Whatever I don't know is not knowledge.[8]

Men in different times, such as Lord Acton and the American Theodore Parker, Erasmus and Einstein, Bertrand Russell and a legion of others, have been seriously considered as virtually omniscient. The brilliance of the polymath may be conceded, while noting that reading everything (not to mention "knowing everything") would seem to leave little time for the business of living.

A tricky intellectual construction surrounds the claims of historical objectivity. Admitting our three perspectives, the construction nevertheless posits that once the evidence is in, the skilled historian is forced to assemble materials in one way and one way only. The method is certain, and the resulting assemblage is "history." Fustel de Coulanges, a nineteenth-century French historian

---

[7] John Lukacs, *A New History of the Cold War*, 3rd ed. (Garden City, N.Y.: Anchor Books, 1966), p. xii.

[8] Andrew Dickson White, *Autobiography of Andrew Dickson White* II (New York: Century, 1905), pp. 398, 412.

and by most accounts an exceptional teacher, responded one day to a class of applauding students by saying, "Do not applaud me. It is not I who speaks to you, but history which speaks through my mouth."[9] Fustel's is a convenient assertion, one that goes beyond allowing the historian to believe that results emerge virtually independently of his efforts and certainly of his biases. Here is a history above criticism, because it is *the* history. Dilutions of Fustel still infiltrate historical writing today. Consider the recent introduction by two excellent American historians to the work of yet a third: "He takes nothing for granted, but searches out all things thoroughly and allows what we now see as the most tragic decade of our history to unfold *in its own way*."[10]

So persistent is this quest for certainty and objectivity in the historical profession, so consistently is it hammered home during incubation periods of historical training, that it would almost appear to be a deep-seated psychological compensation for the obvious subjectivity implied by the human condition. Wilhelm Dilthey was convinced that there existed an "objective mind," contained in things like books or buildings, that made the past endure for us in the present.[11] We might ponder whether it is the books and buildings per se that count or our subjective appreciation of them.

At the opposite pole from the scientific, objective approach lies historical nihilism, opinion uninformed by any canon of historical research. Complete subjectivity has been called a "counsel of despair"[12] that discounts patterns to be found in historical events, even if the patterns themselves are subjective in nature. To argue the case for complete subjectivity is to claim the total irrelevance of historical thought and research; this no rational historian could do, for that would then negate the historian's professional existence. The choice between objectivism and subjectivism fortunately is not mutually exclusive. It is a question of where on the

[9] David Hackett Fischer, *Historians' Fallacies: Toward a Logic of Historical Thought* (New York: Harper and Row, 1970), pp. 6–7.

[10] Henry Steele Commager and Richard B. Morris, Introduction to David Potter, *The Impending Crisis, 1848–1861*, comp. and ed. Don E. Fehrenbacher (New York: Harper and Row, 1976), p. viii (my emphasis).

[11] Dilthey, *Pattern and Meaning in History*, p. 120.

[12] This phrase is used both by H. P. Rickman in his Introduction to Dilthey, *Pattern and Meaning in History*, p. 29, and by Cushing Strout in his description of Carl Becker's relativism. See Strout, *The Pragmatic Revolt in American History: Carl Becker and Charles Beard* (Ithaca, N.Y.: Cornell University Press, 1966 [1958]), p. 48.

scale between objectivity and subjectivity one thinks oneself to be positioned—the question of *relativism*.[13]

But again, say the skeptics, by the burden of the word a thing is either "true" or it is not. Conclusions based on evidence are certain, or they are not. History by this exclusionary principle becomes "an entertaining art whose special appeal is that its material is true."[14] Here we enter again the field staked out by scientific claims and objective thought. Historians like Dilthey have discounted personal experience, calling it feeble, selfish, and egocentric as a standard of historical judgment.[15] There is in this vision room for only one history, one truth. No certain way exists to identify writers who use this approach, but one clue is their tendency to use "history" as the subject of a declarative sentence: "History reveals," "History discloses," "History teaches." Statements like these should immediately put the reader on guard, for the ghost of Fustel looms over the reader's shoulder. "Learning from history" is very differerent from "history teaches."

Many Histories, Many Truths

It is difficult to become reconciled to uncertainty. Intellectually such a reconciliation runs against the general pattern of our education; we are taught to be sure more than we are taught to doubt. Further, "giving in" to uncertainty carries the onus of "giving up" on our mentality. We would all like to see ourselves as people of principles and convictions derived from certainties that in themselves are true. Augustine admonished his son not to judge the father's work by requiring proof of every exception, "For so you would become like those silly women of whom the apostle says that they are 'always learning, and never able to come to the knowledge of the truth.'"[16]

---

[13] To compound the confusion, "relativism" as a concept, if itself true, is also itself relative. See Louis Gottschalk, *Understanding History: A Primer of Historical Method*, 2nd ed. (New York: Alfred A. Knopf, 1969), p. 256. Further, Leon Goldstein has argued that there is an alternative between "realism" and relativism, one that avoids "subjectivist skepticisms" and "provides the criteria for historical truth." *Historical Knowing* (Austin: University of Texas Press, 1976), p. 61.

[14] Daniels, *Studying History*, p. 6.

[15] Dilthey, *Pattern and Meaning in History*, p. 154.

[16] Peter Gay and Gerald J. Cavanaugh, eds., *Historians at Work*, I: *Herodotus to Froissart* (New York: Harper and Row, 1972), p. 276.

Yet life allows the comfort of complete knowledge more to the ignorant than the thoughtful. We are not devoid of principles because we think, but in thinking we tend to reach our principles by a surer path. If we still lack conviction by thinking, we have nevertheless tried to work our way through issues and problems by considering all sides. The art of living thus is not divorced from the art of thinking. William Allen White had a "black abolition Republican" for a mother and a "Stephen Douglas Copperhead Democrat" for a father; no wonder he grew up and profited by that "certain lack of conviction which comes from seeing both sides well presented." [17]

Lack of conviction need not imply a lack of interest in truth. But truth is a rare commodity, and absolute historical truth the rarest. In writing of the Athenian leader Pericles, the biographer Plutarch paused to observe, "So very difficult a matter is it to trace and find out the truth of anything by history." [18] The root of Plutarch's problem, one that has bedeviled and tantalized historians before and since, is that history, in spite of the scientific claims made for it, is *humanistic*—by which we simply mean that it concerns the study of people. Different people, different angles of vision; yet disparity need not reduce history to chaos. Benjamin Franklin believed that "the opinions of men are almost as various as their faces; an observation general enough to become a common proverb, *So many men so many minds*." [19] To which we add, "So many histories, so many truths."

Obviously, on some issues some people think alike. This lessens the possibility of conflicting truths but does not resolve the problem. We again find ourselves on the relativity scale, but in a special dilemma. Ruth Benedict, as a young woman years away from her insightful anthropological writings, described the core of this dilemma with the anguish of a thinking person:

> The trouble with life isn't that there is no answer, it's that there are so many answers. There's the answer of Christ and of Buddha, of

[17] William Allen White, *The Autobiography of William Allen White* (New York: Macmillan, 1946), p. 61.

[18] *Plutarch's Lives*, trans. Dryden (New York: Modern Library, n.d.), p. 194. For an excellent case study of the problems of objectively discerning truth in history, in this instance involving the Dead Sea Scrolls, see Goldstein, *Historical Knowing*, pp. 93–137.

[19] Verner W. Crane, *Benjamin Franklin and a Rising People* (Boston: Little, Brown, 1954), p. 25.

Thomas à Kempis and of Elbert Hubbard, of Browning, Keats and of Spinoza, of Thoreau and of Walt Whitman, of Kant and of Theodore Roosevelt. By turns their answers fit my needs. And yet, because I am I and not any one of them, they can none of them be completely mine.[20]

The dilemma is that of choice, something rarely allowed by science. We do not choose between 3, 4, and 5 as the result of 2+2. But we do choose as to the answer to the question of the causes, actualities, and results of Napoleon's Egyptian Expedition in 1798. Often, historical choice is compounded as a dilemma because the alternatives offered us may be personally repugnant or in some way unsatisfying. Worse, historians may be forced by their evidence not merely to select and define a truth but to choose the truest truth or rate different truths as to their historical merit. The thoughtful reconciliation of these difficulties is the necessary art of history.

These troubles arise because the human being, the subject matter of humanistic thought and of our modern social sciences, will not remain an object. Psychologically and individually we resist classification, despite the claims of actuaries and other impediments to a sane life. Bishop Bossuet, court chaplain to Louis XIV, confidentially asserted that if one only knew how to fix the point "from which things have to be viewed," then all would be well, and wisdom would replace disorder. The great dream of Condorcet, one of the extreme rationalists of the Enlightenment, was a true mathematical science of man's past, based on statistics and probability.[21] The good bishop believed God underlay all history; the French mathematician, that mathematical laws could serve as explanation. Yet both of them sought forms of classification to explain the past.

Beyond the attempts to categorize us, we are in addition a tricky and deceitful lot. Carl Becker told a story that illustrates the point. It seems a team of anthropologists once debouched from an eastern university to study the customs of the Navajo Indians. In the field the experts found the Indians to be fully conversant with the latest anthropological theories and jargon, simply because they had been favored "objects" of study for years. Members of the

[20] Margaret Mead, *Ruth Benedict* (New York: Columbia University Press, 1974), p. 2.
[21] Bossuet quoted in Karl Löwith, *Meaning in History* (Chicago: University of Chicago Press, 1949), p. 137; Mazlish, *The Riddle of History*, p. 96.

tribe were quite willing to give the desired answers to questions as soon as they discerned the university (and hence the anthropological school of thought) the researchers represented.[22]

Becker formulated from examples like this the admittedly extreme relativist view that "the past will provide humanity with any fate you like to imagine. O History, how many truths have been committed in thy name!"[23] The variety of historical subjects is indeed infinite—an author note in a scholarly journal once informed the reader that the writer's most recent project was a history of the condom[24]—yet the importance of historical subjects will obviously vary. Although it might be fun to read of Josephine's dalliances while her husband was away in Egypt, there is no argument as to which events are the more historically relevant. *Does the relevance of an historical event influence the nature of its historical truth?*

Our initial question may be recalled as whether history is that which has been, or the reflection of what has been. Suppose we consider this question in the light of our discussion of historical truth. Two opposed possibilities immediately present themselves. First, there is the notion that historical facts of themselves are powerful enough, by virtue of their truth, to overwhelm the historian and pass through the pen to the reader virtually undistorted and undiluted. The second possibility elevates the historian to the position of final arbiter, both as to the nature of historical fact and the nature of historical truth in the arrangement of fact. In the first instance, historical facts make their own order, shaping themselves into coherent patterns. In the second instance, the historian creates historical order by a specific arrangement of the facts.[25] A partially scientific mode of thought impels the former instance; an artistic mode, the latter.

If the primary duty of the historian, in the philosopher R. G.

[22] Charlotte Watkins Smith, *Carl Becker: On History and the Climate of Opinion* (Carbondale: Southern Illinois University Press, 1973 [1956]), p. 204. My former colleague Parks Coble tells me a similar situation pertains with Hong Kong's perennial refugee population, the members of which have become adept at fielding the queries of American graduate students. One might quarrel that the subjects of historians are usually quite dead and thus not able to fool the researcher. Those who believe this have never seriously conducted historical research.

[23] Carl Becker, *Everyman His Own Historian: Essays on History and Politics* (Chicago: Quadrangle Books, 1966 [1935]), p. 169.

[24] *Journal of Popular Culture* 9 (Fall, 1975): 314.

[25] There are complexities of epistemology undiscussed here; I merely mean to stake out two opposing positions for consideration.

Collingwood's words, is a "willingness to bestow infinite pains on discovering what actually happened,"[26] then the delineation of what an historical fact actually consists of is clearly paramount. But what if the historian's primary duty lies elsewhere, in the interpretation of what the historical facts mean, or, more probably, in a combination of the two processes? One thing is certain: if the historian does not interpret, there are always others whose willingness to do so is matched only by their meager historical knowledge. At its most confined, historical order is considered to derive simply from fact alone. Such a view sometimes leads to historical "knowing" and antiquarianism, but by itself it is no substitute for historical thought, which has imbedded in it the interpretive instinct.

A distinction must be made, however, between the literary skills inherent in historical interpretation and the time-honored wish "to make history live." The great gentleman amateurs of nineteenth-century American historiography were widely and justly admired for their literary skills, by which is meant their ability to enable their readers to imagine that about which they were reading. But for a later literary critic and historian like Van Wyck Brooks, where giants like Prescott, Motley, and Parkman had "recreated" the past, the lesser mortals in their shadows could only describe and explain it.[27]

Although literary recreation is *a* mode of creating historical order, it is not *the* mode, except in the sense that it is that mode the author chooses. Prescott's Cortez is not the Cortez of other historians; Motley's Dutch Republic is seen differently by others; and Parkman's French and Indian War has its varying interpreters. Not all of these other historians, in addition, have selected narrative history as their vehicle. If the past comes alive, it comes alive in our minds, primarily through our appreciation of physical remains and the written or printed word. Any other "re-creation" is impossible, short of fiction.[28]

It is possible, however, merely to list things and create a kind of order, a chronology. But even such a list implies either choice

[26] R. G. Collingwood, *The Idea of History* (New York: Oxford University Press, 1956 [1946]), p. 55.

[27] Van Wyck Brooks, *New England: Indian Summer, 1865–1915* (New York: E. P. Dutton, 1940), p. 474.

[28] I have taken a specific philosophical stance here. The reader should be cautioned that an alternate construction would perceive reality as existing independently of the mind.

(since the compiler might choose to omit some facts and include others) or the limitations of research (since some historical facts are beyond retrieval). No one is any longer in a position to write an historical life of Jesus, for example. Compilers of lists are important, because they are engaged in making the building blocks of historical study. It is, nevertheless, a mistake to infer from this that somehow lists are neutral. Note the ideal of Ssǔ-ma Ch'ien, who modestly said in 100 B.C. of his own memoirs concerning Chinese history that "my narrative consists of no more than a systematization of the material that has been handed down to us. There is therefore no creation; only a faithful representation."[29] We would argue that in systematization there is creation; Ssǔ-ma was both more and less than an East Asian Fustel.

In the ideal, the proudest boast of most historians is their objectivity, though in reality they cannot escape completely the bonds of their own experience and culture.[30] Different cultural configurations will present differing senses of history. Thus, the authors of the Pali Chronicle of Ceylon had no clear notion of historical accuracy. To them, truth existed not so much in the event but in the intention behind the event, which might be religious, aesthetic, or emotional.[31]

The question is not so much how to prevent experience from hampering the historian's judgment; it is how the historian may make experience work for, not against, him. This is no empty challenge. The historian's responsibility to the past should be honorable and his attitude toward the present responsible, for Lord Byron's canto from *Don Juan* is always there, haunting:

> And glory long has made the sages
>   smile,
> 'Tis something, nothing, words, illusion,
>   wind—

[29] Günter Bornkamm, *Jesus of Nazareth*, trans. Irene and Fraser McLuskey, with James M. Robinson (New York: Harper and Row, 1975 [1956]), p. 13; Ssǔ-ma quoted in L. Carrington Goodrich, *A Short History of the Chinese People*, 3rd ed. (New York: Harper and Row, 1963 [1959]), p. 52.

[30] Even reliance on "common sense" is culture-bound. See in particular Murray G. Murphey, *Our Knowledge of the Historical Past* (Indianapolis: Bobbs-Merrill, 1973), p. 83.

[31] L. S. Perera, "The Pali Chronicle of Ceylon," in C. H. Philips, ed., *Historians of India, Pakistan and Ceylon* (London: Oxford University Press, 1961), pp. 37–38.

Depending more upon the historian's
    style
Than on the name a person leaves
    behind.

Experience and Historical Subjectivism

The world of experience is by definition subjective. Each of us
has made a life of mistakes, successes, triumphs, disasters, pleasure, and pain. We draw on the memories as we live, some conscious, some not. So do the historians—they must, since they, like
their subjects, are of the world of experience, not outside it.

Experience and knowledge are usually kept separate by
thinkers. The former usually symbolizes a more mundane, even
trivial, catalog of everyday living; but the latter is implicitly seen as
the product of intellectual processes, or "thought." In practice this
separation breaks down. Each of us is his own historian, in the
limited sense that one's personal experience is one's personal history. This is probably all Carl Becker meant when he used his famous phrase, "Everyman His Own Historian." When we think
about the past, we are in an equally limited sense "thinking history," and this history is "what we know it to be." [32] As knowledge,
and in contrast to what may have actually happened, it may be
continuously refined, increased, or (as arteries harden) decreased
as well.

Even if thinking can be isolated as a purely intellectual process, it is not the only resource aiding historical thought. In other
words, the act of thinking and the concept of historical thought do
not form a tautology. Memory, the storehouse of life's experience,
is always in the background—prodding, cajoling, instructing, testing—and often emerges at the most unexpected times. In the historian who is engaged with a topic, indifference is at least a lia-
bility and probably an impossibility. A historian's own experience
is the most important analytical tool; far from standing above the
battle, the historian participates—but with a difference. The historian tries to fight on all sides, then render judgment. Whether, as
Becker argued, a lack of disinterest is what makes a good historian
is a moot point; [33] but a good historian is a good thinker.

[32] Becker, *Everyman His Own Historian*, p. 234.
[33] Ibid., p. 244. Harold Nicolson has argued, apropos of biographical writing, that if "a biography is to come alive . . . there must exist between the artist

A humbler phrase to describe the quality of experience is "common sense." It has been claimed that sustained common sense has been the property of all great historians. Although such a term will not hold water as a complete definition of historical greatness, it is beyond doubt the saving grace of many historians and of other folk who think about history. "I was watchin' and listenin'," recalled "Nate Shaw" after his many decades sharecropping the southern land. "As the years come and go it leaves me with a better understandin' of history."[34]

A case may be made for experience as the historian's key to relevance; that is, personal experience makes the writing more relevant for oneself, if not for others. Hypothetically, the writer who has suffered a duodenal ulcer might give much more emphasis to Napoleon's stomach problems on the day of Waterloo. This does not mean such an analysis is right or wrong; historical balance is merely shifted to bring it into line with personal experience.[35] Experience may also help as it aids in formulating theory. There is nothing wrong with approaching historical questions theory first, so long as the theory does not bludgeon the evidence.

There is a major peril, however, in putting too much weight on experience alone. Inductive logic, a term used here to imply the overemphasis of personal experience in historical writing, has trapped many historians. Experience has the potential of becoming a handicap as well as an aid to historical thinking. It has been written that "the mind's bent to make much out of little is, of course, the secret of human genius."[36] Perhaps; yet caution and prudence, if not the hallmarks of genius, are nevertheless attributes of the skilled historian.

If man is the measure of all things, then let us say with Prescott that man's understanding must be ripened by reflection

---

and his sitter something more than ordinary interest, something more even than respect; there must exist ardent sympathy." See his Introduction to Christopher Hobhouse, *Fox*, 2nd ed. (London: John Murray, 1947), p. xxii.

[34] Jacques Barzun, *Clio and the Doctors: Psycho-History, Quanto-History, and History* (Chicago: University of Chicago Press, 1974), p. 103; "Shaw" quoted in Theodore Rosengarten, *All God's Dangers: The Life of Nate Shaw* (New York: Avon Books, 1975), p. 37.

[35] See Smith, *Carl Becker*, p. 53, for Becker on this point; for a specific example of experience belying the statements of trained historians, in this case over the condition of post–World War II Europe, see Henry Fairlie, *The Kennedy Promise* (New York: Dell Publishing, 1974), p. 102.

[36] Harold R. Isaacs, *Images of Asia: American Views of China and India* (New York: Harper and Row, 1972 [1958]), p. 380.

and experience. "Poets may be born, but historians are made."[37] The phrase remains salient, although in Prescott's case it is somewhat ironic, since he never visited the scenes of his vivid histories of Mexico or Peru. The "making" of an historical prodigy is almost unknown. Gauss, Mozart, and their like were maturing in their fields of interest (math for Gauss, music for Mozart) before the age of ten. Many of the great discoveries in modern science, such as relativity or DNA, have been made by individuals not too far removed from their teens. But the sort of experience needed by the historian takes time to acquire—flashes of insight may occur, of course—but in general, history and its practitioners must be geared for the long haul.

Modern scientific rationalism has convinced many that man is more the master than the measure of all things. The suspicion lingers that historical writing often overreaches itself in its pretense to be scientific. Therein lurks the notion that history is akin to a solid mass of digestible knowledge, a giant cheese with assiduous seekers of the truth endlessly gnawing at its contours. Hence the current stress on "method," or how one approaches and chews the cheese. Historians overly concerned with method, whether they be quantifiers, "psycho-historians," or what-have-you, at times let their approach shape their material, rather than vice versa.[38]

We will look at the problem from the differing perspectives of two men, one a household word, the other, in the vernacular of the popular culture, a complete unknown. The unknown is the Italian-born philosopher and anti-Fascist Benedetto Croce; while he is widely read in history and philosophy circles, Croce is an excellent example of an intellectual whose thought does not percolate down to the masses. The household word is sportscaster Howard Cosell, whose voice and manner are well known to contemporary American sports fans. Where Croce moved skillfully through his examinations of the philosophy of history on a continuously high intellectual plane, Cosell has become "known" primarily through his exposure in the national media. The latter's most obnoxious phrase, "telling it like it is," may be taken to be the most complete vulgarization of the scientific view of history.

On the side of Cosell is certainty, the pretense to honesty, and

[37] C. Harvey Gardiner, *William Hickling Prescott: A Biography* (Austin: University of Texas Press, 1969), p. 67.

[38] For extended comment on the drawbacks of letting "method" dominate conceptualizations in history, see Barzun, *Clio and the Doctors*, pp. 39–41, 56.

the claim of omniscience. These are all components of the complete scientific view of history, although they have been thoroughly debased in the modern popular culture. Against this endless barrage of media-supported platitudes Croce, who died in 1952, could have offered only uncertainty. "There is no history that completely satisfies us," he once wrote, "because any construction of ours generates new facts and new problems and solicits new solutions."[39] In Croce's historical world there are no secrets, no keys to wisdom—only an endless quest defined by thought. While human mental processes still retain the necessary air of mystery, nothing can ever be "the way it is" except to the perceiving individual. When Becker said that our history was "what we know it to be," he did not mean that his history was our history. Cosell's offense against our reason is not his boorishness but his shallow conviction that through his courageous efforts a contemporary "truth" is being created for all of us. There is no room in this vision for "the *ways* it is."

It should be noted in our remarks on this odd couple that no artificial definition between the worlds of history and journalism is intended. Cosell does not represent contemporary journalism any more than Croce is the only voice of modern historical thought. But perceptive practitioners of journalism, which for our purposes might be called immediate history, would agree with Norman Mailer that there is no history without nuance.[40] In turn, this implies that history, whatever shape it takes, cannot in itself become *absolute*—that is, complete, final, and forever. The search, in Becker's thinking, is not to tell it like it is but to seek truer truths on the relative scale of judgment.[41]

Withal, such statements do not necessarily detract from the plausibility of historical order, so long as it is recognized that such order is always personalized and subjective to a greater or lesser degree. Truth may be relative; this does not mean it cannot be distinguished from that which is either false or not true. In this act of discernment lies the limiting principles of subjective historical thought. A man who has perceived more than most concerning the

---

[39] Benedetto Croce, *History: Its Theory and Practice*, trans. Douglas Ainslie (New York: Russell and Russell, 1920), p. 46. I have eliminated the obvious Hegelian analysis of such a view, which would bore the experienced reader and needlessly puzzle the novice.

[40] Norman Mailer, *Miami and the Siege of Chicago* (New York: Signet Books, 1968), p. 56.

[41] Smith, *Carl Becker*, p. 110.

historical problem of slavery, David Brion Davis, has correctly noted that "there must be some limits, after all, to what a culture can allow one to perceive."[42] But our cultures do not thereby necessarily bind us to falsities on our judgment scale. Though we cannot transcend our humanity, we yet may move outside our culture; in this possibility lies the saving grace of objective historical thought.[43]

Historical order is, then, pattern without doctrine and system without dogma. Practicality, common sense, empiricism, experience—all play an indispensable role in its creation. Each of us has our notion of order; it is part of our humanity. But according to his critics, Becker stretched things too far when he created the paradigm of Mr. Everyman settling his coal bill as an example of the performance of all the essential operations involved in historical research. How one quarries does not wholly define the mining operation. It is what is done with the product, as well as the operations that produce the product, that counts. "If Mr. Everyman had undertaken these researches in order to write a book instead of to pay a bill," claimed Becker, "no one would think of denying that he was an historian."[44] Given the subject and the lack of analysis, not so—Mr. Everyman would be either a charlatan or a fool.

Becker also infuriated many practitioners of his craft when he further asserted that the secret of historical success was not to repeat the past but to use it. "We are surely under bond to be as honest and intelligent as human frailty permits, but [the secret] in the long run is in conforming to the temper of Mr. Everyman, which we seem to guide only because we are so sure, eventually, to follow it."[45] Perhaps he was trying to say, in his gentle way, that the historian, like Mr. Everyman, is a prisoner of the human condition.

Where Becker's stance freely admits, and even glories in, the cultural bonds that limit objective history, his position has been described as a dilemma. That is, if cultural bonds (of which the overworked and vague phrase "climate of opinion" forms a part)

[42] David Brion Davis, *The Problem of Slavery in the Age of Revolution*, 1770–1823 (Ithaca, N.Y.: Cornell University Press, 1975), p. 280, n. 40.

[43] Of course, for an historian to examine a culture other than his own intensifies the problems under discussion. Increased familiarity (experience) may produce better critical analysis. But then again. . . .

[44] The most available source of Becker's classic essay "Everyman His Own Historian" is in Becker, *Everyman His Own Historian*, pp. 233–55. See in particular p. 239.

[45] Ibid., p. 253.

make historians time-bound, their visions of the past are necessarily bankrupt in terms of understanding.[46] Clearly, researchers
who realize their own culturally induced biases are a step ahead of
the game. They would like to lessen the subjective qualities in their
creation of historical order, and self-recognition in this sense sig-
nifies introspection of a high and reasonably honest level. *Is it possible for historians to transcend their culture and fairly judge a past
period independently of their own?*

The problems of relativism, subjectivity, and the limits of cultural transcendence are important and omnipresent. Taken to their
logical ends, they bring a cessation of historical thought or, in a
word, chaos. Such a result runs directly counter to the rational side
of human nature, and thus historical order becomes not only a
possible but a necessary part of the human condition. Without order, no comprehension; without comprehension, no sense of yesterday; without yesterday, a bewildering and perhaps terrifying
today.

[46] See, for example, Strout, *The Pragmatic Revolt in American History*,
pp. 42–43, 83. Strout sees Becker as bedeviled by the impotence of pragmatic
relativism as a basis for his liberal creed and by the weakness of his philosophy as
a guide to history (p. 130). It is possible that Strout has confused Becker's gentle
curiosity and skepticism with a lack of historical virility.

CHAPTER THREE

The Outlines of Historical Order

The necessity for historical order does not in itself define the nature of that order. As one might expect, given the subjectivity of historical thought, the approaches to this problem vary. The possibilities, though several, are not without limit either in number or potential, but they all share a fundamental organizing principle: the concept of time.

Time and Historical Order

The human past should at the minimum make sense to the present, else history in every way becomes useless. This urge to reason amounts almost to a psychological imperative, a deeply sensed desire to shape what has already happened into coherent patterns. We insist that our histories appear in a definite form—a form, in the words of a leading universal historian, that contains elements that are "calculable, definable, and, often, controllable as well."[1]

The form, whatever its final shape, rests on the fundamental concept, time. To most of western civilization, at least, time has been the basic organizing principle of history for millennia. In fact, many thinkers consider the concepts of time and history to be so interlinked as to be inseparable. An initiation to historical reading means an introduction—not to personal memory or to a sense of time, but to historical time, the kind of time that gives the past

[1] William H. McNeill, *Plagues and Peoples* (Garden City, N.Y.: Anchor Press, 1976), p. 4.

dimension in relation to the present. Historical time is relatively brief. The time scale of recorded human activity pales alongside the span of geological time, yet we may understand the latter in a temporal sense as well. An eon may provide order as well as an hour, though neither in itself comprises thinking. Edward Gibbon's "vague and multifarious" reading as a youth did not teach him to think, but it did give him "an early and rational application to the order of time and place."[2]

Though often regarded by physicists and science fiction writers as the fourth dimension, time is of a somewhat different concern to historians. Physicists usually have agreed on standards for measuring time. For years this standard was the rate of the earth's rotation on its axis. After some vicissitudes, the vibration rate of the cesium atom became generally accepted. Historical time elicits no such standard of agreement. Humans have a sense of time that we, in our subjective certainty, claim elevates us above all other species. Lower orders of animals (we think) are timeless. They have no idea of a past beyond their own, they live only in an eternal present, and beyond instinct they have no inkling of their own mortality. On the other hand, people carry a sense of past, present, and future with them always. Because of this sense of time, it is appropriate to say that we live *within* rather than outside history.

At first glance such a basic organizing principle might appear the one truly objective component of historical order. Yet, given our previous discussion, it should come as no surprise that to a great degree we have invented time for our own uses. We share a sense of the flow of events, a pattern we divide into "before," "now," and "after." These impressions can be quantified: into hours, into mathematical formulas, into measurement.

The possibility of quantification gives us a notion of objectivity, yet the conceptualization of time is in itself subjective, developed by us to provide order for our world. Different cultures keep time in different ways; the fact that western civilizations have impressed their sense of time (B.C., A.D., and all that) on other cultures should not blind us to the essential subjectivity of the concept. We are used to the time-scale of Christianity, which reckons time from a central event with both a "before" and an "after." But

<hr>

[2]Jacques Barzun, *Clio and the Doctors: Psycho-History, Quanto-History, and History* (Chicago: University of Chicago Press, 1974), pp. 92–93; Edward Gibbon, *Memoirs of My Life*, ed. Georges Bonnard (New York: Funk and Wagnalls, 1969), p. 43.

pagan history reckoned time from a beginning, usually a foundation story, like the tale of Romulus and Remus. The scales used to measure time have differed as well. The Chinese, for example, have not traditionally counted time by centuries; their historical divisions have instead been keyed to the ruling periods of dynasties. Julius Caesar noticed that the Gauls, based on Druidic teaching, measured their intervals of time in nights rather than days.[3]

Because of this subjectivity, it is by no means certain that time is an indispensable prerequisite to history. This doubt runs contrary to our common sense; it is difficult to perceive how thinking of the past may be sustained without the concept of time. We might fudge this difficulty by noting that in the cultures of the West the passage of time has usually connoted change. Yesterday was different from today, as today differs from what tomorrow will be. But suppose some cultures, some people, may deny the possibility of change, on whatever grounds. Yesterday was as today, and so will be tomorrow. Thus, to examine today is to examine yesterday.

Even so, the critical reader might observe, yet humans are themselves temporal; man lives and dies in time and has an individuality that cannot be recovered except by a sense of the past. The response might be that human qualities are changeless. The individual counts for little, but the species is perpetual. History might thus be separated from time as an organizing principle. To be sure, this is not the way we see it in our culture. *Is it possible that history may be examined without a sense of time?*

To us the essential use of time is to provide pattern and order for our lives and to support our sense of both past and future. To cultures infused with myth and the qualities of the irrational (common to all cultures but not dominant in all), time does not have these dimensions—or, it is more correct to say, time as a mental construct may contain all these dimensions at once. But we, culture-bound as we are, regard time as having a linear dimension, moving from past through present to future.

Historians deal with this linear dimension as they choose or as their evidence suggests, or both. At one end of the spectrum a universal historian like William H. McNeill might sweep over whole

[3] Jeremy Bernstein, *Einstein* (New York: Viking Press, 1973), p. 58; Peter Gay and Gerald J. Cavanaugh, eds., *Historians at Work*, I: *Herodotus to Froissart* (New York: Harper and Row, 1972), p. 147. For the discovery of the concept of time, see the intriguing work by David S. Landes, *Revolution in Time: Clocks and the Making of the Modern World* (Cambridge: Harvard University Press, 1983), esp. pp. 1-82.

centuries in a few paragraphs. At the other end, a popular historian like Jim Bishop might gain an audience by dramatically analyzing only one day, such as the day Abraham Lincoln was assassinated.[4]

The inevitable problem historians face in this regard is that by choosing their time frame, they have unavoidably given order to their vision. The solitary thinker must then decide what components of a time frame made it unique—for if the frame is not unique in important ways, it is difficult to find justification for its use. Often these time frames become chiseled in granite and loom as massive obstacles rather than friendly guideposts for the dedicated researcher. "Dark Ages," "Napoleonic Era," and the "Age of Jackson" are a few of the better known examples. "It is the most serious difficulty of the history of civilization," remarked the brilliant Swiss historian Jacob Burkhardt, "that a great intellectual process must be broken up into single, and often into what seem arbitrary, categories in order to be in any way intelligible."[5]

The editor of a survey of the American 1950s has claimed that recent presidential administrations "possessed a personality that . . . remained unique and identifiable."[6] Americans have had a tendency to write their history in time frames consonant with presidential terms. Put another way, political leadership many times has determined the choice of time frame. We might ponder if the uniqueness claimed for these presidential administrations is possessed by broader patterns of culture as well; further, if political life should provide the primary skeleton for historical time frames.

Terms such as "watershed," when used historically, set off differing time frames from one another. Given the unilinearity of time, the watershed concept implies that before the watershed, the basic components of historical description tend to differ from those used after. American history in particular is so full of these subjective divisions it often seems the nation is in full flood. The American Revolution, the Civil War, the decade of the 1890s—

---

[4]See, for example, William H. McNeill, *The Rise of the West: A History of the Human Community* (Chicago: University of Chicago Press, 1963) and Jim Bishop, *The Day Lincoln Was Shot* (New York: Harper and Row, 1955) for these different forms of ordering the unilinearity of time.

[5]Peter Gay and Victor G. Wexler, eds., *Historians at Work*, III: *Niebuhr to Maitland* (New York: Harper and Row, 1975), p. 157.

[6]Warren F. Kimball, Foreword to Charles C. Alexander, *Holding the Line: The Eisenhower Era, 1952–1961* (Bloomington: Indiana University Press, 1975), p. xi.

take your pick, each period has its adherents. September 3, 1929, the day bullishness on the stock market reached its height, has been described as one of the great divides of national history.[7] On the one side, the hedonistic and optimistic bustle of the 1920s; on the other, the gloom, inertia, and frightening uncertainty of economic depression. The decade of the American 1920s, in fact, exists in a time-frame pocket all its own: Jazz Age, Aspirin Age, Era of Wonderful Nonsense, Dry Decade—the descriptions are endless and indicate a choice marriage between a given time frame and the opportunities for bold, incisive historical description.

With such a welter of possibilities, the problem of sorting out the relative importance of differing time frames is obvious. For many years, the study of Puritan America was regarded in some circles as a tedious bore, until the revivification of Puritan Studies during the last four decades. Louis XIV, the Sun King of France, possesses along with his reign endless fascination, whereas the reigns of lesser lights, such as that of his great-grandson, Louis XV, have not had the same attention. Differing emphases like these, though seemingly natural in relation to the ebb and flow of human affairs, have not met with approval in all quarters. Benedetto Croce, for one, believed that every historical fact and every historical epoch was productive in its own way. All ages, all time frames, as it were, should thus be "praised and venerated." A fact or an epoch that is repugnant or condemned was, to Croce, beneath history: "Hardly even the premise of a historical problem to be formulated."[8] He probably meant by this only that as we share our humanity with those who have lived before us, by denigrating them and their time we only debase ourselves.

Units of time are basic, then, to our conceptions of order. By themselves, they have no value, as when some rash fellow might make a claim that the period 1861–65 was "worse" than 1941–45, and leave it at that. What counts is what gives shape and texture to the time frame: the human action within it.

[7] Frederick Lewis Allen, *Since Yesterday: The 1930's in America, September 3, 1929–September 3, 1939* (New York: Harper and Row, 1972 [1939]), pp. 8, 105. For a specific historiographical example of this type of order, see Richard S. Kirkendall, "The New Deal as Watershed: The Recent Literature," *Journal of American History* 54, no. 4 (March, 1968): 829–52. For a general analysis, see Marcus Cunliffe, "American Watersheds," *American Quarterly* 13 (Winter, 1961): 480–94.

[8] Benedetto Croce, *History: Its Theory and Practice*, trans. Douglas Ainslie (New York: Russell and Russell, 1920), pp. 90–91.

Some Possibilities of Historical Order

We will hold in abeyance the consideration of the *movement* of history, sometimes called history as process. Presently we are concerned with some basic (and differing) conceptions of what shape history might take as a static consideration.

The initial possibility might be the nihilistic one that time frames are meaningless skeletons upon which to build order, for history itself is unordered. Further, the past is beyond the possibility of being ordered either by its inhabitants or by ourselves; it defies any conceptualization whatsoever. The past is chaos, its pattern and meaning perpetually unclear. To admit this possibility is of course to negate historical function. Historians selecting this alternative would be engaging in a contradiction in terms, but they would still be thinking about history, if only in a negative sense.

A second possibility is that history, seen in the broadest sense, is cyclical. The components of its time frames (or any other form of organization) recur in a periodic fashion. The concept of *organicism* is usually, although not always, implicit in this view. The themes and evidentiary material commonly mentioned to "prove" the cyclic possibility are those that describe the rise, apogee, decline, and fall of civilizations. One growing, healthy culture conquers an older, decadent one, and then it in its turn grows old and falls prey to the next virile aggressor. The "cycle" appears very much like the life of one person, which is understandably finite and periodicized. Thus civilizations, perceived in various "stages," have been described as "infant," "young," "mature," and "old." The themes of birth, growth, decay, and death are the elements that usually define the cyclical time frame.

In the first instance, seeing history as a succession of cycles conjures up the hoary idea of history repeating itself. The repetition notion is the most extreme variant of the cyclical view, but it is by no means the only or even the prevalent one. In other instances, historians have seen elements of cycles occurring in differing civilizations, but these cycles have different starting and ending points and differing components within their respective time frames. Thus, the cycles are not identical. For example, the decline of the Roman Empire took place amidst a European scene vastly different from that which accompanied the decline of the Ottoman Empire some 1,500 years later. Although the two events may in no way be described as identical in their entirety, some analysts might see a certain cyclical identity in the similar organic situations of decay and death.

Yet another possibility is that the structure of history, being perceived as unilinear, permits history to develop in only one direction. Not only does history not circle back upon itself, it continually carves out new paths into the future. The directions these paths take may be considered as predetermined, or only dimly sensed, or fatalistically awaited. But for those who think about history in this guise, the past is past. Though it serves as the foundation for the future, it can never be regained in actuality.

A culture may perceive its history as developing in different directions through time. Islam, for instance, sees its past in the structure of a mountain, ascending through prophets like Adam, Moses, and Jesus to the pinnacle represented by Muhammad. The descent follows from the early generation of the great conquests to the barbarous influx of the Mongols from the East and the Crusaders from the West. But for the faithful, the mountain may be climbed again.

It would be a grim business if the direction in which history tended was downward, or backward, or on some other pessimistically oriented heading. Some moderns, looking at such gifts of recent technology as mass crematoria and nuclear weapons, have reasoned precisely so. The prevailing view, however, in the western world at least, has for over two centuries seen history as equivalent to progress. Progress may be defined in many ways, but it usually has been linked to a materialism based on technological improvement and to the achievement of a higher collective standard of living. This advance may be variously realized or rationalized (economic competition, war, state regulation of some kind), but however it is achieved, the presence of the progress ideal means that history, like fine wine and sex, improves with age. Here is an optimistic view of historical order; whatever has been is inferior to whatever lies around the corner.

Each of these possibilities leads to further options. One might snatch a smidgeon of order from an unwieldy chaos, or define cycles in a wide variety of ways, or despite the vicissitudes of war and economic cataclysm still see the sun of progress shining over all. But essentially the reconciliation of any of these three modes of thought is most difficult. In the words of Charles Beard, historians make an "act of faith" when they choose their frame of reference.[9] Most historical writing in recent centuries has clung to the idea that history, whatever it is, appears to move onward and upward,

[9] Charles Beard, "Written History as an Act of Faith," *American Historical Review* 39, No. 2 (Jan., 1934): 219–29.

bearing a perhaps unrepentant human race with it. But optimism is the child of good times, and so, too, are many optimistic histories. The world wars of the twentieth century have influenced a dilution of this trend.

Although history may fall into patterns after the fact, its component events as they occur might rest only on chance. History in this guise is thus seen as a form of dice rolling, with an infinite number of dots on each die. Late in his life the psychologist A. A. Brill remarked that "whatever we did depended, not as we think, on ourselves, but on accidental factors which we ourselves did not control." "History, instead of being governed by reason and providence, seems to be governed by chance and by fate," glumly concluded an examination of meaning in history.[10] Uncertainty is elevated into a principle, and with it comes a fatalism delineated more fully by novelists than historians. Accept fate, for it cannot be controlled.

On the other hand, human free will may actually inhibit historical order. Only the action of forces outside the control of the individual, in this view, gives shape to the past. Otherwise, myriad discrete human atoms, all operating to different purposes, would leave historical order in such ruins as to be beyond retrieval. "If the will of every man were free, that is, if every man could act as he chose," wrote Tolstoy in *War and Peace*, "the whole of history would be a tissue of disconnected accidents."

Beyond these fundamentally philosophical variants of order, more mundane patterns are possible. Historical study has been described as having three dimensions: chronological, geographical, and topical.[11] These dimensions might often overlap. Napoleon's expedition to Egypt in 1798 may be marked by chronology (the year 1798), by geography (the French invading Egypt by sailing across the Mediterranean), and by topic (the fact of the expedition itself). Chronology simply orders historical information and divides history into discrete units of time. Geography classifies history by location or territory. Topical history concentrates on human action and enables historical study to specialize—to study diplomacy, economics, religion, or any other shred of the past

---

[10] Brill quoted in Nathan G. Hale, Jr., *Freud and the Americans: The Beginnings of Psychoanalysis in the United States, 1876–1917* (New York: Oxford University Press, 1971), p. 396; Karl Löwith, *Meaning in History* (Chicago: University of Chicago Press, 1949), p. 199.

[11] Robert V. Daniels, *Studying History: How and Why*, 2nd ed. (Englewood Cliffs, N.J.: Prentice-Hall, 1972), pp. 57–58.

imaginable. All of these are modes of historical order; their selection or combination by the historian also implies choice, although the choice does not impose the philosophical problems implicit in Beard's "act of faith."

All this is a thorny business, difficult to grasp and in many ways intellectually painful to contemplate. It would be nice if history possessed an "inner logic" that we could objectively discover and evaluate. We have already denied this premise on subjective grounds, but what if we are (1) wrong or (2) lying to you? Some very fine minds have induced precisely such order in history. The possibility that historical order is logical and systematic has piqued the interest of thinkers for hundreds of years.

Today, the view of history as a system has very few takers and even fewer proselytes. A system must operate logically to operate at all, yet relativists like Carl Becker have sneered at such a possibility. Though there may be a very interesting history of logic, Becker claimed, there most certainly was no logic of history. Most contemporaries probably take a middle ground, such as that staked out by Jacques Barzun: "The principal effect of history is to show the past not as orderly and logical but as a confusion that up to a point can be sorted out and understood." [12] Unfortunately, especially in textbooks, the aspect of confusion often becomes buried, and history appears to possess an inherent logical pattern.

Until very recently in the recorded past of western civilization, probably the most common appreciation of an inner logic for history held that a divine plan of some sort underlay the unfolding patterns of existence. Both unity and continuity were provided by a master hand. This view requires faith, and more than a bit of fatalism as well, but its logic is inherently rational.

Historical research could be reconciled with faith by arguing that research discoveries merely reveal the divine plan, or such parts as the Maker permits. George Bancroft's work was largely a product of this thought. "Things proceed as they were ordered, in their nice, and well-adjusted, and perfect harmony," he observed. "As the hand of the skillful artist gathers music from the harpstrings, history gathers it from the well-tuned chord of time." Bancroft's goal was that "historic truth may establish itself as a science" and that by this careful, rigorous method, "the principles

[12] Charlotte Watkins Smith, *Carl Becker: On History and the Climate of Opinion* (Carbondale: Southern Illinois University Press, 1973 [1956]), p. 47; Barzun, *Clio and the Doctors*, p. 98.

that govern human affairs, extending like a path of light from century to century, become the highest demonstration of the superintending providence of God." Even Ranke, prime mover of the scientific approach to research, believed in the presence of God in history. "I am certain of the omnipresence of God and think that one can grasp him definitely with one's hands," he wrote at an early age to his clerical brother. "In my present mood I swear to myself a thousand times that I shall spend my life in the fear of God and in history." [13]

Although the ideal of Bancroft and Ranke, two very different types of historians, was a common one in modern Christian cultures, and stripped of its scientific rationalism an even more common outlook in medieval times, it is a mistake to assume that divine order is a product of Christianity. Many ancient cultures saw divine wishes in history and in everyday affairs. A culture does not have to espouse monotheism to believe in divine order, either. An entire pantheon of gods may be assigned responsibility for events on earth. The notion of divine order is independent of any particular religion or form of religious practice. Call the Master God, Jehovah, Allah, or the combined residents of Olympus, the principle still holds.

Cultures in which religion was a central binding force usually depended on analyses of divine plans for the sense of their past as well as auguries of their future. These emanations did not necessarily rest solely on a mythical or metaphysical base. Mustafa Naima Efendi, one of the most skilled of the court historians to the Ottoman Sultan, wrote early in the eighteenth century that foolish statements and spurious tales were not the stuff of history. "Historians ought first to inform themselves, from those who have proper information concerning the question at hand, of what was the divinely ordained condition of any age in history." [14]

An inner logic based on humans, not on spiritual mysteries, developed with the growing rationalism of the modern world. Organicism as historical logic was known to the ancients, but it was usually sublimated to divine plans. In more recent times, it became common to compare history with the stages of development in the

[13] Bancroft quoted in Russel B. Nye, *George Bancroft* (New York: Washington Square Press, 1964), p. 155; Ranke quoted in Leonard Krieger, *Ranke: The Meaning of History* (Chicago: University of Chicago Press, 1977), p. 26.

[14] Stanford J. Shaw, *History of the Ottoman Empire and Modern Turkey*, I: *Empire of the Gazis: The Rise and Decline of the Ottoman Empire, 1280–1808* (New York: Cambridge University Press, 1976), p. 289.

individual. These stages are not so much willed by external power as they are a product of "natural" forces. Just as humans are born, age, and pass away, so too do civilizations follow the organic chain of birth, life, and death. The task of the historian in this case is not to discern divine will but to determine where in this organic spectrum the subject of analysis best fits.

The basic objection to schemes of divine or organic order, or any other objective pattern of historical logic, is of course their contention that the periodization of history is somehow external, natural, and independent of human perception.[15] This objection is avoided in a third pattern of order, which argues that events impress themselves so powerfully on the historian that their pattern in itself compels inner logic. The historian does not respond to spiritual or organicist blueprints, but nevertheless must order the narrative, or story, as the logic of events dictates.

Here is a conception that conceives history as a tunnel, and a very narrow one at that. Many of those who pursue the art of historical narrative have admitted that in practice trying to heed the gentle whisper of historical events saying "place me here," "I go before this," "I caused that," and so on, might be a good thing for mediums, but not for historians. Frederick Lewis Allen, one of the more adept practitioners of the craft, frankly confessed that if he could figure out a way to write several stories at once and construct them in parallel columns so some special human brain could follow all of the threads in the stories at the same time, then he might have a chance to help the reader sense the multiplicity, heterogeneity, and simultaneity of events. It would be simpler, sighed John Hicks, if historical synthesis (the art of tying all the threads into a coherent narrative web) could follow the example of a symphony orchestra, where various instruments of different tonal qualities blend together to produce a harmonious whole. Narrative history, he concluded, was necessarily unitonal.[16] We would add this need not imply it is monotonal as well.

Obviously one's own patterns of thought and belief play a significant role in the decision to select or deny various patterns of historical order. The decision is an important one, for without our own ideas of order, we have no really basic conceptions of history

---

[15] See Croce, *History: Its Theory and Practice*, p. 115, for this type of rebuttal.

[16] Allen, *Since Yesterday*, p. 241; John Hicks, *My Life with History: An Autobiography* (Lincoln: University of Nebraska Press, 1968), p. 166.

upon which to build. *Is there an "inner logic" of history? How would one go about proving or disproving such an assertion?*

The Limits of Historical Order

As we have noted, it is difficult to deny historical order, else chaos ensues. Once established, such a concept simply eludes final definition, just as does "history" itself. Yet it is possible to hedge the thing in a bit or, to use current jargon, to establish parameters. History with too much order is generally history that in some way has been tortured into shape.

Order, once admitted, transcends the irrational. One may readily concede the element of the irrational in human nature while noting the urge to rationalize past events. "The historian's compulsion is the passion for pattern," Arthur Schlesinger, Jr., has noted.[17] The peril lies not in the possibility of order, for that is necessity itself, but in extending types of order in such ways as to blot out alternatives. A rigid scheme tends to invite historians to pigeonhole their evidence, to fit it to a dominant conceptualization. Such schemes often sow the seeds of their own destruction.

The historian hopes, in approaching a subject, that it will lend itself to rational explanation. For some, the feeling may be more than hope—a deep-seated psychological need, intensely personal, for patterns to emerge. Recalcitrant evidence may thus be overridden and made to speak in the voice of the historian-ventriloquist. This is one of the perils of utilizing "models" of historical behavior. Economic historians in particular have accomplished much fruitful analysis using a modular approach (testing their evidence against the model as a measure of historical truth), but in general the use of models is at present limited to conceptualizations of historical problems.

At their most extreme, these hopes and needs for pattern freeze into system, where theory masters fact in the contest for knowledge. "Closed" systems—those that have a beginning, an end, and a rational, causal connection between the two—necessarily exclude competing theories. They either accept historical facts on the system's own terms or reject the facts as incompatible

[17] Arthur Schlesinger, Jr., "The Historian as Participant," *Daedalus* 100, no. 2 (Spring, 1971): 354.

with the fundamental assumptions of the system. Benedetto Croce might charge that closed systems are "cosmological romances,"[18] yet these romances have been alluring enough to entice some of the finest minds in recent centuries: Kant, Hegel, and Marx, to name only a few.

The historian who believes in a system of some type is placed in a quandary when evidence pops up that does not seem to fit the system. The choices then become: (1) ignore the evidence, hardly appropriate action for an historian; (2) fit the evidence to the scheme of the system, in which case theory bears the burden of rational explanation; (3) reshape the system to account for the evidence, in which case the binding elements of the system may be shattered; or (4) destroy the system and build anew with the fresh evidence, not necessarily in a systematic way. "Everything happens in life," as Van Wyck Brooks has observed, "but an author reveals his tendency in his habitual choice of the things that happen."[19]

In confronting a past stripped to the bare bones of reasoning, those who think about history are virtually forced to choose the skeleton of order on which to build their ideas. Isaiah Berlin, in a justifiably well-known essay, quotes a line from the fragments of the Greek poet Archilochus to the effect that while the sum of the hedgehog's knowledge is one big thing, the fox knows many things. Berlin goes on majestically to divide the world of historical reasoning between the hedgehogs and the foxes, between those who on the one hand relate every historical event to a single unifying vision and those who manifest "scattered and diffused" thought, contradictory and disconnected though it may be.[20] Berlin identifies such diverse figures as Dante, Plato, and Ibsen as hedgehogs; Shakespeare, Montaigne, and Erasmus are foxes.

Whether we choose to accept this colorful nomenclature or not, we note that Berlin intended the hedgehog and the fox to serve as suggestive symbols, not as archetypes. Some historical thinkers, like the novelist Tolstoy, might realistically be foxes but yearn for the unifying vision that would make them hedgehogs. There is perhaps a bit of hedgehog and a bit of fox in every vision

[18] Croce, *History: Its Theory and Practice*, p. 62.

[19] Van Wyck Brooks, *New England: Indian Summer, 1865–1915* (New York: E. P. Dutton, 1940), p. 383.

[20] Isaiah Berlin, *The Hedgehog and the Fox: An Essay on Tolstoy's View of History* (New York: Simon and Schuster, 1970), pp. 1–2. The entire essay well repays careful reading, even if the reader does something less than nod agreement.

of historical order, but on principle the basic choice is still there, commanding attention and placing limits on the nature of the order itself.

The possibility of some sort of natural order in history is tantalizing in the extreme. We might get our own inclinations mixed up with conceptions of natural order, as did the noted American historian J. Franklin Jameson when he described American historiography as falling "naturally" into four periods. Jameson went on to argue that these four time frames held true whether we regarded historical writing as literary or as scientific; in other words, the time frames were independent of interpretation. Likewise, as she assembled the materials that were to become the highly regarded *Patterns of Culture*, anthropologist Ruth Benedict expressed amazement as to "how all the points I've worked on all fall into the same outline." [21]

The mistake is in confusing the natural order subjectivism often provides with the wish for the one objective truth. We do not know if Jameson and Benedict made this mistake in the cases cited, although it is most unlikely that they did. But the temptation to see the mirror-image of our own rationality stamped on the human action around us is strong. "To him who looks upon the world rationally," intoned Hegel, "the world in its turn presents a rational aspect." [22] For different visions of order, different reflections of order.

Indeed, the same mind harbors different orders of history. Consider the specialist on Napoleon. He is familiar with the Egyptian Expedition, probably in many instances to the day and the hour. But this same individual may maintain only a casual interest in, say, the history of the Byzantine Empire. Here his order is framed by centuries, not days and hours, and punctuated by memorable events, such as the fall of Constantinople to the Ottoman Turks in 1453. Further, the same mind may harbor differing orders concerning the same subject. For example, a recent analysis of France has argued that early modern France may be described both as a part of the growing Atlantic commercial economy and as

[21] J. Franklin Jameson, *The History of Historical Writing in America* (Boston: Houghton Mifflin, 1891), pp. 1–2; Margaret Mead, *Ruth Benedict* (New York: Columbia University Press, 1974), p. 39.

[22] Georg Wilhelm Friedrich Hegel, *The Philosophy of History*, trans. J. Sibree (New York: Dover Publications, 1956), p. 11.

a monarchical society.[23] Such complexity need not imply confusion, but it does circumscribe the chances for the one big vision.

Moderation and uncertainty tend to make the historian duller than usual, in spite of the fact that the rashest statement generally attracts the largest audience. But caution should precede reflection: "The beginning of wisdom is a sense of proportion."[24] A rigid scheme of historical order is a stifling influence, while cut-and-dried conceptualizations inhibit whatever art there is in historical research and writing.

Yet in our concern for proportion and balance, we must always make room for the visionary. Yesterday's oddballs have a disconcerting way of becoming today's accepted prophets. Visions and prophecies are not in themselves history, but those who dwell on the unknowable and transfer their sense of wonder and mystery to scholars are allies, not enemies. Moreover, regularities in history do not attract as much attention as the abnormal.[25] The unknown and the irregular will always issue to mankind varying edicts concerning the order of things, and people will be found who will repond eagerly. For who knows when one of the offbeat visions may be the real McCoy?

Still, the search for order at times is the pursuit of the will-o'-the-wisp. In looking too hard for order, we run the risk of seeing history as it never was, even as it never could have been. Order, like meaning, is not omnipresent in history, though we may fervently wish it were. As a young man, the sixteenth-century Chinese philosopher Wang Yang-ming spent seven days staring at a grove of bamboos, seeking the fundamental principle of Being. A friend of Wang's named Ch'ien succumbed to exhaustion after three days; Wang himself "reflected deeply . . . but got nothing. Subsequently he fell sick."[26] Few things in life are so intellectually

[23] Edward Whiting Fox, *History in Geographic Perspective: The Other France* (New York: W. W. Norton, 1971), pp. 70–71.

[24] Howard Zinn, *The Politics of History* (Boston: Beacon Press, 1970), p. 165. It is ironic that this comment should come from Zinn, who as a highly politicized historian has had his share of critics charging that he lacks precisely this sense of proportion.

[25] For comment on this point, see Theodore Roszak, *Where the Wasteland Ends: Politics and Transcendence in Postindustrial Society* (Garden City, N.Y.: Anchor Books, 1973), p. 297; Barzun, *Clio and the Doctors*, p. 75.

[26] Frederic Wakeman, Jr., *History and Will: Philosophical Perspectives of Mao Tse-Tung's Thought* (Berkeley: University of California Press, 1975 [1973]), pp. 245–46. This example is slightly out of context because of the cultural differ-

disheartening as the prolonged concentration upon a knotty problem that in the end yields nothing.

Estimating the appropriateness of differing conceptions of historical order is a fine art—seldom recognized, never mastered, but always a necessary component of historical thinking. To reason about order is to think about history in a critical way. The mind that holds to one concept, one order, is in this sense a caged mind. While order may be time-bound, it by no means is constrained by people, cultures, or civilizations. It is both the anchor and the full sail of history.

---

entiation involved. Whether the principle is one of "order" or of "Being," the point remains.

CHAPTER FOUR

The Institutionalization of Historical Order

Concepts of historical order transcend the isolated individual. If it were possible for Robinson Crusoe to have been born and lived all his life alone, and then suddenly to have been deposited in the midst of a teeming street in seventeenth-century London, he would in a very real sense have been without history, with no conception of the past of his own kind. All of us take our ideas of historical order, to greater or lesser degree, from sources outside ourselves. Left on our own, we generally do an indifferent job of reasoning things through, especially in our younger years, when our experience is more limited.

Educational institutions have been around for centuries, some of the time serving their proper function as conduits and stimulants rather than repressors of thought. They provide, in part, surrogate experience and distillations of life for us to ponder, emulate, or avoid. There exist both advantages and disadvantages in formal schooling as a vehicle for transmitting notions of historical order. The problems involved are not of the philosophical kind previously discussed, but since most of us have been educated or miseducated in this formal environment, the problems sometimes tend to escape our notice and remain buried in the avalanche of "received wisdom."

Historical Research: The Path to Professionalism

At its furthest reach the search for truth through history, which means seeking truth through historical research, has been judged capable of complete realization. Upon accepting an offer to edit the monumental *Cambridge Modern History*, Lord Acton in a letter to his contributors argued that a "final stage" in the conditions of historical learning was near. All information was within reach, he claimed, and "every problem has become capable of solution."[1] We are not so sanguine as Acton. He looked to a new professional class of historians to root out the answers buried deep in the past. A later generation of researchers, while profiting from a professional approach to their craft, has been more cautious in extolling the potential of professionalism.

Research is the historian's métier. Here logic, imagination, and common sense come into full play. Ego involvement attends this process also; as Arthur Schlesinger has noted, the best results in historical investigation have almost always been attained by the "lone man [or woman] thinking."[2] As a camel is a horse designed by a committee, so a group effort devoted to a single topic and thesis is liable to be disjointed and uneven. One must not discount the many compendia and cooperative efforts made necessary by the nature and amount of the material, such as the massive and important *Dictionary of American Biography*. But minds completely tuned to one another, while not an impossibility, are rare enough in the historical field to elicit comment when they merge successfully in research and writing. It is scarcely necessary to observe that cooperative endeavors where separate individuals each write one chapter, and someone else oversees the "meshing" of the whole, do not represent this sort of cooperation.

From the earliest introduction to the treadmill of graduate education, the budding historian is urged to be "original" in research. The need for originality, fresh discoveries, and new interpretations is omnipresent, but there is little likelihood that lasting discoveries or interpretations will come from unseasoned pens. Younger historians in training (ideally, this sort of training never stops) are well-advised to familiarize themselves with basic works in their fields of interest and build on the most secure foundation possible. There is an old chestnut to the effect that if you take it out of one book, it is plagiarism; if you take it out of many books, it is research. Fair enough, but in our haste to be "original," we at times forget the constant riches held by familiar material. Casting

[1] Gertrude Himmelfarb, *Lord Acton: A Study in Conscience and Politics* (Chicago: University of Chicago Press, 1962 [1952]), p. 223.
[2] Arthur M. Schlesinger, *In Retrospect: The History of a Historian* (New York: Harcourt, Brace and World, 1963), p. 118.

the common or the mundane in fresh molds is thinking about history also.

The essential rewards of research in unfamiliar sources are undeniable. History includes its source material—in this it is akin to mathematics, where one could observe that 4 "contains" 2 and 2. But unlike lower orders of mathematics, history is not necessarily the sum of its component parts. From another angle, history cannot be developed from sources separate from itself; thus, the necessity of research.

A corollary argument concerns the correctness of the source material. If all the sources are valid, that is, considered to be of some historical truth, then the accretion of these sources, in whatever form, is itself true—so the argument runs. Yet from our discussion of subjectivism this does not logically follow. Sources by themselves do not determine the shape of the product into which they are molded; if they did, we would have not history, but mere chronicle. As R. G. Collingwood noted, you cannot collect your evidence before you begin thinking, because nothing is evidence unless in relationship to a definite question.[3]

For the committed historian, then, research is far more than exhuming evidence as an end. There is, first of all, the excitement of the search itself, as perverse as this may sound to students who view library assignments as veritable sentences to the rack. It is fun to be a detective, to "find things out." Those choosing to regard historical research as dullness relieved by occasional intervals of boredom may note that many historians function in precisely this way, as detectives, and thoroughly enjoy doing so. The economist-historian John R. Commons not only devoured detective novels but confided to his students that were he to start all over again, his first textbook would be a detective novel. The thrill of the successful chase should not be slighted; R. W. B. Lewis was once reduced to trembling anticipation when he finally tracked down a suitcase of materials concerning the life of author Edith Wharton. The hunt is all the more potentially rewarding when the witnesses are no longer available for direct interrogation.[4]

[3] For comment on this point, see Benedetto Croce, *History: Its Theory and Practice*, trans. Douglas Ainslie (New York: Russell and Russell, 1920), pp. 23–24; J. Franklin Jameson, *The History of Historical Writing in America* (Boston: Houghton Mifflin, 1891), p. 154; and R. G. Collingwood, *The Idea of History* (London: Oxford University Press, 1956 [1946]), p. 281.

[4] Robin W. Winks, ed., *The Historian as Detective: Essays on Evidence* (New York: Harper and Row, 1968), is a fascinating collection of writings about

Evidence is where you find it. Some historical detective work goes unrewarded for years, as in archeologist Heinrich Schliemann's tenacious search for the ancient city of Troy. At other times needed or useful information comes accidentally; one stumbles across the unexpected in a dusty tome or, like E. Digby Baltzell, eavesdrops on a discussion in a campus drugstore for evidence on the American caste system. Of course, hard digging may never be rewarded. "Rejecting vague opinions, I have studiously sought for chronicles far and near," the medieval monk William of Malmesbury resignedly wrote, "though I confess I have scarcely profited anything by this industry." To his credit, though he remained "poor in information," William doggedly kept at it "as long as I could find any thing to read."[5]

The historian more fortunate than William of Malmesbury has only begun research once the evidence is bagged, so to speak. There remain the problems of evaluating the evidence as to its authenticity and deciding precisely how to use it.[6] The record of events by itself is rich and rewarding. But behind the events are people. We would like to know not only how they thought and felt before, during, and after the events, but also how their thoughts and feelings conditioned their actions, and vice versa.[7] Here, thinking about history becomes tantamount to nailing jelly to a

---

historical detection. See also William O. Aydelotte, "The Detective Story as a Historical Source," *Yale Review* 39 (Sept., 1949): 76–95. John R. Commons, *Myself: The Autobiography of John R. Commons* (Madison: University of Wisconsin Press, 1964 [1934]), p. 135; R. W. B. Lewis, "Edith Wharton: The Beckoning Quarry," *American Heritage* 26, no. 6 (Oct., 1975): 56. No prospective historian should ignore Josephine Tey's exceptional novel of historical detection, *The Daughter of Time* (New York: Berkley, 1975), nor an excellent display of factual detection recounted by Ben Weider and David Hapgood, *The Murder of Napoleon* (New York: Berkley, 1983).

[5] E. Digby Baltzell, *The Protestant Establishment: Aristocracy and Caste in America* (New York: Vintage Books, 1964), pp. 358–59; Peter Gay and Gerald J. Cavanaugh, eds., *Historians at Work*, I: *Herodotus to Froissart* (New York: Harper and Row, 1972), p. 353.

[6] Although these processes involve thinking logically and conceptually, they do not necessarily involve considering history in the broad and generalized scope of our concern. The interested reader is referred to Louis Gottschalk, *Understanding History: A Primer of Historical Method*, 2nd ed. (New York: Alfred A. Knopf, 1969 [1950]); Jacques Barzun and Henry F. Graff, *The Modern Researcher*, 3rd ed. (New York: Harcourt, Brace and Jovanovich, 1977 [1957]); and James West Davidson and Mark Hamilton Lytle, *After the Fact: The Art of Historical Detection* (New York: Alfred A. Knopf, 1982).

[7] Carl Becker, *Everyman His Own Historian: Essays on History and Politics* (Chicago: Quadrangle Books, 1966 [1935]), p. 299.

wall. The use of evidence evolves into a tricky business, a matter of *interpretation*, which in turn is a major criterion by which the historian's skills may be evaluated.

It is all so difficult, and thus challenging, because the deck is stacked against the researcher from the beginning. Most evidence from the past has vanished forever—dead with the people who carried it in their memories, crumbled with the buildings of ancient civilizations, dissolved with the countless written records lost in the passage of time. Castiglione, in his handbook of courtly perfection for the Renaissance man, details a discussion on ancient history, in the midst of which signor Gasparo sighs that "God alone knows just how all these things happened; for those centuries are so remote from us that many lies can be told, and there is no one to gainsay them."[8]

More recent history carries no guarantee of increased veracity. Today the historian dealing with modern materials is liable to be smothered in paper, microfilm, and the like. The profusion of records has become a handicap as well as a great aid; more is not necessarily better. Plenty of potential historical material never gets into record form, particularly in this age where the telephone makes ephemeral much that would have been committed to paper a century ago. To complicate matters further, evidence on paper may lie or distort. Bismarck, the architect of German unification, is supposed to have said apropos of diplomatic documents that they were for the most part only paper smeared with ink. Main points never got into the records.[9]

Even with evidence that is verified and as complete as the researcher can assemble, the problem of what to do next still looms. It has been argued that to understand the historical pattern of events (the way the evidence "falls into place"), the historian must be able to relate intent, action, and consequence. Of these, unfortunately for the scientifically minded, action is most likely to possess documentation, and even here the record is often far from adequate. Consequence usually appears in somewhat smudged but still definable forms and often allows historians the full play of their critical skills. The third partner in the trio, intent, is the hardest to dredge out of the available documentation and is the area most often misinterpreted or ignored.

[8] Baldesar Castiglione, *The Book of the Courtier*, trans. Charles S. Singleton (Garden City, N.Y.: Anchor Books, 1959), p. 235.
[9] Fritz Stern, *Gold and Iron: Bismarck, Bleichröder, and the Building of the German Empire* (New York: Alfred A. Knopf, 1977), p. 304.

To relate all three is to trace the most difficult historical problem of all—*causation*. Voltaire was given to asserting that "historical truths are merely probabilities," and although he overstated his case a bit, as usual, he nevertheless cautioned us that clear tracks through the underbrush of historical evidence are few and far between. Even before Voltaire, the extremely conscientious Benedictine, Jean Mabillon, had admitted the impossibility of complete certitude. He had called instead for an agreement by experts, based on empirical investigation—the foundation stone of modern historical generalization.[10]

Researchers in command of a body of evidence possess in a certain sense great power. Historical hindsight most certainly is not "20-20," for if it were we would have one history, and one only. The shapers of the evidence, however, must be aware that the wisdom of hindsight may often become "arrogant and hypercritical."[11] They must also be able to judge which evidence is useful and which not and be prepared to justify either the inclusion or exclusion of material in their creation of history.

What constitutes valid historical evidence? Each researcher will have an answer dependent on individual interests and the scope of the work, although there are tests for validity that are common to virtually all forms of evidence.[12] The usefulness of the evidence differentiates history from chronicle: "History is principally an act of thought, chronicle an act of will."[13] As we make history through research and writing, we necessarily think about it. Unlike Rousseau, who was too clever by half when he urged his readers to begin by ignoring the facts, as they did not affect the question, the historian is continually aware that facts may define, answer, or change the nature of the question. The omitted fact or the fact taken for granted may be the most crucial of all.[14]

A final devilish touch: historians sometimes confront options

[10] See H. P. Rickman, Introduction to Wilhelm Dilthey, *Pattern and Meaning in History*, ed. H. P. Rickman (New York: Harper and Row, 1962), p. 45; Bruce Mazlish, *The Riddle of History: The Great Speculators from Vico to Freud* (New York: Minerva Press, 1968 [1966]), p. 64; Peter Gay and Victor G. Wexler, eds., *Historians at Work*, II: *Valla to Gibbon* (New York: Harper and Row, 1972), pp. 161–63.

[11] Paul Knaplund, *Moorings Old and New: Entries in an Immigrant's Log* (Madison: State Historical Society of Wisconsin, 1963), p. 247.

[12] See Gottschalk, *Understanding History*, and Barzun and Graff, *The Modern Researcher*, for material on this point.

[13] Croce, *History: Its Theory and Practice*, p. 19.

[14] Walter L. Dorn, *Competition for Empire, 1740–1763* (New York: Harper and Row, 1963 [1940]), p. 232; Commons, *Myself*, p. 28.

in the presentation of evidence of seemingly equal validity. The "paths not taken" by historical action, though obviously not appropriate for research based on historical records, should be kept in mind as the evidence is evaluated. The thorough researcher wants to know what all the reasonable options were in any given situation, in order to more reasonably evaluate the choice taken.

The problems inherent in the establishing and handling of historical evidence became the primary goads urging the growing professionalization of the craft in the nineteenth century. The professional approach to human affairs, broadly construed, is itself a form of order, since it implies that under whatever conditions, the game is to be played by certain rules.

The Rules of the Game: Professionalization and Order

As creatures, historians are often identified today by the initials dangling off the ends of their names: M.A., Ph.D., and so on. These are the professionals—educated in the discipline, usually committed to it as a lifetime endeavor, and generally a reasonable if not exactly a jolly lot. Almost one hundred years ago, one of the first of the new American professionals pondered the nature of his training and found it wanting. "It may almost be said that the historian, like the poet, is born, not made," ventured J. Franklin Jameson. "But if he is made," he added in a burst of qualification, "he is not made by machinery."[15]

Sensitivity to the past is highly individualized, but as we have noted earlier, there is much common ground among youngsters who went on to do some type of historical work. "The fact is there are some who are historians by the Grace of God," reflected Albert Schweitzer, "who from their mother's womb have an instinctive feeling for the real." A modern professional, Roy F. Nichols, spoke of his career in history as "determinism," which he was accustomed to think of in religious terms that became more mystical as he grew older. The comments of Schweitzer and Nichols recall Samuel Eliot Morison's high estimate of Winston Churchill as an historian. No plodding graduate student could ever catch up with the heritage Churchill had from birth. "Call this snobbery if you will," Morison loftily proclaimed. "It is the truth."[16]

[15] Jameson, *History of Historical Writing in America*, pp. 154–55.

[16] Albert Schweitzer, *The Quest of the Historical Jesus: A Critical Study of Its Progress from Reimarus to Wrede* (New York: Macmillan, 1961 [1906]), p. 25; Roy F. Nichols, *A Historian's Progress* (New York: Alfred A. Knopf, 1968),

Andrew Dickson White, like Jameson an early professional, argued that without an original spark of interest to be kindled into a lifelong flame, all the professional schooling in the world would not help. To those who cared, however, White believed history offered training in thought far transcending the narrow interests of the classroom. His main aim as a teacher was "to set my audience or readers at thinking, and to give them fruitful historical projects to think upon."[17] Although we have balked at defining history, then, we will consider an historian to be *that individual whose primary business is thinking critically about history.*

Such persons, obviously, need not necessarily burden their names with the heavy freight of initials. Jameson was forced to fudge his statements on the origins of historians because the ability to think critically is not the equivalent of a formal education. James Truslow Adams, one of the most popular American historians during the 1920s and 1930s, attended a technological college and stayed at Yale only long enough to think the place deadening. He turned to history only after almost two decades on Wall Street, yet his escape from "graduate school pedantry" probably was an asset. Adams, in short, had cultivated his abilities as a critical thinker in the "real world."[18] Critical thinking is both an art born of experience and a talent that may be cultivated by the study of certain rules. The second path, though not especially independent of the first, is the way of the professional.

Since historians are critical thinkers, they face a general problem that confronts individuals in any society. The problem centers on the nature of the engagement of intellectuals with their social order. The major (and contrasting) possibilities are two: (1) remain as disengaged as possible from society, since involvement increases bias and impairs critical judgment; or (2) engage as much as possible in society, since social leadership and social development profit from knowledge, especially knowledge gained from critical reasoning. Each possibility has its varieties of involvement and its ad hominem arguments taken from the history books. One side might contend that "there are times when a man of learning must withdraw from political and social involvement, from all ac-

---

p. 298; Emily Morison Beck, ed., *Sailor Historian: The Best of Samuel Eliot Morison* (Boston: Houghton Mifflin, 1977), p. 378.

[17] Andrew Dickson White, *Autobiography of Andrew Dickson White* I (New York: Century Company, 1905), pp. 262, 83.

[18] Allen Nevins, *James Truslow Adams: Historian of the American Dream* (Urbana: University of Illinois Press, 1968), p. 24.

tion, and wait patiently for the appropriate historical moment." [19] To which the committed activist might rejoin that by that time our hero would be dead, and his ability to influence action would be buried with him.

In spite of periods of academic turmoil and student-faculty activism, it has been a venerable tradition that learned people tend to hold back from taking an active part in contemporary issues. The seclusion and aloofness inherent in the ivory-tower syndrome does have some basis in fact. Most of us like to be considered special in some way, and more than a few academics regard a detached relationship to the crowd as an elevation rather than a simple separation. Disdain often runs rampant even within learned communities. Scientists and humanists ponder their inabilities to get along; sociologists puzzle over what it is exactly that historians are trying to do, a bewilderment reciprocated; and philosophers wonder why the home economists are on the campus in the first place. Differences such as these are as much human as institutional and predate modern academia by many years—witness the historian Vico's loathing at the displacement of humanistic letters by Cartesian philosophy in the seventeenth century.[20] The humanists, constantly beleaguered, survive still; the Cartesians are interesting curiosities of an age long gone.

One's choice of historical study may be conditioned, in part, precisely by this desire to be special. At the not-so-tender age of thirty-two, the well-traveled George Bancroft confidently asserted that every young man must choose between the "vulgar ambition of personal power" and the life of the mind. Unfortunately for ideals such as these (which tend to flatten out under the hammer blows of living), history is about humans. Since historians are presumably more effective in interpreting the experiences of others if they have more varied experiences of their own upon which to draw, the life of the mind lived in a vacuum may produce just that—a vacuum. Doubtless, it was the observation of this situation that goaded Morison into his splenetic comment that graduate schools are a "chain reaction of dullness," in which professors who write "dull, solid, valuable monographs," which no one outside the profession reads, teach their students to do the same.[21]

[19] William Irwin Thompson, *At the Edge of History: Speculations on the Transformation of Culture* (New York: Harper and Row, 1972 [1971]), p. 103.

[20] Mazlish, *The Riddle of History*, p. 18.

[21] Russel B. Nye, *George Bancroft* (New York: Washington Square Press, 1964), pp. 144–45; Beck, ed., *Sailor Historian*, p. 385.

The professionalization of the historical discipline did not aim at this type of seclusion. History shared in the growing professionalization of many areas of western culture, such as the social sciences, medicine, and the law. Beginning in Europe in the middle of the nineteenth century, canons of professional practice traveled across the Atlantic in the intellectual baggage of the few American scholars trained abroad, mostly in German universities. Andrew Dickson White could applaud the German Empire as "the greatest Continental home of civilization,"[22] and Herbert Baxter Adams of Johns Hopkins could teach a Teutonized theory of trans-Atlantic cultural transmission, both without seeming alien to Americans.

Graduate training rapidly took hold in the United States. By 1900 the doctoral degree was the badge of acceptance for historians in the better universities. Insofar as the new professionalism tended to apply critical reason to "rules of evidence" and inculcated students with careful method, it was a brilliant success. The benefits of the professionalization of history resulted in greater attention to historical "problem-solving" and a diminution of the tradition of the historical narrative. A professional group having widely varied interests developed, today only numbering a few thousand at most, yet with a presumed common dedication to the best instincts of professionalism.

Unfortunately, "amateurs" persisted in researching and writing history. Nothing elicited anger in the committed professional scholar more than the amateurs, who, not knowing they had outlived their golden age, continued to produce for a wide and appreciative audience. While deep in the making of *The Outline of History*, which became a best-seller from the pen of an Englishman best known for his science fiction, H. G. Wells predicted that "this book will rouse everybody in the history textbook & history teaching line to blind fury. It is a serious raid into various departments of special knowledge (and my God! how badly they do it). . . . There will be a sustained attempt to represent me as an ignorant interloper and dispose of me in that way."[23]

---

[22] White, *Autobiography*, I, 535. The best examination of American history as a profession is John Higham, with Leonard Krieger and Felix Gilbert, *History: The Development of Historical Studies in the United States* (Englewood Cliffs, N.J.: Prentice-Hall, 1965). For a more general treatment, see Burton J. Bledstein, *The Culture of Professionalism: The Middle Class and the Development of Higher Education in America* (Norton, 1976).

[23] Norman MacKenzie and Jeanne MacKenzie, *H. G. Wells: A Biography* (New York: Simon and Schuster, 1973), p. 321.

On their part, professional historians have generally considered that only specialized training could develop and deepen historical insight. Amateurs, it was claimed, often emphasized the personal and the bizarre at the expense of the larger picture and of the more stable, if less lively, arrays of facts. Worst of all, they usually did it for money and tended to "popularize" for their audiences; indeed, the process had been going on for centuries. "The majority of writers bring to the undertaking no spirit of fairness at all: nothing but dishonesty, impudence and unscrupulousness," sourly commented the Greek Polybius, historian of ancient Rome. "Like vendors of drugs, their aim is to catch popular credit and favor, and to seize every opportunity of enriching themselves. About such writers it is not worth while to say more."[24]

Conscious of the wide gap that they claim separates them from amateurs, professionals as a group have strongly contributed to the institutionalization of historical order in the twentieth century. While cultivating a studied disdain for popularizers, most professionals have been as acquisitive and money-conscious as the next person, although it is considered good form to keep this sort of thing under wraps. John Hicks, who made a comfortable profit from his textbook, remembered learning early the virtues of hard work and keeping free from debt. The lessons of financial integrity and personal responsibility taught by his mother remained with him all his life. In summing up his career Hicks half-painfully and half-proudly confessed, "I will not deny that in writing *The American Nation* I was interested in royalties."[25]

There remains the possibility of the historian too arrogant, too disinterested, or too inept to compete in the marketplace. But professions are businesses as well as ideals, and ignoring the situation does not make it vanish. Like businessmen, historians many times depend on others for information; certain "names" are regarded as pacesetters or leaders; conventions are held where gossip, opinion, and substantive material are exchanged. As in business, entrenched interests may develop, and it is axiomatic that they resist new ideas, both from within and without the profession. After noting that a university faculty is a collection of individuals, each with differing opinions, John Commons asserted that the University of Wisconsin, an institution highly regarded by Pro-

[24] Gay and Cavanaugh, eds., *Historians at Work*, I, 127.
[25] John D. Hicks, *My Life with History: An Autobiography* (Lincoln: University of Nebraska Press, 1968), pp. 17–18, 33, 194.

gressive reformers, had a faculty that "has always been perhaps nine-tenths on the conservative or reactionary side."[26] Rarely is the imp of the perverse found in faculty life. Iconoclastic talk abounds, to be sure—but the gap between thought and action is usually measured in the conservative morality of the middle class, to which most academics belong.

The professional investment in order is high. The stakes include not only the natural egocentrism held by any possessor of a body of discrete and certified knowledge but also the related order of the academic world. This latter universe is as prone to feuds, jealousies, and vanities as any professional (or for that matter human) group. It may be, as John Hicks believed, that "in history . . . everyone poaches at will on everyone else's preserve,"[27] yet historians are far from a lasting band of brothers and sisters. The many fragmentations of the discipline into specialties and subspecialties have created the paradox of a profession that, in the process of improving itself in parts, has been weakened as regards the whole.

Beyond the appeal of order itself, the individual is bound to professionalism by other strong ties. The achievement of the professional license may be equated by some with successful struggle. In the pattern made familiar since Charles Darwin's epochal writings on evolution, the act of survival seems to insure not only the perpetuation but the improvement of the profession. Education has been equated with the survival of the fittest; it is the "system of nature."[28] The objection may be made that such views are outmoded today. One must then be prepared to explain contemporary practices of ranking students through grades and the correlation between grades and employment eligibility.

Struggle, for the professional, does not end with the degree. The arguments over whether academic historians should be researchers-writers, teachers, or both have been waged for decades and are beyond resolution. For the writers, the arena of competition lies in publishing. To them, "the authoring of books consti-

[26] For similarities between business and history (the latter as a surrogate for practically all of academia), see Frederick Lewis Allen, *The Big Change: America Transforms Itself, 1900–1950* (New York: Harper and Row, 1969 [1952]), pp. 214–15. Commons, *Myself*, p. 110. In fairness to the University of Wisconsin, we should note that Paul Knaplund, a contemporary and faculty colleague of Commons, described the history department as "democratically organized" and responsive to younger members. See Knaplund, *Moorings Old and New*, p. 232.
[27] Hicks, *My Life with History*, p. 209.
[28] White, *Autobiography*, I, 393.

tutes the highest function of the historian," because teaching communicates only to a limited audience, whereas a book addresses a
potentially unlimited audience.[29] If this be the case, the psychological investment in the creation and publication of a book is
enormous, since what is between the covers is ostensibly the best
one's mind can produce. The more rash among the profession may
project their ego-involvement into the realm of eternal historical
truth. The more timid, on the other hand, usually know too much.
Abundance, rather than paucity, of knowledge often leads to an
"academic style"—hard to define but instantly recognizable to
those with experience of the soporific. As Carl Becker once remarked, this style is overcautious, overgeneralized, and hedged in
by "triple quantifications, remote historical allusions, and parenthetical cross references."[30]

The arena of competition promotes both variety and sameness. Historical styles of analyses come and go. The narrative stubbornly thrives, biography holds its own, quantifiers boldly assert
their numbers, and areas of research interest change with time. As
in other academic fields, the variety of historical thought is great.
Some historians, like other people, are quick, or trendy, or ready
to roll with the next new idea; some are not. Many historians take
themselves much too seriously—some do not. Some historians
have a sense of humor, while many do not. Variety makes the
arena potentially disputatious at all times. Men are always divided
on more issues than they know, Lord Acton once proclaimed pessimistically. It is only a matter of time until differences surface;
"Every colleague of today is a future opponent, if he only lives a
few years."[31]

The drawbacks of professionalism are not directly connected
to the rigorous training implied. But professionalization inevitably
means organization, and organization is often a deadening influence, the archfoe of inquiry. The tendency of organization, sighed
the nineteenth-century feminist and abolitionist Angelina Grimké
Weld, is to kill the spirit that gave it birth. As order, organization inhibits those intangible qualities so necessary to historical
thought and yet so hard to measure. The difference might be suggested by the poet Emily Dickinson's comment concerning some

---

[29] Schlesinger, *In Retrospect*, p. 116.
[30] Charlotte Watkins Smith, *Carl Becker: On History and the Climate of Opinion* (Carbondale: Southern Illinois University Press, 1973 [1956]), p. 161.
[31] Himmelfarb, *Lord Acton*, p. 148.

scholarly person; "He has the facts, but not the phosphorescence of learning." [32]

Educational institutions, wherein most academic professionals practice their crafts, are in the broadest sense organized for two purposes;: inquiry into the unknown and the transmission and criticism of the known. The spirit of inquiry is a perpetually frail reed. The impulse to stay inside the secure universe of revealed knowledge is always correspondingly strong. For students, the conflict between these tendencies is best revealed in the classroom.

Teaching History: The Transmission of Order

Students usually begin to perceive historical order in a formal educational environment. The transmission of order thus becomes largely dependent on the experience, skills, and enthusiasm of the teacher and on the nature of the teacher-student relationship. Teaching holds unlimited potential for the expression of personality and character, but this potential is too often stifled by trite reiteration (the dull pedagogue), bureaucratic interference (the large class, grades), and basic student lack of interest in a topic. [33]

The good teacher may make history "exciting" or "relevant," two words that raise hackles throughout the profession. Nevertheless, there will always be those who remain beatific in their unenlightened state, even after the teacher gives it his best shot. Students are akin to army mules. Not being personally engaged with the task at hand, they have to be driven (fear of bad grades). Being driven, they submit stubbornly if at all. The experience being completed, the entire process must be endured again when fresh educational freight weighs them down.

As part of the fundamentals, like the alphabet and the rules of the art of grammar, children are usually told that the younger they are

[32] Gerda Lerner, *The Grimké Sisters from South Carolina: Pioneers for Woman's Rights and Abolition* (New York: Schocken Books, 1971 [1967]), p. 333; Dickinson quoted in Van Wyck Brooks, *New England: Indian Summer, 1865–1915* (New York: E. P. Dutton, 1940), p. 234.

[33] For some trenchant remarks on teaching history at the university level, see Norman Graebner, "Observations on University Teaching and History," *AHA Newsletter* 13, no. 9 (Dec. 1975): 5–7. See also the journal *The History Teacher*, passim.

so much the more observant they are. This I think is not aptly said, since we are on the one hand trained by the writings and institutions of our ancestors, who devoted themselves to wisdom before us, and by the passage of time and the resultant experience in life, yes, trained the more quickly the more advanced the age of the world is in which we are set; on the other hand, after mastering for ourselves the things that are discovered before us, we can devise new things with the same inspiration as those of old.[34]

So wrote the philosophical German bishop Otto of Freising eight hundred years ago. There is a relationship between learning and experience, although grasping the hard edges of definition has always proven elusive. In China there are words for the situation, to the effect that while the educated believe nothing, the uneducated believe everything. At times, though, far from providing an empty sack into which the wisdom of the ages may be dumped, youth voices its dissatisfaction with the given order of things.

Student criticisms of the shortcomings of history as it is taught are more common than one might guess. Generations are prone to distrust the purposes and abilities of one another; the interplay often enmeshes in the classroom. "Each oracle denies his predecessor, each magician breaks the wand of the one who went before him," wrote Oliver Wendell Holmes.[35] Instructors who fail to measure up stay in the mind fully as long as the good ones. Even late in life Arthur Schlesinger remembered his teacher George Wells Knight, head of the Department of American History at Ohio State, as a man who habitually polarized complex historical issues. "One felt that his was the only possible view, that only the stupid or the malevolent at the time of the event could ever have thought differently. To his students Knight seemed a peerless teacher, an opinion which he gave evidence of sharing himself."[36]

Teachers, of course, operate under certain institutional pressures. They require listeners; at advanced levels, they many times must compete for students, and here the awards often go to the golden-tongued actors rather than the substantial (but dull) plodders. Even Ranke had to cancel his last lecture course in 1871 because of lack of students. The actors proceed as if in response to

[34] Gay and Cavanaugh, eds., *Historians at Work*, I, 387.
[35] Arthur Cotterell and David Morgan, *China's Civilization: A Survey of Its History, Arts, and Technology* (New York: Praeger, 1975), p. 127; Holmes quoted in Brooks, *New England*, p. 252.
[36] Schlesinger, *In Retrospect*, pp. 20–21.

the advice given Andrew Dickson White as a young lecturer—
never stop dead, but keep saying *something*. Communication is essential, yet substance alone will usually not suffice. All that James
Truslow Adams remembered of Professor Ladd at Yale was the te-
dium of listening to a "mere unapproachable oral textbook."[37]

Historical teaching is too easily given over to rote memorization and the tiresome recitation of names, dates, figures. Thomas
Edison was so bored by such schooling that he later said he would
not give a penny for the ordinary college graduate. The famous in-
ventor opined that after practical engineers, business managers,
and industrialists had had their way with America, there would be
time for literary men—perhaps in three or four centuries. For
Mark Sullivan, memorizing lists was no education at all. Historical
trivia could be found in encyclopedias and should not burden
classroom transactions. John Commons, who never achieved the
doctoral degree, felt throughout his life that exams gave preference
to memorizers and penalized independent thinking.[38]

The rebellion against history taught in this fashion may extend too far, and in this way mistaught history achieves its most
negative effects. Boring is the neighbor of useless. Further, through
poor teaching the discipline may bring discredit upon itself. As a
carefree youngster, Lincoln Steffens balked at history taught as a
revealed fact. He was astonished that history was not a science,
proceeding to infer that "historians did not know!"[39] To the intellectually curious, approaches to history that penalize or ignore
thinking, even the most speculative variety, make the classroom a
continuous torment. Albert Einstein was amazed that modern
methods of instruction had not yet succeeded in completely stran-
gling free inquiry. Clearly, coercion and insistence on dutiful obe-
dience were not the answer.[40] *What is the appropriate role of the
historian in the classroom environment?*

Good teachers are the more notable for their scarcity. The

[37] Leonard Krieger, *Ranke: The Meaning of History* (Chicago: University of
Chicago Press, 1977), p. 291; White, *Autobiography*, I, 261; James Truslow
Adams, *Our Business Civilization: Some Aspects of American Culture* (New
York: AMS Press, 1969 [1929]), pp. 149–50.
[38] Matthew Josephson, *Edison: A Biography* (New York: McGraw-Hill,
1959), p. 440; Mark Sullivan, *The Education of an American* (New York: Doubleday, Doran, 1938), pp. 90–91; Commons, *Myself*, p. 42.
[39] Lincoln Steffens, *The Autobiography of Lincoln Steffens* I (New York:
Harcourt, Brace and World, 1958 [1931]), pp. 124–25.
[40] Jeremy Bernstein, *Einstein* (New York: Viking Press, 1973), p. 78.

habit developed by John Commons of inviting his graduate students to his home for "Friday Niters" of general conversation would seem to be not an idealized but a reasonable pedagogical approach. To imprint one's mind on another in a relationship such as this is a remarkable happenstance, to be especially prized when the results are positive. Carl Becker had never been interested in history before he took his first course with Frederick Jackson Turner at the University of Wisconsin in 1894. After that, he never lost interest. And one of Herbert Baxter Adams's students later fondly spoke of the "comradeliness in him, as if he had been an older and wiser fellow student."[41]

Some of the problems connected with the institutionalization of history are unavoidable. Older people *can* be wiser; not all wisdom is whelped from the spontaneous sensate impulses of teenage peer groups. Predigested knowledge *does* have some merits, but where it inhibits inquiry or channels it into paths well-worn by years of avoiding "difficult" or "unnecessary" questions, it becomes a barrier to historical learning. To maintain successfully the order of the teacher-student relationship is necessarily to tune continuously a delicate mechanism. Everyone prattles about keeping an open mind, yet historical study and thought require discipline as well as wide-ranging intuition and speculation. To put the problem in a common metaphor of American life, the study of history requires precise line play as well as spectacular rushes by the running backs.

We must accentuate the difficulties of managing a different kind of historical order. Historians who are aware of the environment in which they took their first tentative steps toward professionalism are ahead of the game. They may use the advantages their education gives them in method and mastery of material. They should always be aware, however, that some of the restrictions in the marketplace of ideas are inhibitions to historical thought. These, one hopes, may be transcended or ignored. Self-recognition of this caliber is a milestone on the way to intellectual maturity, not only in thinking about history but in life itself.

[41] Commons, *Myself*, pp. 5–6; Smith, *Carl Becker*, p. 6. For the impact of the Turner-Becker relationship on Becker, see Carl Becker, "Frederick Jackson Turner," in *Everyman His Own Historian*, pp. 191–232. See also Frederic C. Howe, *The Confessions of a Reformer* (Chicago: Quadrangle Books, 1967 [1925]), pp. 29–30.

II. Process

CHAPTER FIVE

Historical Change

Order is not the only ingredient in the mix of history. History is made comprehensible through pattern, but were we to regard the past as a series of static configurations we would deny its life—which is to say, ourselves. Human events make history; the framework in which they occur, whether spatial or temporal, is neutral until people occupy it. "Time in itself does nothing," a leading historian of American culture has claimed. "What counts is what goes on during the passage of time."[1]

The movement of the human past through time we will call "process." The word is sometimes used to denote rigid schemes or systems in motion. We use it to mean only movement, nothing more. Movement and continuity are the conceptions with which historians work, as G. M. Young has noted. As the painter passionately apprehends form, so the historian regards process.

The idea of process has been weighted at times with mystical qualities. The human being is perceived as the merest chip afloat on a vast and turbulent sea, tossed about in ways unfathomable in the whole of things that he could never understand, only make his peace with his world.[2] Clearly, any vision of history as process is liable to the subjectivism mentioned previously. With a respectful bow in the direction of mystery, which the historian never can overcome, we assert that analyzing process is both a possible and a reasonable way of thinking about history.

[1] Carl N. Degler, *Neither Black Nor White: Slavery and Race Relations in Brazil and the United States* (New York: Macmillan, 1971), p. 223.

[2] Carl G. Gustavson, *The Mansion of History* (New York: McGraw-Hill, 1976), p. 106; Isaiah Berlin, *The Hedgehog and the Fox: An Essay on Tolstoy's View of History* (New York: Simon and Schuster, 1970), p. 72.

To discuss history in this way, as process, we must immediately discard any claims to mathematical precision (although leaving room for logic and empirical thought). Thus we do not mean "process" in Jacques Barzun's sense: "Activities are what we do and can imagine others having done; processes are what goes on unwilled or unknown."[3] The inquiry rests, rather, on whether human activity through time may be described in terms of patterned movement. Being subjective, we do not regard "process" as a term embodying historical actuality. The word connotes instead the possibility of historical imagination and understanding.

Let us rehearse. If we deny *all* pattern to history, we endorse chaos. If we insist *all* history is pattern, we deny humanity. Our position is somewhere in the infinite middle ground, where people struggle to make sense of their past and to widen the possibilities for their future. If such reasoning seems fuzzy at the outset, it is (no mathematical precision, remember). Yet history has an amazing way of becoming beveled and shaped within the historian's brain. John Hicks was given to wondering if history were akin to a series of unrelated explosions of differing intensity, with historians hopelessly trying to pick up the pieces between blasts. Despite his pessimism, he frankly confessed to a mild structuralism of his own. Hicks was an organicist: history appeared to him as seedtime, growth, decay, new life—all embodied in the notion of progress. While skeptical about the abilities of the modern human in relation to predecessors, Hicks nevertheless reshaped his history, as we all do. "When I pour it in sour—it always comes out sweet."[4]

The Idea of Change

"Things change." No statement encompassing human experience is so trite. Its threadbare nature aside, the idea of change or the sense of change is crucial to historians. Without the concept, they would be out of business. The more things change, the more they do *not* remain the same. The narrative historian in particular is positively in love with the idea; the more change, the better the story. We have all read pretty phrases in this regard that rest easy on our minds, so long as they are not examined too closely. For

[3] Jacques Barzun, *Clio and the Doctors: Psycho-History, Quanto-History, and History* (Chicago: University of Chicago Press, 1974), p. 96.
[4] John D. Hicks, *My Life with History: An Autobiography* (Lincoln: University of Nebraska Press, 1968), p. 78.

example, "the stream of time often doubles on its course, but always it makes for itself a new channel." Or, apropos of American colonial warfare, "the sun of History in its relentless march across the heavens of time was beginning to throw a shadow toward Lexington Green."[5]

Nothing seems more complex than our contemporary world, a condition which has reflected human bewilderment for millenia. "It will appear from countless examples how unstable are human affairs—like a sea driven by the winds," remarked the Renaissance historian Francesco Guicciardini.[6] Change, whether understood or not, adds to this bewilderment far more than resolving it. Historians assume that change is a virtually constant condition, but before we begin to consider change and historical process, we must consider the possibility of a world without change. Such a possibility is partially a matter of semantics. Environments change, human physical characteristics change, kingdoms rise and fall; all seems in flux to a greater or lesser degree, especially in our post-Darwinian world. These continuous changes, however, may mask a greater constancy—centered perhaps on human nature, or on the universe (Einstein notwithstanding). These are big questions, some would say metaphysical, and thus of no concern to the historian. As subjects of historical speculation, though, they do lend themselves to analyses of historical process, as we shall see.

Common sense helps us affirm that although change occurs, newer patterns of life contain elements of the old. There is no total difference with the past, just as there is no total similarity. What gives history value, according to one thinker, is "change within likeness and likeness within change."[7]

Again, we are dealing with a subjective component of human reason. Change to one observer will not be considered change to another, and estimates of rates of change vary as well. Consider two baseball catchers, primed to receive two fireballs. One catcher has an orthodox mitt; the other boldly squats behind the plate barehanded. As the respective pitchers begin to increase their ve-

[5] Frederick Lewis Allen, *Only Yesterday: An Informal History of the 1920's* (New York: Harper and Row, 1964 [1931]), p. 297; Douglas Edward Leach, *Arms for Empire: A Military History of the British Colonies in North America, 1607–1763* (New York: Macmillan, 1972), p. 147.

[6] Donald J. Wilcox, *In Search of God and Self: Renaissance and Reformation Thought* (Boston: Houghton Mifflin, 1975), p. 196.

[7] Pardon E. Tillinghast, quoted in Bernard Sternsher, *Consensus, Conflict, and American Historians* (Bloomington: Indiana University Press, 1975), p. 337.

locity, say to 90 mph, the bemitted one is cushioned against the shock, while the barehander may be rewarded with a broken hand. The event is the same; the results vary. So historians vary wildly in their estimates as they ask questions concerning change: (1) what are the important factors defining change? (2) at what pace did change occur? (3) what caused change? and (4) what were the results of change?

Some things in history are not as important as others. Napoleon's hairline receded through time; this is change, although not quite of world-historical importance. Napoleonic domestic reforms altered the course of French history—here is change that would seem to count more. No hard-and-fast rules exist for accepting one factor as a crucial component, or one facet of change as important and others not. If someone were so perverse as to write a *History of Baldness*, the Napoleonic hairline would doubtless take its place with other celebrated chromedomes—Ben Franklin, Kojak, Mr. Clean—and would doubtless emerge as more important than the emperor's domestic reforms. While the imperial pate is *sui generis*, Napoleon might conceivably be used to fit an evolutionary pattern of baldness throughout the ages (men were less bald in 1600, more bald in 1950).

In general, historians assert factors in human action as either direct or indirect agents of change. Not always, of course; earthquakes kill, plague decimates whole populations, a sudden rain changes the shape of a battle. Sometimes change may be a combination of intention and accident. By analyzing *before* and *after*, and carefully comparing the two, the historian might make a good guess at the components of change. Unfortunately, the business seldom comes easily.

A ludicrously simple example: Charles I of England was alive on January 30, 1649. The headsman's ax descended, and the king's severed head was held aloft. Change had occurred; *the king was executed*. A far from simple example: In A.D. 180, so Gibbon tells us, the Roman Empire "comprehended the fairest part of the earth, and the most civilized portion of mankind."[8] Three centuries later the Empire lay in shambles. Change had occurred; *the Roman Empire "fell."* But the difference is obvious. No sane historian would assert that Charles was machine-gunned in 1649. We have direct testimony (eyewitness) and indirect testimony (automatic weap-

[8] Edward Gibbon, *The Decline and Fall of the Roman Empire* I (New York: Modern Library, n.d.), p. 1.

ons were not invented until the nineteenth century) to the contrary. On the other hand, historians continually refresh themselves by debating the components of change involved in the fall of the Roman Empire; unlike Marcus Antoninus, these questions never grow old. The first question has been decided within reason; the second remains open. Both processes had far-reaching historical results, but in only the one instance is the analysis of the change itself reasonably beyond debate.

The *pace* of change is another question altogether. Many times change may occur in an instant (Charles's head was not sawed off with a pen-knife). At the other end of the scale geological change, which is of historical importance when connected with the human element, may be measured in eons. We will use the terms "reactionary," "revolutionary," and "conservative" to denote three differing ideas of the pace of change. These terms usually indicate political preferences, but as used here they refer only to conceptions of the pace of change. We are not trying to exhaust the possibilities, only to suggest some.

To reactionaries, any change bringing the new or strange, regardless of amount, is too much. An ounce means revolution, a pound anarchy. For them, the past is better. The dream of turning back the clock always glows, the brighter the more change bearing the unfamiliar accelerates. At the very least, reactionaries wish history to halt. At best, they would like it to recede. The seeming impossibility of the dream does not deter people from wishing it were so. The last Bourbon kings of France yearned for the years of royal absolutism that had vanished with Louix XIV over a century before. Reaction is a holding action against change. In reality it can be no more, although often the reactionary provides a powerful governor on the pace of change. Reactionaries have long been out of favor with the historical community. The reactionary tends to advance ideas of divine right and absolute power, methods of social control that seem outmoded to the modern liberal—but then, few historians have worn a crown.

At the other extreme, change may be considered as occurring too fast—breathless, jumbled, out of control. Revolutionary change involves the notions of time and effect. The beheading of Charles I was not a revolution, it was an event. Its *effect* may have been revolutionary; let historians debate. The sense of rapidity enters here. How fast did change occur? If in a relatively short period of time, possibly a revolution. But the amount of time involved in change cannot alone compose a revolution. Perceivably it took a relatively short time to shear Napoleon's hair; the balder he got, the less time involved. But the effect would only make historians yawn, not to mention Josephine. The effects of change must be of "historical importance." Here again criteria are unstable. Consider the series of events lumped under the rubric of "Industrial Revolution." The results changed the world, yet the events themselves did not happen overnight or even within the span of one life. More than semantics is at issue here; the question is *by what yardsticks should we measure historical change and its importance?*

Revolutionary change is complicated for historians because violence of some sort is usually perceived as connected with it. We tend to regard political revolutions with the attendant coups, countercoups, and other assorted treacheries as the models of revolutionary change, but these are only a few of the possibilities. Rapid change may be completely free of violence and yet of considered historical importance. Think of the occasional diplomatic rapprochement or the harnessing of electricity to steam power. A further complication lies in the possibility that a big change may consist of smaller changes, by themselves insubstantial but cumulatively of note. A major task of the critical historian lies in attempting to determine relative importance and in weighing the various factors as well as possible, looking at results as well as causes.

There remains a position we loosely denote as conservative, one that sees change and continuity existing together. Conservatives, unlike reactionaries, will admit the seeming inevitability of change. Unlike revolutionaries, who want to make tomorrow out of today, conservatives are cautious, Janus-faced. They look to the past not for a negative on the future, but for guidance. The past is their sea anchor as they seek the steadiest course ahead. For them, change must be controlled and its best aspects distilled to make a better future.

The classic conservative position was best stated by Gibbon's contemporary, Edmund Burke. Reaction and revolution, for Burke, were both mad chases in search of a fool's paradise. Change was mandatory; "a state without the means of some change is without the means of its conservation." On the other hand, not so fast. Burke believed that the two great principles of European civilization were, first, the learning and manners implicit in the code of a gentleman, and second, the order inherent in religion. Both these principles Burke saw being consumed in the fires of the French Revolution raging across the Channel. It was too much. Let the pace of change be slow and the middle way protected. "A disposition to preserve, and an ability to improve, would be my standard of a statesman."[9]

Reaction, revolution, and conservatism are variable, subjective components reflecting the pace of change. Unfortunately for the historian's peace of mind, however, change does not occur in a vacuum. The "before" and "after," cause and result, are what make change approachable analytically as well as substantively. We may readily observe in many instances the *fact* of change; we still want to know "why?" and "to what effect?"

Engines of Change: Questions of Cause

Give me a lever, Plutarch has Archimedes figuratively boast, and I can move the world.[10] Historians search for prime movers also, although usually not as part of so grand a scheme. Logically, the search for first causes in history may be carried out ad nauseam as well as ad infinitum. A simplistic person might credit the French Directory and its wishes for Napoleon to leave France, along with the young Corsican's ambition, as major causes of the Egyptian Expedition, but the meticulous logician would argue that there are primary causes for Napoleon's very existence, without which no expedition at all. So are Napoleon's mother and father responsible, then, for the event? The quest could rapidly become an endless process of unraveling genealogical tables.

Of lesser import, but still within the bounds of plausibility, is the chance that causes might be so intertwined as to be indistinguishable. In popular discourse, this is the "chicken and egg" question: which came first? Some historians are continuously concerned with the relationship of the chicken and the egg; others are not. Either way, the researcher who recedes into the infinite past or moves in circles looking for cause is on an errand of little promise. The practical, realistic approach usually ascribes causes to any number of antecedent factors that have a calculable and direct bearing on what ensues. There is very little scientific precision

[9] Edmund Burke, *Reflections on the Revolution in France* (New York: Everyman's Library, 1910), pp. 19–20, 76, 153. "Liberalism," in this scheme, would be ordered change as well, but a type of change enlisting, perhaps, the sympathy of masses rather than elites. Anyway, he who asserts constant definable differences between conservative and liberal is making bold with the evidence.

[10] *Plutarch's Lives*, trans. Dryden (New York: Modern Library, n.d.), p. 376.

here, although philosophers continually conjure up rules most historians ignore, perhaps a bit too blithely. The best advice, perhaps, is that change begins at home, as Leopold von Ranke, the influential German historian, once argued. Authority and opinion rarely encounter change from without, he asserted; "the hostilities by which they are overthrown are usually generated and nurtured within their own sphere."[11]

Change may be the product of a multiplicity of causes, or of a few, or of one, or, to the frustration of the historian, no cause can be ascertained reasonably. Change may be planned, and then (wonder of wonders) happen just that way. The planned change may go awry. Accidents intrude, more often than rational persons would like to admit. The historians must sort out these aspects, based on their evidence and their powers of reasoning.

What do you make, for instance, of the following famous but hypothetical example? Shakespeare's Richard III stands alone at Bosworth Field screaming "A horse! A horse! My kingdom for a horse!"[12] The Bard's younger contemporary, George Herbert, then pens his famous lines to the effect that there was no horse because the beast had not been shod, no shoeing because no nails could be found. Was the kingdom, then, lost for want of a nail? Or because of the lack of horseshoes? Or would Henry Tudor have defeated Richard anyway, horse or no? Although the example is from the Elizabethan stage, the stakes in real life were on a scale sufficient to engage the attention of historians. Richard and Henry contested for the Crown of England, and thus the search for causes, why Richard lost at Bosworth while Henry won, are important in a way they would not be had the two simply played a friendly game of chess.

The historian immersed in such complexities sometimes imagines too much. The temptation to overstep one's evidence and see causes where the evidence does not point may be most inviting, particularly so when the researcher has a pet theory to be tested against the evidence. Approaching historical problems theory first may be useful conceptually, but sidling up to the evidence in this way often puts cart before horse. Many historians have theories they wish to test against evidence, but the better ones do not let evidence truckle to theory, regardless of the situation.

---

[11] Peter Gay and Victor G. Wexler, eds., *Historians at Work*, III: *Niebuhr to Maitland* (New York: Harper and Row, 1975), p. 48.

[12] *King Richard III*, act V, scene 4, line 7.

Put another way, theory is not cause, and vice versa. We may theorize as to what a certain cause was, to be sure, but unknown causes cannot be summoned forth by theory—only by historical evidence. True, theory may make the causes coherent and inter-related in a meaningful pattern. But first, the questions eliciting the evidence must be asked, and these may be theory-directed or not, with the risks previously mentioned.

A trite example should make the point. The "devil theory" of war has enjoyed a long and somewhat indecent career among historians. Though it comes in several variant forms, the devil theory generally holds that in a war, it is the enemy who (1) caused the war; (2) seeks to profit inordinately by the war, usually through world conquest; and (3) wages the war with a bestial ferocity beyond the bounds of civilization. Strained as they are, these concepts still make up a theory, one that attempts to postulate the nature of the enemy in a war situation. Many Americans, for instance, felt precisely this way about Imperial Germany in 1917 and 1918.

History can be and has been written, mostly along nationalist lines, to agree with the devil theory of war. Armed with the theory, the researcher can sift out evidence that is not in accord. Material implying that Imperial Germany was not the only instigator of World War I, for example, could then be discarded. The result, of course, would not be history, but a polemic—yet many "histories" have been written under these or like circumstances. The devil theory is slick enough to transcend shooting wars. "It was borne in upon us, with increasing ominousness," wrote Frederick Lewis Allen in the wake of World War II, "that Soviet Russia in her turn was bent upon world conquest."[13] Everything the Soviet Union did during this period could thus be interpreted in this light—and often was.

Establishing cause is such a tricky business because the written record, upon which the historian relies so strongly, is not in itself a complete basis for causal analysis. "Words and deeds are not the same thing; if they were, we would all be under arrest."[14] Words often give us *reasons* for historical action, the justification for the event. Reasons may tell us the explanation for an event or

[13] Frederick Lewis Allen, *The Big Change: America Transforms Itself, 1900–1950* (New York: Harper and Row, 1969 [1952]), p. 153.
[14] George Wolfskill, *Happy Days Are Here Again! A Short Interpretive History of the New Deal* (Hinsdale, Ill.: Dryden Press, 1974), p. 121.

the purpose for which an event was designed. But reasons are not causes; if they were, the truth value of historical documents would be virtually 100 percent, and when the documents disagree, as they invariably do, historians would have no recourse but to drop back fifteen yards and punt. Another simple hypothetical example will illustrate the difference.

Say we wish to analyze a military battle, to see what caused the battle to happen and how the course of the battle went. We have before us the orders of the various commanders, issued before the contest was joined. To write the history of the battle from these orders, that is, a priori, would obviously be logically fallacious. Yet the orders, while not the deeper *causes* of the battle, afford us some of the *reasons* why the battle took the shape it did. For the rest, we rely on eyewitness accounts, orders issued during the fighting, the inevitable memoirs of generals or admirals, and our knowledge of terrain, military capacity of the contenders, and the like.

To complicate matters further, many causes are "hidden." That is, the causes of a certain event may be unrecognizable or only dimly sensed to contemporaries who offer the historian evidence. Their ideas of cause may not satisfy the historian, who knows what the contemporaries could not know—the long-range *results* of the event. What could not be distinguished up close many times emerges clearly with hindsight, which, if not always "20-20," has a certain capacity for accuracy often (but not always) denied contemporaries. The folksinger Pete Seeger has allegorized for us:

> A big steel cargo ship carried a full load of soy beans. There was a leak in the boat, but the captain didn't know about it. Every day when they checked the bilge, it was dry. The water was being absorbed by the beans as it leaked out. One day that ship just split in half and sank. The beans had gradually swelled and swelled, until the pressure was too much; the steel plates cracked, just like that. Snap.[15]

The assertion of a hidden cause does not, of course, free the historian from the responsibility to judge contemporaries in the light of their knowledge. Perhaps the captain was ignorant of the water-retentive capacity of soybeans.

Because history is about people, the analysis of cause cannot

[15] Jerome L. Rodnitzky, *Minstrels of the Dawn: The Folk-Protest Singer as a Cultural Hero* (Chicago: Nelson-Hall, 1976), pp. 19–20.

always be judged as a logical operation. Just as people may behave irrationally, so causes may be of an irrational rather than rational nature. Ideology and interest, for instance, may mesh to the point where they are virtually impossible to sift out through historical analysis. The rational and the irrational are not poles apart in human behavior. The irrational cause, we hasten to add, may influence history as much or more than the rational one. Many historical events have occurred under the influence of human faith, or anger, or insanity. Divine causes, whether they emanate from pagan concepts of Fortune or Christian ideas of God and Christ, must be given historical weight. Developments that the ancients could not explain in any other way they attributed to the gods. Hebrews, Greeks, and Romans all regarded history as a mixture of human unpredictability and divine providence. The historian must always be cognizant that people will, on occasion, *act* on their beliefs. That rage, anger, or any other emotional excess departing from the norm have influenced history is plentifully indicated, if only by consideration of the ongoing prevalence of political assassinations.

On the borders of the irrational, and tenuously connected with cause, exists a concept called the "spirit of an age." The "spirit" is a very fuzzy idea, yet one that enjoyed a great deal of popularity during the nineteenth century. The spirit has been used to explain practically everything; for example, Van Wyck Brooks credits the "time-spirit of Western civilization" as a major cause of post–Civil War change in the United States.[16] As surface analysis, the utilization of such concepts relates more to belief than fact. Upon closer inspection, the "spirit of an age" and its somewhat more constricted little brother, the "climate of opinion," are extremely frail foundations upon which to build causal relationships. Historians immersed in these concepts must immediately defend themselves against not-so-frivolous questioning as to what such "spirit" or "climate" consists of. Once these questions have been addressed, the concept tends to evaporate, unless a researcher is already operating within the frontiers of faith.

The need to establish cause will not vanish. Thinkers have often yearned for some kind of system that would, once and for all, logically link cause and effect in such a way that history might become a true science, even if only a "social" science. The urge to empirical reasoning is thus always strong, the more enticing the

[16] Van Wyck Brooks, *New England: Indian Summer, 1865–1915* (New York: E. P. Dutton, 1940), p. 94.

more empiricism implies formula. At the furthest reaches, as in the thought of the nineteenth-century French philosopher Auguste Comte, historical narrative vanishes in favor of a totally scientific reconstruction of the past. History in this sense becomes cause piled upon cause, and that only. The tale history tells then unfolds logically and rationally, welded together by cause from past to present.

No historian has yet been able to achieve this kind of perfection, save by self-delusion. When the researcher shapes evidence into a story, some of the incidents may be causally related. But the story can still make sense even if incidents are not causally connected.[17] Historians of thought, in particular, often tell effective stories in which causation is either held in abeyance or ignored completely.

We cling to analyses of causation in the hope that establishing probable cause will make history "true," or at the very least "probably true." Cause helps us explain change rationally. And yet, Robert Frost can still tell us something with lines like these:

> For dear me, why abandon a belief
> Merely because it ceases to be true?
> Cling to it long enough, it will turn true again,
> For so it goes.
> Most of the change we think we see in life
> Is due to truths being in and out of Favor.[18]

Historians who overlook cause altogether are neglecting one of the most challenging aspects of their craft. Others may agree with James Harvey Robinson of Columbia University, who early in this century asserted confidentially that it was not the real business of the historian to determine *what* had happened. Rather, the historian should be concerned with *how* things happened—that is, establish cause. Once achieved in this way, history would then possess, perhaps, a "logic" all its own. The possibilities have intrigued speculators on the past for centuries; they pave the way for historians traveling the high road to determinism.

[17] For comment on this point, see Haskell Fain, *Between Philosophy and History: The Resurrection of Speculative Philosophy of History within the Analytic Tradition* (Princeton: Princeton University Press, 1970), pp. 277–308.

[18] Wilson Carey McWilliams, *The Idea of Fraternity in America* (Berkeley: University of California Press, 1974 [1973]), p. 517.

CHAPTER SIX

The Lure of Determinism

Logically, determinism is a fairly simple business. We might say "if A, then B, and only B." That is, A *determines* B. Of course, people are not ciphers and continue to be tenacious in their refusal to be so evaluated; yet historical determinism persists.

To be sure, the creed in all its varieties has seen better days. The hope once prevailed in some quarters that history could be reduced to a set of laws, or master themes. These laws would hold not only for the past, but for the future as well. Usually, determinism implied that nature behaves in a predictable fashion, rather than by change. Effects would follow from conditions that determine their qualities. Applied to history, determinism thus was potentially a science of human historical development, although it did not necessarily rule out free will.[1] The idea may come to the fore again, since totalitarian or authoritarian regimes in particular admire the deterministic view of history, so long as the view substantiates the supremacy of the rulers.

"Determinism" as a concept has a relatively brief history. It is a Kantian term, from the late eighteenth century, but its future lay in the 1800s. The nineteenth century percolated with confidence in science and the scientific method. Every year the frontiers of the mind expanded, and rapidly—in physics, biology, medicine, and a host of other disciplines. The new social sciences, already laggards by custom, in general strove mightily to avoid being left behind in the race for the empirical diadem. The "discovery" of "social laws" made the presses hum, particularly after Darwin's epochal mid-

[1] Franklin L. Baumer, *Modern European Thought: Continuity and Change in Ideas, 1600–1950* (New York: Macmillan, 1977), pp. 311–12.

century writings, which were to be so abused by the social sciences. If the laws that governed human development were hidden, their revelation would be only a matter of time. Witness the moody yet still hopeful Henry Adams, writing to fellow Brahmin Francis Parkman: "The purely mechanical development of the human mind in society must appear in a great democracy so clearly, for want of disturbing elements, that in another generation psychology, physiology, and history will join in proving man to have as fixed and necessary development as that of a tree; and almost as unconscious."[2]

Believing this, people had only to ascertain the secrets of history. Once uncovered, these secrets would unlock all the mysteries. Human development, the course of entire civilizations, indeed, the very shape of the future, could all be registered in the discerning mind of the empirical historian. The truth *was* there; that in claiming its existence they were indulging in speculation, not science, did not trouble those who looked for the laws. Like the black radical Malcolm X, a late convert to the Moslem religion, the determinists could have advanced the ultimate argument from faith: "Everything is written."[3] But is it?

The Environment and Determinism

Only a fool discounts nature. Our age, surrounded by an endless assortment of electrically powered devices, artificial flavorings, spray deodorants, and all sorts of other paraphernalia that tend to isolate man from his surroundings, often indulges in the vain claim that the environment can be mastered. Space flight in particular has led moderns toward a certain contempt for nature, the environmentalist movement notwithstanding. Space and time seem either to have vanished or to have been controlled.

Only slight reflection is needed to establish the nonsensical aspects of such conceit. If clouds can be seeded, still the floods or droughts come; if men can move mountains, so can earthquakes. For virtually all history, people have been at the mercy of the en-

[2] Peter Gay and Victor G. Wexler, eds., *Historians at Work*, III: *Niebuhr to Maitland* (New York: Harper and Row, 1975), p. 246. Adams, in the final twenty-five years of his life, grew disenchanted with the possibility of scientific history, even criticizing his own highly regarded historical work as a failure.

[3] Malcolm X, *The Autobiography of Malcolm X* (New York: Grove Press, 1964), p. 149.

vironment. Their slow steps toward accommodation with their surroundings, most of which have occurred very recently, pale beside the power of nature. The relationship of the environment toward the humans it tolerates is the seed of geographic determinism.

A classic example of geographic determinism may be found in American history, where several historians have argued that the American environment—rich, vast, underpopulated—led directly to a certain type of American political development—individualistic and democratic.[4] In short, geographic preconditions explained American development, in a way that geography could not do for established European or Asian cultures.

The connection between history and geography, perceived in this way, has been until recently a common one. The two were once assumed to be virtually inseparable sciences, with history taking its cue from geography. Geographers were arrogant enough to assume that history was produced by the environment, that geography was the necessary precondition for history. Historians naturally found this argument somewhat less than irresistible, yet they could not avoid the obvious influences that geography has had upon historical development. "The fundamental reality of any civilization must be in its geographic cradle," Fernand Braudel has concluded.[5]

Any researcher dealing with population movements, wars, economic patterns, and numerous other topics must necessarily consider geography. So strong is the impact of the environment in many major cases of historical analysis that some thinkers have concluded that the natural dimension is everything; somewhere the German philosopher Herder wrote that history was only geography set in motion. Jules Michelet, as he began his famous hymn to the French people in the *History of France*, asserted that at first, "history is altogether geography." The political division of France was founded on its natural division. "From the point of view where we are about to place ourselves," Michelet wrote, "we shall predict

---

[4] A critical review of this reasoning, concentrating on the work of Daniel Boorstin and Louis Hartz, may be found in Bernard Sternsher, *Consensus, Conflict, and American Historians* (Bloomington: Indiana University Press, 1975), pp. 28–60. Beginning students should not ignore the classic exposition of the theme in Frederick Jackson Turner, *The Frontier in American History* (New York: Holt, Rinehart, and Winston, 1965 [1920]).

[5] Edward Whiting Fox, *History in Geographic Perspective: The Other France* (New York: W. W. Norton, 1971), p. 19; Fernand Braudel, *The Mediterranean and the Mediterranean World in the Age of Philip II*, II, rev. ed., trans. Siân Reynolds (New York: Harper and Row, 1976 [1966]), p. 773.

what each of [the political divisions] will do and produce; we shall indicate to them their destiny, and dower them in the cradle." Jaime Vicens Vives, who almost alone modernized the Spanish historical tradition, began one of his best studies by boldly stating that the nature of the Spanish land masses "determined" the infrastructure of Spain's economic history. For Walter Prescott Webb, historian of the American Great Plains, there was a law in human affairs higher than man's law—the "law of nature," which controlled the settlement and development of his region.[6]

The historical emphasis on geographical factors is usually traced to the eighteenth century, when Enlightenment thinkers, notably Baron Montesquieu, argued that geography and climate directly affected both political institutions and legal systems. Heretofore war had been thought to be the major trauma for mankind. Montesquieu, whose impact on his fellow savants was considerable, advanced the notion that man was directed as much or more by the environment. These themes have persisted to the present day, although modern technology has tended to diminish their power in relation to recent history. A modern survey of Europe in Montesquieu's own time, for example, includes the phrase "Sardinia, like Prussia, presented the case of geography making conscience impossible." Likewise, Webb wrote that the environment in the American West was an "overwhelming force" that caused men and institutions to "bend to its imperious influence."[7]

In America, continuing our original example, geographic emphasis has played a major role in the work of historians such as Daniel Boorstin. For Boorstin, American society was produced by the particularities of the American environment. Climate, soil, mineral wealth—all are direct influences on the American experience. The problem, when one confronts thinkers like Montesquieu, Michelet, Webb, or Boorstin, is to assess *to what degree* geography influences history in their thought. Is geography everything? If so, then geography (for them) does determine history.

Unfortunately for the geographical determinists, the environment, while clearly limiting human action, still allows consider-

[6] Gay and Wexler, ed., *Historians at Work*, III, 70–71; Peter Gay and Gerald J. Cavanaugh, eds., *Historians at Work*, IV: *Dilthey to Hofstadter* (New York: Harper and Row, 1975), p. 220; Necah Stewart Furman, *Walter Prescott Webb: His Life and Impact* (Albuquerque: University of New Mexico Press, 1976), p. 90.
[7] Walter L. Dorn, *Competition for Empire, 1740–1763* (New York: Harper and Row, 1963 [1940]), p. 154; Furman, *Walter Prescott Webb*, p. 14.

able independence for that action. To a great degree, people choose among environmental alternatives. Napoleon sailed to Egypt in 1798 across the Mediterranean; conceivably he could have marched his men most of the way—a foolhardy choice, perhaps, but one that was available.

More to the point, geography, like time, is inert. Once living creatures, such as the grizzly, or plant life, like the cactus, are added, we might style the result environment. In this sense, both geography and the environment, when they interact with humans, retain their capability of influencing human action. "It is worth repeating," commented Braudel, "that history is not made by geographical features, but by the men who control or discover them."[8]

Humans may make geography respond, just as geography may condition their response. Such interaction, however, is not determinism. The determinist would argue that influence is a one-way street, running from geography to history. But to the degree the environment is malleable, the influence is more correctly two-way, and the researcher who ignores environmental factors (one can almost hear Samuel Eliot Morison, who personally traced many of the great voyages about which he wrote, snorting "Armchair sailors!") does so at his own peril.

The environment in which we live extends beyond geography. Only recently have historians begun to emphasize the historical influence of disease. Different environments, different diseases; Eskimos rarely get yellow fever. Until the medical revolution of the last century, diseases periodically eliminated entire populations and even today retain their potential for havoc in much of the world. Regular trade contacts between European and Asian civilizations around the time of Christ created what William McNeill calls a "uniform disease pool" in which patterns of infectious disease spread throughout the known world. By the tenth century, Chinese and European populations that were relatively resistant to certain diseases began to outgrow the populations of the Middle East and India. McNeill concludes that "subsequent world history could in fact be written around this fact,"[9] a statement that skirts the edges of determinism.

That disease has influenced history in major ways is obvious.

[8] Braudel, *The Mediterranean and the Mediterranean World in the Age of Philip II*, I, 225. Braudel's leisurely discussion of the relationship of Mediterranean geography to its history is in many ways a model account.

[9] William H. McNeill, *Plagues and Peoples* (Garden City, N.Y.: Anchor Press, 1976), p. 145.

Disease can kill off whole populations; in the fourteenth century the Black Death, or bubonic plague, eradicated probably one-third of the population of England, an equal percentage in France, and probably as high as 60 percent of the urban residents of Italy. The plague directly influenced social and economic life, education, agriculture, even architecture. Psychologically, the disease was a terrible blow, the effects of which lasted well beyond the lives of those spared its ravages. Centuries later, the rise of England and the decline of France in the eighteenth century have been traced to England's greater ability to control plague, malaria, and smallpox.[10] Examples could be multiplied endlessly.

There is something seductive about ascribing major historical results to tiny microbes and their interaction with humans. McNeill has argued that early on in our relationship with epidemic and endemic diseases, "parasitic gradients" were created in which different climates fostered different types of parasitic organisms. Populations from warmer, wetter climates could travel to cooler, drier areas and run little danger of being infested by unfamiliar parasites; the opposite was not true. Cold and dry climates fostered an ecological balance with plants and animals, not with parasitic organisms. Tropical diseases long kept European cultures from infiltrating warmer, wetter gradients. A corollary is that Africa, for example, has in the minds of whites remained "backward" in terms of its civilization. Its history has been *determined* largely by its differing disease patterns. Disease, then, may be a greater weapon among civilizations than the mightiest army. Diseased or disease-resistant populations, in confrontation with populations susceptible to disease, have every advantage.[11] Several Indian tribes on the east coast of North America were literally obliterated by their contact with European diseases within a generation of the European landings.

Disease patterns in both their individual and collective sense are well within the concern of the historian. We want to know how important Napoleon's famous tummy-ache actually was—not because he suffered it after a bout with Josephine, but on the field at Waterloo. Likewise, the spread of infectious disease has been of major importance in the development of our entire history. Yet limits exist here, also. While McNeill correctly argues that infec-

[10] Philip Ziegler, *The Black Death* (New York: Harper and Row, 1971 [1969]), pp. 224–31; McNeill, *Plagues and Peoples*, pp. 256–57.
[11] McNeill, *Plagues and Peoples*, pp. 30, 48, 76.

tious disease will remain "one of the fundamental parameters and determinants of human history," [12] the balance between the human race and disease is not static. Some killers of the past—cholera, smallpox, plague, yellow fever, polio—no longer have the capacity to devastate whole populations, if treated properly. Indeed, the world population explosion, a cruelly ironic partial result of our successes against disease, has become a factor of crucial historical importance.

Disease, like geography and the broader environment, is a critical component of human history. As a unilateral determinant, however, it falls short. Microbes do not concern themselves with the laws of history, any more than do the mountains and the rivers. It is we who make these laws, and who then busily provide the action that undoes them.

The Guiding Hand: Determinism and the Irrational

Thinking has its limits. The world more often than not seems out of control, at least out of human control. Just as order may be perceived in the irrational, so too may process be considered, as part of a vast scheme no one can comprehend but of which everyone is a part.

The power of the irrational in shaping our vision of our past is unquestioned. Over and over again the chorus has swelled, for example among the Romanticists of the early nineteenth century, that human emotions are the moving force in human destiny. We only delude ourselves with our reason, for instinct is the surest guide.

While the Romanticists have had their day, their insistence on the primacy of instinct over intellect has gained new depth and ostensible scientific justification from psychology. To Sigmund Freud, standing at the fountainhead of the new "science," history had a first cause, a "primal event." The primal event created societies and specified patterns of morality. More importantly, it *determined* all subsequent human action. Freud thus denied the possibility of fundamental change for either the human race or society. We are wedded to our nature for eternity. [13]

[12] Ibid., p. 291.
[13] Bruce Mazlish, *The Riddle of History: The Great Speculators from Vico to Freud* (New York: Minerva Press, 1968), p. 424.

Although both the Romanticists and the Freudians centered their attention on the irrational aspects of human behavior, the Freudians and their followers tried to explore the irrational with rational methods. Others placidly regarded human intellect as ineffectual. Leo Tolstoy believed that rationalism was a cover-up for that which people could not explain. All human action, for him, was directed by "natural law." This condition so offends our reason, however, that we must delude ourselves by believing that life is a succession of free choices.[14] Mysticism is elevated to a philosophy of quiescent acceptance, one that obviously does not sit well with the dynamic industrial nations of the West.

Geography aside, the most common focus of history as irrational process has centered on the divine. In most divine plans, history is *teleological*: it has a purpose and operates to a final, predestined end. No matter that the irascible Mark Twain could call teleological theories of history "lies of silent assertion."[15] Millions of people have not only believed such theories; they have tried to live their lives in accordance with them. The pagan concept of "Fortune" functioned in this manner. "Just as Fortune made almost all the affairs of the world incline in one direction, and forced them to converge upon one and the same point," earnestly wrote Polybius, "so it is my task as an historian to put before my readers a compendious view of the part played by Fortune in bringing about her general purpose."[16]

With the coming of the Christian era, western civilization thus was prepared to accept the notion of a single divinity (as opposed to the ideas of most pantheistic pagan cultures) determining human affairs. The Jewish but pro-Roman historian Josephus, writing in the first century A.D., introduced the providence of God into human destiny. He is perhaps the first historian to separate our baser nature from our higher instincts. God shows the way to salvation, while people "owe their destruction to folly and calamities of their own choosing."[17] Such a distinction, impinging as it does on the fundamental question of whether people possess a "free

[14] Isaiah Berlin, *The Hedgehog and the Fox: An Essay on Tolstoy's View of History* (New York: Simon and Schuster, 1970), p. 27.

[15] Wilson Carey McWilliams, *The Idea of Fraternity in America* (Berkeley: University of California Press, 1974 [1973]), p. 453.

[16] Peter Gay and Gerald J. Cavanaugh, eds., *Historians at Work*, I: *Herodotus to Froissart* (New York: Harper and Row, 1972), p. 112. See also Herbert Butterfield, *The Origins of History* (New York: Basic Books, 1981).

[17] Gay and Cavanaugh, eds., *Historians at Work*, I, 202.

will," allows God an omnipotent benevolence at the same time it accounts for all the horrors people visit upon themselves.

As Christianity triumphed throughout most of Europe, much of its strength came from historical determinism. Eusebius, sometimes called "the father of ecclesiastical history," wrote in his *Chronicle* (c. 303–25) that history tended in one direction; even before Christ, the Christian era was foreshadowed. Whether one speaks of mathematics, literature, or history, God directed these tools of the human race toward the creation and perfection of Christianity.

By the time of Augustine the universal church had begun to emerge from dream to institutional reality. Augustine's masterpiece, *The City of God* (413–26), was a defense of Christianity within the decaying Roman Empire. Herein he postulated the existence of two historical worlds, the temporal city and the City of God. The history of the temporal city is of passing importance; what counts is eternal life in the eternal city. History, for Augustine, was a Christian morality play par excellence. The great events are not the temporal ones—the Persian Wars, the rise of Rome—but the spiritual. Thus the stories of the Garden of Eden, the Resurrection, the promise of the Second Coming of Christ became the true history of humanity. The basis of history, in other words, was not the worldly activities of men and women but the progressive unfolding of God's plan.[18]

What was God's plan, and in what direction did it tend? Although there have been many minor variations, the general scheme of things decreed humanity's spiritual salvation. Theologians debated, in the centuries following Augustine, in exactly what fashion the earthly millennium would be achieved. For example, Joachim of Fiore, a medieval Calabrian abbot, perceived in history a pattern that enabled him to prophesy its future stages. There would come an age of the Father or of the Law, an age of the Son or of the Gospel, and finally an age of the Spirit, wherein the human race would realize a mystic happiness lasting until the Last Judgment.[19] What was not in doubt was the impending fact of the millennium itself, which had been determined by Christ's existence. In the view of certain New Testament authors, history moves toward a definite climax, or *eschaton*. The Book of Revelation advances the

---

[18] Ibid., pp. 253–54, 270–71.
[19] Norman Cohn, *The Pursuit of the Millennium*, rev. ed. (New York: Oxford University Press, 1970), pp. 108–109. See also p. 155.

idea of *chiliasm*, in which Christ will rule on earth while the identity of anti-Christ is at last revealed. Christ's return marks an end to history and the inauguration of spiritual perfection for eternity.

Pending this development, human temporal existence continued to be underwritten with spiritual justifications. Not until empirical science grew strong enough to contest religion (and this did not begin to occur prior to the seventeenth century) did men venture an historical alternative to divinely conditioned process. Jacques Bénigne Bossuet, court priest to Louis XIV, offers us an excellent illustration of the intermingling of Augustine's two cities. For Bossuet (who once began a sermon before his king by equating Louis with God), church, state, and crown were one and the same. God is the true principle of history, and the hand of God sustains the authority of religion. Every historical event was the product of God's will, to the end that the "chosen people" might flourish. Obviously, this vision is extremely malleable, as any culture might regard itself as "chosen." But for Bossuet, his chosen "nation" was the Roman Catholic Church, which as he wrote had been enduring 150 years of Protestant schism. The temporal crown and the spiritual church, through the king, spoke as one.[20] "Divine right" monarchy was thus the logical culmination of history.

Lest we become convinced that history brings happiness only to kings, we should note that religious determinism, for political purposes, has tended in other directions as well. Even a skeptic like Pierre Bayle, who certainly disagreed with his contemporary Bossuet over the latter's ideas of God's intervention in history, could think of divine providence as a force for historical order. For Bayle, Providence was a "restraining grace which, like a strong dike, holds back the waters of sin as much as is necessary to prevent a general inundation."[21]

Despite being a set of laws, determinism is marvelously plastic. For some, God wears a crown; for others, He is a democrat. The onset of democratic revolutions brought in its wake historical assessments that saw God's imprint everywhere. George Bancroft, writing in the euphoric years of youthful American nationalism, perceived God's design in history just as had Bossuet. But Bancroft believed that human faith in discovering God's truth led to faith in human ability to be self-governing. Church and state were still

[20] Peter Gay and Victor G. Wexler, eds., *Historians at Work*, II: *Valla to Gibbon* (New York: Harper and Row, 1972), pp. 203, 199, 213–14.
[21] Baumer, *Modern European Thought*, pp. 120–21.

connected, only now both were democratic. The state affirmed and protected the "universal verities" of Christianity, just as Christianity taught the morality necessary to sustain self-government. Such faith had caused the American Revolution and had led directly to the type of government that followed.[22] America was truly a nation under God (just as France had been under Louis).

The irrational modes of determinism grew progressively weaker as the march of science rolled on. After Darwin, after Marx, after Freud, determinism itself gained new life in some quarters, girded now by empiricism rather than belief. Today, historians all but ignore the kind of faith that illuminated the view of history held by the Bossuets and Bancrofts. Yet the historical community as much as any branch of scholarship has been forced to reflect on the relationship of its discipline with the polar gods of science and faith. Reason and emotion conduct eternal war; perhaps this is the truest determinism of all.

The Varieties of Scientific Determinism

The "laws" of the physical world, as they began to be "discovered" in the seventeenth and eighteenth centuries, seemed to spawn a host of possibilities for analyzing not only human environment but humanity itself. Even history, studied scientifically, could be made to yield laws concerning our biological, intellectual, cultural, and spiritual development, Science would simplify and explain, according to its advocates. People began to search for the keys to historical laws, keys that would be secular, turning at the behest of reason rather than faith.

The hopes for a scientific history had brightened for decades before an almost unknown German thinker, Karl Marx, began to write in the 1840s. Perhaps typical of the ideas of the Age of Reason was the proposal of the mathematician Pierre Laplace. Laplace's universe is devoid of uncertainty. All history is fixed in a rigid mold of cause and effect. Laplace admits the possibility of change, but change does not alter the basics of the universe; it produces nothing new. His scheme was the logical culmination of Newtonian physics applied to history.[23]

[22] Russel B. Nye, *George Bancroft* (New York: Washington Square Press, 1964), pp. 134–35.
[23] Baumer, *Modern European Thought*, pp. 460–61.

While he was thus not the first of the scientific determinists, Marx is beyond doubt the most important. Marxist thought is complex and at times contradictory, but Marx's basic deterministic ideas seem relatively clear. After emigrating to England in 1849, Marx experienced at first hand the developing labor-capital relationship in the world's most industrialized economy. Building on his earlier observations on the Continent, he attempted to develop a theory that in the last analysis would rest on science and that would explain human social development. Marx was extremely conscious of change and its effects; he saw the results all around him in England's "dark, satanic mills," and he did not like what he saw.

For Marx, the task of history "is to establish the truth of this world." Once established, the truth would become the engine of worldwide revolution. An earlier German philosopher, Georg W. F. Hegel, served as the younger man's sounding board in establishing Marx's truth. Hegel had argued that laws indeed govern history, but Hegel's system rested on ideas and a rather vague concept of "absolute will" overshadowing all. Marx kept the substance of the famous Hegelian dialectic, which accounts for change in an orderly, patterned way: thesis-counterthesis-synthesis. But Marx and his lifelong friend and collaborator, Friedrich Engels, rejected Hegelian mysticism. In contrast to "German philosophy" (by which they largely meant Hegel), "which descends from heaven to earth, here we ascend from earth to heaven."[24]

History is determined materialistically; this was Marx's truth. Meshing the notion of changing cultural patterns with the evolutionary concept of life itself as a struggle, Marx centered his attention on the "dismal science" of economics. He reasoned that those who control the means of production also determine what classes of society would dominate at any given historical moment. Social classes continually are in contention, for the material rewards are great and the seemingly ancillary benefits by way of social control greater still. The laboring classes, for Marx, are the children of destiny. As they are the fundamental agents of production, so would they inevitably reap the benefits that are rightfully theirs. This proletariat would not succeed immediately, however; the dominant classes would never surrender meekly all that had sustained them for myriad generations.

[24] Mazlish, *The Riddle of History*, p. 250; Gay and Wexler, eds., *Historians at Work*, III, 120.

Here is Marx's "great law," which, with even greater distortions, would indeed change the world in the twentieth century, although certainly not as Marx himself had ordained. Engels confidently described his hero's achievement:

> It was precisely Marx who had first discovered the great law of motion of history, the law according to which all historical struggles, whether they proceed in the political, religious, philosophical or some other ideological domain, are in fact only the more or less clear expression of struggles of social classes, and that the existence and thereby the collisions, too, between these classes are in turn conditioned by the degree of development of their economic position, by the mode of their production and of their exchange determined by it.[25]

The weaknesses of Marxist thought are fundamentally those of all determinist schemes: if events do not develop as predicted, the thesis tends to be weakened. Yet Marx spoke powerfully to the have-nots of the world, and millions of them have responded. The great twentieth-century revolutions in Russia and China did not fit the orthodox Marxist pattern (the revolution was to come first in those areas that had experienced the apogee of capitalism), but Marxist writings, in the liturgical sense, have made him the god of modern revolution. Marx to a great degree perceived humanity as one-dimensional, an economic entity. His materialistic emphasis is his greatest strength, because his formula appeals so potently to the disadvantaged, but it is his greatest weakness historically, for he downplays or ignores the role of ideas in history and rejects completely the irrational as a factor.

So great has been the influence of Marx during the past century that alternate "scientific" views of the human past have tended to lose force by comparison, particularly among the peoples of the nonindustrialized nations. These views might be lumped, somewhat unfairly, under the title of "cultural determinism," since they all perceive humanity as proceeding along lines of development indicated by human environment. Cultural determinism reflects not so much on production, distribution, or consumption as it does on behavior, attitudes, and value systems. Anthropology has fostered cultural determinism to a certain degree; anthropologists like Ruth

[25] Haskell Fain, *Between Philosophy and History: The Resurrection of Speculative Philosophy of History within the Analytic Tradition* (Princeton: Princeton University Press, 1970), pp. 233–34.

Benedict believed that in any culture the institutionalized forms of behavior available to the deviant or unstable individual are culturally determined.[26]

The two strongest examples of cultural determinism rest on the concepts of race and nationalism. Racism as a philosophy that both explains and predicts human development was elevated to "scientific" status in the nineteenth century, primarily by such archtheorists of racial discrimination as Arthur Count de Gobineau. Like religious determinism, racial determinism takes several variant forms but almost always favors European and American white people (naturally enough, since it is usually these types who are doing the theorizing). In Gobineau's pessimistic vision, the superior white race, the "Nordics," had had their day, and white-structured civilization was on the road to disintegration. Others who did not share Gobineau's gloomy outlook promoted periodic campaigns to keep the white race from becoming "mongrelized."[27] An avalanche of pseudo-scientific prattle was unleashed in these crusades, ranging from the analysis of skull shapes to the supposed climatic adaptability of the various races.

Despite its shaky empirical stance, racism has had considerable historical effect. The results may be seen in authoritarian social systems, slavery, the fevers of nationalism, and anti-immigration laws, to mention only a few examples. To the convinced, the situation seemed obvious. "The basic factor in human affairs is not politics, but race," proclaimed Lothrop Stoddard, a Harvard Ph.D., in 1920. Here is Stoddard's fundamental truth; using it as a guide, he could describe World War I as "nothing short of a headlong plunge into white race—suicide." Human marks of distinction—hair, skin color, eyes—became indices of behavior and, more importantly, of civilization.

Only posterity will know if racial determinism reached its final, horrible climax in Hitler's Third Reich. For the present, we hold with Lord Acton's criticism that racial determinism denies both human identity and individual liberty. Gobineau, for Acton, had concocted only "one of many schemes to deny free will, responsibility, and guilt, and to supplant moral by physical forces."[28]

[26] Margaret Mead, *Ruth Benedict* (New York: Columbia University Press, 1974), p. 44.

[27] Thomas F. Gossett, *Race: The History of an Idea in America* (New York: Schocken Books, 1965 [1963]), pp. 352–53.

[28] Lothrop Stoddard, *The Rising Tide of Color against White World-Supremacy* (New York: Blue Ribbon Books, 1920), pp. 5, 179; Gertude Him-

Nationalism is a somewhat vaguer concept than race, but no less influential for that. There was a time, not all that remote from ours, when "national character" was a theme of overriding importance for many historians. National and racial stereotypes were the almost inevitable results, not only in the common coin of popular discourse but among professional scholars as well. The German word *Volksgeist* was a powerful term, implying that national character in itself impelled change. Historians of all nationalities have adhered to the idea—the American Bancroft, the Frenchman Michelet, the Englishman Macaulay, and the German Treitschke are conspicuous examples—and have done so with the devoted encouragement of the nations and national aspects they have championed. National histories, though somewhat diminished from their high fervor of a century ago, still are unrivaled today as a central mode of historical interpretation, unless it be by the Marxist approach.

Classic national determinism held that the growth of national institutions, such as the American presidency, English parliament, or Prussian General Staff, determined human character and hence historical development. Obviously, nationalism could not be used to analyze those cultures where the concept and its practice were unknown, like the Egypt of the Pharaohs or the Scandinavia of the Vikings. Yet national interpretations seemed both to explain and sustain the modern course of history.

Not everyone ran with the crowd, by any means. National character could be admitted as a concept—"nobody doubts it who knows schools or armies," Acton sourly commented—but this did not mean it was a determinant in history. For Acton, the advance of civilization went beyond nationality; nationality inhibited the real goal of human existence, which was liberty.[29] Twentieth-century historians, with the results of overweening nationalism in front of them in the shape of catastrophic world wars, have cause to ponder these thoughts anew.

Whether perceived as class struggle, racial destiny, or national character, human existence was predicated essentially on observable historical "facts." Far from depending on the irrational, these varieties of determinism rest, so they claim, on reason and have thus been in this degree irrefutable. Historical action conditioned

melfarb, *Lord Acton: A Study in Conscience and Politics* (Chicago: University of Chicago Press, 1962 [1952]), p. 183.
[29] Himmelfarb, *Lord Acton*, p. 183.

by determinism has been considerable, particularly in the numerous offshoots of Marxism. Yet science now makes us wary as well as hopeful. If scientific determinism no longer enjoys the power to influence minds that it once did, it is because history has intervened and because historians, like their predecessors, are ever eager to refute what has gone before.

The Problems of Determinism

The rationalists of the Enlightenment affirmed the supremacy of reason to history; the Abbé Sieyès was unwilling to write his memoirs because he believed each generation must learn from its own experience, not that of the past. Not so with the historicists. For them, science is a tool for explaining the historical process. Historical research is primarily a search for values, the past speaking to the present in a didactic mode.

"Historicism" is a big word, one of the most slippery in historical discourse. As a term, it has been described as predominantly of European origin, inclining toward the concepts of determinism and historical laws. Humanity itself, at any given time, is a product of the historical process, and our actions can be understood only by placing them in their historical context. The basis of the evaluation of anything is to be found in its past. Therefore, historical knowledge is the basic, or only, requirement necessary to understand the present.[30]

Thus historicism may be described fairly as "the use of historical epochs as a metaphor of the present." These epochs, or historical configurations, are unique, although related to each other by the processes of growth and change. The intellectual godfather of this view is often taken to be Leopold von Ranke, although elements of historicism may be found in earlier writers, such as the Italian Giambattista Vico. Ranke and his disciples, particularly Friedrich Meinecke, have advanced a history that stresses "the ineffable, inimitable, and impartial in the recounting of human events."[31]

[30] Louis Gottschalk, *Understanding History: A Primer of Historical Method*, 2nd ed. (New York: Alfred A. Knopf, 1969 [1950]), pp. 231–32; Robert V. Daniels, *Studying History: How and Why*, 2nd ed. (Englewood Cliffs, N.J.: Prentice-Hall, 1972 [1966]), pp. 94–95. For a compact discussion of the concept of historicism, see Dwight E. Lee and Robert N. Beck, "The Meaning of Historicism," *American Historical Review* 59, no. 3 (April, 1954): 568–77.

[31] Kenneth Silverman, *A Cultural History of the American Revolution*

Unfortunately, even historicists are human. Impartiality, though a noble pose and scientific to a fault, was a condition even the illustrious Ranke never attained, rooted as he was in conservatism and Protestantism. The continuing pretense of historicists to impartiality enrages their opponents; that, plus the inclination of historicists to see history as a predictive science.[32] The central thesis of historicism, that history is discoverable law that extends from past to future, is for critics the supreme egocentricity and mystical folly of historical scholarship.

Benedetto Croce once described historical thought as "dialectic of development." He meant that historical change occurs without determinism, because determinism is incapable of *explaining*. The determinist model has difficulty with historical relativism, because in borrowing "laws" from either the physical or social sciences to explain its data, the model ignores the possibility that these laws might not apply to the historical case in question.[33] Put another way, laws in history have no intrinsic device for explaining historical events that do not appear to fit the pattern of the law.

The difficulty of explanation was not immediately realized by the empirically oriented historians of the nineteenth century and their adherents. For them, the "truth" was itself explanation, and a priori history contained its own logic. Almost unintentionally, the revolution in social consciousness that had been achieved by the Darwinists and Marxists smoothed the path of historical determinism. The many permutations Darwinism took as Darwin's writings entered social discourse cannot concern us here, but the Darwinist evolutionary emphasis on change within pattern left its mark. Marxism had an even greater effect, particularly in political and social life. Marx's legacy remains both a hope and a prediction, the predominant secular religion of the twentieth century.

Yet it was a leading popular analyst of Darwinism, Loren Eiseley, who admitted that in spite of "Darwin's Century," man "is what he is—a reservoir of indeterminism." Human action often *may* be predictable, especially in the aggregate; any actuary will attest to that. But to say that determinism is absolute is to negate

(New York: Thomas Y. Crowell, 1976), p. 130; Mazlish, *The Riddle of History*, pp. 54–55; Gay and Wexler, eds., *Historians at Work*, III, 18.

[32] The most trenchant argument against historicism is the essay by Karl R. Popper, *The Poverty of Historicism*, 3rd ed. (New York: Harper and Row, 1964 [1957]).

[33] Benedetto Croce, *History: Theory and Practice* (New York: Russell and Russell, 1920), p. 179; Murray G. Murphey, *Our Knowledge of the Historical Past* (New York: Bobbs-Merrill, 1973), p. 83.

so much historical evidence that, to its critics at least, any determinist stance is only a hollow shell. The hard-liners take their stand with Jacques Barzun. "Abstract systems spell failure in history *ipso facto*," Barzun declared. "History and ideology wage the Hundred Thousand Years' War."[34]

With all this, we should conclude by observing that determinism is no straw man to be set up and knocked down with regularity, simply to satisfy professorial egos. In its insistence on reason and empiricism, the determinist approach has much to offer. Determinists who care about their evidence almost always stumble over what the philosopher W. B. Gallie called "the crude variety of the world,"[35] but so, too, do all historians worth their salt. The temptation that history can be somehow reduced to law will not die. Laws seem to be the firmest sort of historical generalization and hence the most productive of "truth." The endless material to be found in the storehouses of history, contradictory and exasperating as the evidence often is, makes determinism seem like wish-fulfillment, certainly preferable to chaos. Laws rationalize; but in themselves they are a poor substitute for justice. The seeming order that determinism brings to history-as-process is purchased at considerable cost to historical thought.

Can historical thought, then, function without "laws"? Roy F. Nichols has argued that historians should not be concerned with laws analogous to the physical world, such as those of matter and motion, but with the "processes of adaptation,"[36] or change. The point may be moot, but we must keep in mind that historians usually generalize their evidence in ways their audience understands. Napoleon may be described as taking his expedition across the Mediterranean to Egypt. No evidence exists for the exact speed the fleet made at any given time, but we know roughly how fast the French traveled, because we know when they weighed anchor at Toulon, when they arrived at Malta and left, and when they dropped their hooks off the Egyptian coast. No evidence has come to light that they stopped any place along the way, except Malta,

[34] Loren Eiseley, *Darwin's Century: Evolution and the Men Who Discovered It* (Garden City, N.Y.: Anchor Books, 1961 [1958]), p. 350; Jacques Barzun, *Clio and the Doctors: Psycho-History, Quanto-History, and History* (Chicago: University of Chicago Press, 1974), p. 120.

[35] W. B. Gallie, *Philosophy and the Historical Understanding*, 2nd ed. (New York: Schocken Books, 1968 [1964]), p. 100.

[36] Roy F. Nichols, *A Historian's Progress* (New York: Alfred A. Knopf, 1968), pp. 108–109.

although Lord Nelson certainly tried to effect such a halt. We might generalize as to the sailing speed of Napoleon's ships without fracturing the available evidence. Historians function this way all the time; purists demur, but without such artifice historical communication would become much more difficult.

Determinism, then, should not be confused with the convenience (and perhaps necessity) the historian finds in "law-like generalizations." [37] Common sense cannot help researchers in many historical situations. They must try to explain on the basis of generalities. To the ordained determinist, the use of "unlawful" generalities begs the question of truth. The choice many scholars implicitly have made, however, is to reject determinism as a means of explanation. The restless mind is uncomfortable with laws, and the best histories are produced by restless minds. So the search for alternate modes of expression in the consideration of historical process will continue. *That* is written.

[37] Murphey, *Our Knowledge of the Historical Past*, pp. 98, 84. By this phrase I do not mean to become enmeshed in the "covering law" debate. Essentially, the proponents of covering laws in history argue that historical explanations are not complete until laws that are relevant to them can be formulated. The covering law thesis advances a philosophical and epistemological model, not necessarily a determinist one. See Leon J. Goldstein, *Historical Knowing* (Austin: University of Texas Press, 1976), pp. 148–53.

CHAPTER SEVEN

History in Motion

If determinism has had a checkered career within the historical community, its flaws as an empirical approach to history have not killed the notion of history as process. The concept of historical movement persists despite the unruly course of the past. Perceptions of change, as the one seeming constant in human existence, continually foster fresh speculation: how does history "move"?

The Natural View: Organicism

No special insight is required to equate the stages of human growth and development with social change. The ability to reason implies the skills to analyze both one's surroundings and oneself. Probably our first use of our reason was to perceive mortality, to observe that if life forms seemed perpetual, individual life was not. The organic stages of human life—birth, growth, maturity, decay, death—were common symbols of social communication long before historians began to use them as shorthand description.

But a brief step was required, then, to telescope the course of human social development into an organic mold. Like individuals, societies have their beginnings, their periods of ascendency, and their declines. The series of civilizations, empires, and dominant cultures that parade through the pages of history fall easily, almost too easily, inside the metaphor of organicism. We speak of the youthful swagger of nationalistic America, the mature dominance of Antonine Rome, or the prolonged death throes of the Ottoman Empire.

The underlying concept of organic movement, at least initially, is one of growth. Growth suggests multiplying strength and an increasing ability to insure favorable outcomes in power relationships. If growth has an organic peak, it is that precarious point at which some kind of social stability is reached and people are as close to contentment as any civilization will allow. The process of growth also implies a move from simplicity in the patterns of life in the direction of complexity. As societies become more complex, they tend to channel their energies in specific directions; such at least is the organicist stance, corresponding to that stage in human development where the individual chooses a life pattern or has one chosen. "Gravitation is the rule, and centralization the natural consequence, in society no less than in physics," asserted Charles Francis Adams, Jr. Charles Francis was inclined, like his brother Henry, to the avowal of laws in history. "Physically, morally, intellectually, in population, wealth, and intelligence, all things tend to concentration."[1]

Historians used organic comparisons long before the impact of evolutionary science began to undermine humanity's vision of itself. But evolution, with its empirical power, became a great bulwark of the organicist view because, above all, evolution seemed to provide a convincing recipe for ordered change. If individual life forms could evolve, why then could not discrete societies be regarded as evolving also? More specifically, the evolutionary emphasis on life as a struggle for survival offered an explanation for the reason some civilizations flourished for long periods of time and others died quickly. The correlation is so tempting that it is much more often stated or assumed than proven. "The slow processes of evolution presumably apply to human societies and their symbolic systems as much as to human bodies, so that when logic cannot decide, survival eventually will."[2]

Growth and evolution override the individual's finite existence. They offer people the hollow assurance of perpetuation—if not of themselves, then of their kind. Societies thus may be considered not only as fluid but creative as well. The web of history, organically, is woven on a linear frame in which father endows son with paternal achievement. "Look at the young rascal!" is the ad-

[1] Charles Francis Adams, Jr., and Henry Adams, *Chapters of Erie* (Ithaca, N.Y.: Cornell University Press, 1956 [1886]), pp. 11–12.
[2] William H. McNeill, *Plagues and Peoples* (Garden City, N.Y.: Anchor Books, 1976), p. 8.

miring cry one historian has the American East exclaim as it regards the youthful West. "[The East] was like a father, watching
his son engage in some deviltry."[3] Even though a society may perish, its legacy is some kind of "lesson" that hoists us all one step
further up the ladder.

The passage of generations may make growth seem continuous and thus perpetual. Psychologically, the belief may be of little
comfort, for the world is full of inscriptions like the one John
Hicks and his wife saw engraved over the entrance to a Swiss ceme-
tery: "What you are, we were; what we are, you will be." In reaction, Hicks mused that the statement might well hold for civilizations as well as individuals. But this was a rare streak of pessimism
for a man who wrote as if history went from seedtime to seedtime,
each harvest a milestone on the march "ever onward and upward."[4]

Organicism may also be used as a metaphor for health. Just as
all systems in the human body, when functioning correctly, presumably produce physical well-being, so a society's component
parts often are described as vital, strong, or weak. We commonly
speak of a robust economy or a vigorous intellectual life. More
than one historian, for instance, has compared the stock market
crash of 1929 to a man of rugged health suffering his first acute
illness. Economic catastrophes and war seem the most popular
subjects for these comparisons, perhaps because their rude shocks
appear directly analogous to physical ailments. Speaking of World
War I, a scholar examining the American role described the coming of war to Europe "as illness comes to a man of advancing years
and weakened constitution, as disaster native to the system."[5]

Warfare in its relationship to entire civilizations seems so akin
to fatal disease operating on the human body that the metaphor
has long been a staple of historical discourse. William McNeill
saw strong parallels between what he called the "microparasitism
of infectious disease" and the "macroparasitism of military operations." He argued that the development of powerful military
or political institutions (the "concentration" of Charles Francis

[3] Robert G. Athearn, *Westward the Briton* (Lincoln: University of Nebraska
Press, 1962 [1953]), p. 152.
[4] John D. Hicks, *My Life with History: An Autobiography* (Lincoln: University of Nebraska Press, 1968), pp. 335, 78.
[5] Frederick Lewis Allen, *Since Yesterday: The 1930's in America, September
3, 1929–September 3, 1939* (New York: Harper and Row, 1972 [1939]), p. 22;
Preston W. Slosson, *The Great Crusade and After, 1914–1928* (Chicago: Quadrangle Books, 1971 [1930]), p. 1.

Adams, Jr.) had its counterpart in the biological defenses erected by human beings when exposed to bacteria and viruses. "Warfare and disease are connected by more than rhetoric."[6]

There can be no real quarrel with the casual use of organic metaphors in historical writing. Used properly, organic themes may make vivid precisely what the historian wants vivified, and communication with the reader is enhanced thereby. When Benedetto Croce likened history to a living being and chronicle to a corpse, his point was clear and so were his sympathies, regardless of the views of his reader.[7] In the sphere of literary discourse alone, organic comparisons may be evocative, so long as one is not constantly being buried under them.

But organicism works in wider arenas as well. As a model for the course of history, the organic view has found takers again and again. Not all organic analyses regard the historical subject as steadily improving through time, either. John Hicks, remember, was a nice man and an optimist. An alternative view sees the course of world history, particularly western history, in decline since the nineteenth century. The perspective is still organic, only now the patient is on a deathbed rather than performing adolescent cartwheels. Moreover, organicism may underlie a clash of cultures, where one waxes at the expense of the other. Typical is this view of Spanish-American relations on the southeastern frontier: "A kind of organic law seemed to decree the continued growth of the United States and the continued decline of Spain."[8]

The basic problem of organicism, as with determinism, is that the evidence that should underlie the thesis is often perverse. The Ottoman Empire, for example, should have "died" years before it actually disintegrated; yet the famous "Sick Man of Europe" was kept alive, in the interest of some of the Great Powers, throughout the nineteenth century. To explain the intrinsic life of civilizations using an organic mold is difficult because there are so many external forces continually operating. *Do civilizations behave like the human body, that is, organically?* If they do, then in the general picture organicism becomes a vague determinism, because humans

[6] McNeill, *Plagues and Peoples*, pp. 53–55.

[7] Benedetto Croce, *History: Its Theory and Practice*, trans. Douglas Ainslie (New York: Russell and Russell, 1920), p. 20.

[8] Arthur Preston Whitaker, *The Spanish-American Frontier, 1783–1795: The Westward Movement and the Spanish Retreat in the Mississippi Valley* (Lincoln: University of Nebraska Press, 1969 [1927]), p. 16.

are mortal and we think we know what the end is. What comes after the end is anyone's guess.

A gloomy picture, for anyone with historical perspective, is that which paints impending decay and death. Fatalists argue it comes to us all; why protest or debate? We might respond with Croce that history is life, not death. To analyze the decline and fall of a civilization is not to analyze the decline and fall of civilization itself. Moreover, who is to say when a civilization is dead? We still live, some of us, using variations of Roman words, conducting our courts along lines set out by Roman law, and, incredibly, still traveling along Roman roads. For Croce, histories that related the death of peoples, states, institutions, and all the rest were either false or poetry.[9] We do not go so far; history is to be found in the descent as well as the ascent.

Organicism finally is rooted in the rhythm of life itself. There is the continual sense of the new, the mature, the old in almost any study of the past. The catch is to determine if social behavior in the aggregate is *inductive*—that is, if societies behave like discrete human beings, not only organically but in the development of "social character." In many instances the rhythm seems to be there. We must ponder not only the possibility of its organic nature but of its cyclic and progressive aspects as well.

History as Repetition

At times, history seeks to repeat itself. The French expression *déjà vu* describes those occasions when we think we are living through experiences that have happened to us previously. Collectively, historical repetition bears this aspect. Nobody learns from history, runs the lament. If we did, because these repeat experiences usually seem to be nasty ones, history would never be able to close the circle.

The Chinese, until recently, compiled their history by dynasties, all of which, according to one noted Asian scholar, presented a "boringly repetitious story." The dynasties would enjoy a heroic founding and a rise to power; then would follow a long decline and eventual collapse. As a result, and in spite of the obvious development of their civilization, the Chinese believed the best fu-

[9]Croce, *History: Its Theory and Practice*, p. 92.

ture was most suitably achieved by the recreation of some past golden age.[10]

The true cyclical view of history is exemplified by the ancient Chinese conception. To see history occurring and recurring in cycles is to assume a start and end point, or *periodicity*, in human affairs. Periodicity may be seen as a rhythmic part of the behavior of political, economic, social, or intellectual life, or, as in the Chinese case, used to describe an entire culture. The classic western statement of the idea perhaps belongs to Polybius, the Greek analyst of the rise of Rome. Polybius asserted that political life went in order through six distinct phases: monarchy, tyranny, aristocracy, oligarchy, democracy, and anarchy. Each of these phases led naturally to the next, until people wearied of anarchic excess and reestablished the institution of kingship to insure social order. From this point the cycle began again.[11]

Cyclic reasoning at its purest has a certain fatalistic component, for there is no allowance for human experience. Everything has happened in the past and will happen again in the future. Different people and different events will be involved, of course, but the form will be essentially the same. To a great degree, cyclic reasoning is plastic as well, because a cyclist usually chooses to accentuate one aspect of history to the exclusion of others, as Polybius did with his political categorizations.

The simplest mode of seeing history as repetition is dualistic. The past is viewed as oscillating between two different poles. For the sociologist Pitirim Sorokin, all history was the tale of two cultures, which he named the ideational and the sensate. The first cultural type tended to locate reality in the supersensory or spiritual aspects of human existence. The second located reality within the scope of our organs of perception. Sorokin's arguments were naturally much more complex, but his vision held that history was composed of the alternation of these two kinds of culture. A second example comes from a recent history of sexual attitudes, in which G. Rattray Taylor asserted that societies may be divided into patristic types, composed of those who model themselves on their fathers, and matristic types, composed of those who find

[10] John K. Fairbank, Edwin O. Reischauer, and Albert M. Craig, *East Asia: Tradition and Transformation* (Boston: Houghton Mifflin, 1973), pp. 70–71. The quote is Reischauer's.

[11] Peter Gay and Gerald J. Cavanaugh, eds., *Historians at Work*, I: *Herodotus to Froissart* (New York: Harper and Row, 1972), pp. 115–16.

their identification in mother-figures. Although this theory seems limited to sexual behavior, Taylor claimed that as societies move from matrism to patrism, or vice versa, attitudes toward other things change as well.[12]

Regardless of the method of categorization, if one believes in history as an endlessly oscillating mechanism, a kind of pendulum, then one believes "history is not a line but a dial."[13] The past is a series of opposites, and so (we must assume) is the future. A considerable part of this sort of speculation is rooted in dualistic perceptions of human nature. As we are children of darkness, so are we children of light. Our past rots or glows as our characters decree.

Cyclic dualism is not generally favored by historians. As a mode of historical explanation, dualities are much too tidy, too schematic. But historians on occasion have adopted more complex cyclical views. One dominant figure is the Italian thinker Giambattista Vico, who wrote almost three hundred years ago.[14] Vico's theme encompassed entire cultures. Through historical analysis he posited that similar historical ages tend to recur in the same order. At first glance, Vico's ideas simply repeat Polybius on a greater scale. Vico's stages, however, were characterized by (1) the age of the gods, where Fate rather than reason held sway; (2) the age of heroes, in which dominant leaders keyed the life of the culture; and (3) the age of men, where popular opinion was supreme, but unstable. He believed there had been two cycles to date, one in antiquity and the second expiring around him in the eighteenth century. Unlike those of the Chinese and Polybius, however, Vico's cycles ended at a higher point than they began. History was an upward spiral rather than just a simple cycle.[15]

---

[12] R. P. Cuzzort, *Humanity and Modern Sociological Thought* (New York: Holt, Rinehart and Winston, 1969), pp. 234–53; G. Rattray Taylor, *Sex in History: The Story of Society's Changing Attitudes to Sex throughout the Ages* (New York: Harper and Row, 1973 [1954]), pp. 77–80.

[13] William Irwin Thompson, *At the Edge of History: Speculations on the Transformation of Culture* (New York: Harper and Row, 1972 [1971]), p. 81.

[14] Vico is a difficult and obtuse thinker. He may best be approached through his autobiography, *The Autobiography of Giambattista Vico*, trans. Max Harold Fisch and Thomas Goddard Bergin (Ithaca, N.Y.: Cornell University Press, 1975 [1944]). His masterwork is *The New Science of Giambattista Vico*, rev. ed., trans. Thomas Goddard Bergin and Max Harold Fisch (Ithaca, N.Y.: Cornell University Press, 1970 [1948]).

[15] Bruce Mazlish, *The Riddle of History: The Great Speculators from Vico to Freud* (New York: Minerva Press, 1968 [1966]), pp. 11–58.

Two hundred years later Oswald Spengler, in his widely discussed *Decline of the West* (1918–23), took what one critic called an "astrological view" of history. As a cyclist, Spengler's vision of history differed from Vico's in direction; for Spengler, the result of historical motion was a downward spiral. He wrote, remember, as an observant European during Europe's bloodiest war to that time. Spengler seemed to see cosmic regularity in human action. As heavenly bodies move through space, an apogee here, a perigee there, so history moves—rise and fall, dawn and evening. Moreover, society's parts are meshed in such a way, like the universal machinery of Newton, that separate aspects do not move independently. Politics do not advance as intellectual life declines. Society, like the heavens, moves as a universe, with a universal rhythm.[16]

Vico and Spengler, along with a third great speculator, Arnold Toynbee (who sought a philosophy of history in the "unity of civilization"), are widely discredited today. Their declining reputation is not due to accusations of stupidity or to a naive outlook on the past. These three were original and penetrating thinkers and what they wrote has fulfilled a basic task: their words have made others think. Like organicism, however, their cyclical theories (Toynbee's is a special case) tend necessarily to mutilate or ignore large amounts of evidence. All three were unhappy with the time in which they lived, which may have conditioned their outlooks on history.[17]

What, then, is the use of grand schemes of historical repetition? For one thing, cyclic ideas force people to think in universal terms when the current fashion tends toward microhistory and the too-facile compartmentalization of historical topics. For another, it is not beyond the realm of possibility that historical *trends*, or "cycles-within-history," do recur. Not with the metronomic regularity of a Polybius or with the mystic cosmic clockwork of a Spengler, perhaps; but many historians will admit likenesses within

[16] Ibid., pp. 320–21. Spengler was not original in his ideas of downward spirals. The Brahmins of India, for example, believed in cycles of deterioration, with the last age being *kali yuga*, the worst. See L. S. Perera, "The Pali Chronicle of Ceylon," in C. H. Philips, ed., *Historians of India, Pakistan and Ceylon* (London: Oxford University Press, 1961), p. 32.

[17] For Spengler, see his obtuse classic *The Decline of the West*, 2 vols. (New York: Alfred A. Knopf, 1980); for a *short* introduction to Toynbee, see Roland N. Stromberg, *Arnold J. Toynbee: Historian for an Age in Crisis* (Carbondale: Southern Illinois University Press, 1972); and for Toynbee's own ideas, Arnold J. Toynbee, *A Study of History* (D. C. Somervell, abridgment of vols. I–VI) (London: Oxford University Press, 1947).

differing time periods. Economic historians in particular would be sorely put in dealing with their subject without some notion of cycles. Many more writers will not blush in drawing analogies from one age to the next. When overdone, as it so often is, this is one of the greater vices of popular historical scholarship.

The urge to study cycles may even be a negative one. By urging change, the critic admits the existence of cycles. Lincoln Steffens once charged with exasperation that Americans tolerate repetitive failures in government because it was ever so. Unwilling to use the experimental method of the sciences (so beloved of Progressives) to break the circle, the country had, by its inaction, created a self-fulfilling prophecy of indifferent government.[18] Steffens's argument is typical of those analyses that see the potential of breaking out of cycles, if only men would will it. Cycles exist, and reform is the way out of the rut.

At times, when we read today's newspapers or turn on our electronic injection of evening news, we get the impression we have been through all this before, especially if we read regularly in historical topics. Consider:

> The people have lost faith in themselves when they cease to have any faith in those whom they uniformly elect to represent them. The change that has taken place in this respect of late years in America has been startling in its rapidity. Legislation is more and more falling into contempt, and this not so much on account of the extreme ignorance manifested in it as because of the corrupt motives which are believed habitually to actuate it.[19]

An outraged citizen bemoaning Watergate or any number of recent congressional scandals? No, only Charles Francis Adams, Jr., giving his opinion of the state of the nation over a century ago.

So doubt exists. Trends do have a habit of recurrence. Americans, like most people with a libertarian tradition, usually are skeptical of claims made for immutable laws in human affairs. The strict idea of cycles affords little chance for improvement, because to where we began we shall return. Even the Viconian spiral, allowing as it did for improvement, still presented the past as regular and the future as predictable in the repetition of the forms of human events. Cycles seem restrictive, confined. They battle human

[18] Lincoln Steffens, *The Autobiography of Lincoln Steffens* II (New York: Harcourt, Brace and World, 1931), p. 718.
[19] Adams and Adams, *Chapters of Erie*, p. 98.

instinct in fundamental ways and thus have never attracted more than a small minority in the historical community.

Painting the past with broad strokes has been of some influence, nonetheless. Arthur Schlesinger, for instance, gave considerable credence to the cyclical theory of American governmental trends, the same trends that had so angered Steffens. Schlesinger was in fact disappointed that historians had not taken their cue from the work economists had done in analyzing business cycles. Historians had not pressed on to examine "analogous recurrences in other fields of thought and action." Among the conclusions in his memoirs was the observation that in religion there seem to have been alternating periods of orthodoxy and heterodoxy, in literature the interplay of realism and romanticism, and in the fine arts the endless war between classicism and experimentalism. Were these merely "haphazard phenomena," he asked, or the "expressions of an inherent and explicable rhythm?"[20] In response to Schlesinger, *how would one investigate the possibility of historical cycles?*

Organicism and cyclic thought, as influential as they have been, are not the principal models of historical process today. For about two hundred years the western world has become increasingly attached to the conception of a history that occurs in a linear and advancing fashion. Modern thinkers find the idea much more to their liking than the biological finitude of organicism or the dreary repetition of cycles. Present-day opinion would seem to break the fetters that had circumscribed human potential for so long. We are now to be allowed our full capacity for both collective and individual improvement. After centuries on a circular or roller-coaster track, history has been shunted onto the mainline. The rails run one way only, and the engine is named Progress.

History as Progress

"Feller citizens," boomed an orator on the Wisconsin frontier in 1849, "the *tail* of civilization is now exactly where the *front* ears was no mor'n sixty years ago."[21] He was telling his audience

[20] Arthur M. Schlesinger, *In Retrospect: The History of a Historian* (New York: Harcourt, Brace and World, 1963), p. 199.

[21] Quoted in Charles E. Rosenberg, *The Cholera Years: The United States in 1832, 1849, and 1866* (Chicago: University of Chicago Press, 1962), p. 226.

what they already knew; things were getting better, and America
was providing a spectacular vision of improvement for all the world
to see. Forget about the millions of slaves, the embryonic urban
slums, the Indians pinched onto harsh reservation lands—the evidence was there. One could even hear it: in the roar of the forge,
the ringing of the cash register, the chugging of the new-fangled
locomotive. Here was progress, and America's endlessly self-
congratulatory slogan was echoed throughout the industrializing
nations of the West.

The triumph of progress as both an ethic and an ideal has
tended to blot out the fact that the concept of history as progress
is, as these things go, of recent birth. Far more common have been
views like those held by the Chinese, who saw tradition as a powerful governor on the pace of change. Where progress looks always
to the future, the leadership of dynasties such as the Ming and
Ch'ing took their models of behavior and social organization from
the past.[22]

The Greeks, who proved themselves time and again as exceptional thinkers concerning the human condition, did not have the
idea of progress. Nor did the Romans, despite their worldly power.
The Greeks were suspicious of change, their outlook on life pessimistic. The might of Rome expanded political frontiers but con-
tracted individual ones. In the wake of the classical decline, moreover, Christian mysticism did not generally concern itself with the
destinies of secular affairs. The medieval world view looked to the
hereafter more than the here-and-now. Only with the increasing
secularization of Europe from the fifteenth through the seventeenth centuries was the groundwork prepared for the idea, as opposed to the fact itself.[23]

During the eighteenth century theory began to overtake actuality, and the idea of progress became both an explanation-model
of western achievement and an inclusive pattern for the future. Immediately, however, complexities in the model developed that lin-
ger today. "To progress" implies that one is moving toward something, and in a certain direction; in short, that all this human
activity has a *goal*. Mere change without an inherent goal-structure
we might simply style "development."[24] The analysis of the idea of

[22] Fairbank, Reischauer, and Craig, *East Asia*, p. 178.
[23] J. B. Bury, *The Idea of Progress: An Inquiry into its Growth and Origin*
(New York: Dover Publications, 1955 [1932]), pp. 1–36. Bury is still the best
introduction to the topic.
[24] In this differentiation, our guide is Wilhelm Dilthey, *Pattern and Meaning*

progress is thus the investigation of the supposed goals toward which progress tends. As we shall see, there has been disagreement as to what these goals are.

In addition, there has been no concurrence on how progress itself moves, the movement of movement. An inexact analogy from the physical world might help. Suppose we regard progress as velocity; then the movement of progress may be likened to acceleration or deceleration. Perhaps progress occurs in fits and starts (as my aging car accelerates). Or perhaps progress is smooth, unperturbed, onward and upward through the loom of time. Croce, for one, believed there was always progress but that we only tend to notice it when "the motion of the spirit seems to become accelerated and the fruit that has been growing ripe for centuries is rapidly plucked."[25]

Regardless of the imperfections and uncertainties in the idea, progress spoke powerfully to the rationalists of the Enlightenment. Constantly they reiterated an essentially optimistic and linear vision of history. Edward Gibbon punctuated his magisterial *Decline and Fall of the Roman Empire* with a resounding affirmation of progress, one with which his readers could readily concur. For Gibbon, our precious cultural benefits had been carried to the corners of the earth by war, commerce, and religion. "We may therefore acquiesce in the pleasing conclusion," he smoothly wrote, "that every age of the world has increased and still increases the real wealth, the happiness, the knowledge, and perhaps the virtue, of the human race."[26]

Gibbon's ingredients for progress might be summed up as the advance (the determinist would say "march") of civilization. In the most abstract view, progress and civilization were linked firmly together. Progress advanced civilization, so that each age could look upon its past and see improvement by comparison. Edmund Burke, the politically minded contemporary of Gibbon, hoped that the people of the nineteenth century would justifiably recoil from the barbarities of their predecessors, for programs implied in this sense a rejected past and a welcome future. Burke, as a conservative, would never disown the past completely, but he was enough of a humanist to discern the necessity for improvement.

in History: Thoughts on History and Society, ed. H. P. Rickman (New York: Harper and Row, 1962 [1961]), p. 105, n. 1.

[25] Croce, *History: Its Theory and Practice*, p. 222.

[26] Edward Gibbon, *The Decline and Fall of the Roman Empire* II (New York: Modern Library, n. d.), pp. 436–44.

At times, progress and civilization seemed to advance in such lockstep order that they appeared identical in the writings of some historians. Generally, however, progress was held to be the process and civilization its product, or goal. Even the downcast Spengler believed that the inevitable end-product of his astronomical phases was civilization. Spengler's civilization, as a goal, was literally the end, the culminating expression of a dying culture-form.[27] After the exploding super-nova, only the black hole.

Beyond the broad and not altogether satisfying establishment of civilization as a goal, different and more specific aspects of progress may be glimpsed. Material progress, dependent upon the continuing miracles of technology and science, is usually the most common expression. Some historians, like the committed internationalist James T. Shotwell, have gone so far as to avow that technology and science have been *the* determining factors in history. While materialism is partially a child of the Industrial Revolution, it has many parents. Flashes of a blend of material and spiritual progress may be seen as early as the fifth century, in the writings of Augustine's disciple Orosius.[28]

Only with the burgeoning consumer economies of the West, though, has the materialism of abundance come to be equated with progress itself. Conversely, ideas centered on the improvement of the human spirit through religion, though still advanced today, have lost much of their holistic force. A far more common practice is to pay lip service to religious ideals while continuing to bathe in a seemingly never-ending river of consumer goods. Efforts to fuse the religious and the material seem only to result in the frequent "how to" best-sellers that America so remorselessly inflicts upon itself and the rest of the world.

During the nineteenth century, the years for which Burke had such high hopes, individual liberty was favored highly as the logical outcome of progress. Lord Acton believed God waited at the end of history, right enough; but on the way, true human liberty would be realized at last. The hope persisted into the following century, but for millions of people it was torn to shreds in the maelstrom of World War I. The Canadian historian Alfred L. Burt,

[27] Edmund Burke, *Reflections on the Revolution in France* (New York: Everyman's Library, 1910), pp. 139–40; Croce, *History: Its Theory and Practice*, pp. 40–41; Mazlish, *The Riddle of History*, p. 342.

[28] Harold Josephson, *James T. Shotwell and the Rise of Internationalism in America* (Rutherford: Fairleigh Dickinson University Press, 1975), pp. 42–43; Gay and Cavanaugh, eds., *Historians at Work*, I, 315–17.

depressed by the vengeful climate surrounding the making of the Treaty of Versailles, expressed his belief that liberty was not a linear component of existence; the war had proven that. Rather, it was cyclic—"liberty awakening, struggling painfully, conquering, misusing its victory, descend [sic] into license and end [sic] in dissolution. . . . Is it not the same as ever?"[29] In Acton's time, liberty was expectation. For the men of Burt's generation, it had become false hope or illusion.

The Age of Enlightenment had its full measure of materialism, spiritual values, and passionate avowals of human liberty, but fundamentally many of the finest minds of the period hoped for the eventual assertion of humanity's rational nature, a triumph of reason. Wishing does not make it so, but everywhere in the West reason seemed to be advancing, superstition and irrational behavior retreating. The ascension of reason was even celebrated in quasi-religious festivals during the French Revolution. By then Voltaire, the archpriest of reason, had gone to his grave, but he had left behind a dilemma for his admirers to consider.

Voltaire's problem, shared by others who had dabbled in Oriental philosophies, lay in his belief that human nature was an eternal constant. Yet a lifetime of warring against ignorance had left him with an equally firm belief in progress. Voltaire reconciled the seeming paradox by arguing that progress is the gradual assertion of reason, of humanity's discovering its true self under the mass of custom, habit, and superstition that had buried it for ages. Had Voltaire lived in the nineteenth century, he might have believed himself vindicated. Reason more than survived the strong onslaught of Romanticism and became the philosophical justification for the victories won by empirical science. Even the pessimistic Freud, with his conviction that progress cannot lead to happiness or perfectability, admitted the concept. "In the long run nothing can withstand reason and experience."[30]

We have been describing progress as an essentially linear concept, but Vico, among others, had seen a kind of progress in historical cycles. The most optimistic have been able to see progress

[29] Gertrude Himmelfarb, *Lord Acton: A Study in Conscience and Politics* (Chicago: University of Chicago Press, 1962 [1952]), p. 204; Lewis H. Thomas, *The Renaissance of Canadian History: A Biography of A. L. Burt* (Toronto: University of Toronto Press, 1975), p. 38.

[30] Walter L. Dorn, *Competition for Empire, 1740–1763* (New York: Harper and Row, 1963 [1940]), pp. 218–19; Freud quoted in Mazlish, *The Riddle of History*, pp. 412–13.

even in a cyclical nadir, a cycle that ends in complete collapse, disaster, or nothingness. Looking at the history of the American frontier, Carl Becker saw a "seed plot" where fresh forms of institutions and thought germinated. The seeming regression of civilization on the frontier was to Becker essential, "the condition of all progress being in a sense a return to the primitive." After all, how better to measure progress than from a zero base, since the distance traveled would seem light-years beyond the infinitesimal generational crawl of tired European or Asian cultures. "One gathered from having read American history," dryly commented novelist Sherwood Anderson, "that there was a sort of advantage to be gained from starting with nothing."[31]

The course of events in the twentieth century has punched several holes in the idea of linear progress. Those who argue that if history can never be a straight line, then its course on the average nonetheless is upward, must deal with the hideous facts of modern existence. Recent wars have not only taken lives in the many millions, whereas a European princeling would count one thousand dead a calamity two hundred years ago; these wars also have been sustained by science and technology, the once-undisputed motors that drove the engine of progress.

For some, the good life exists today. For many more, life is lived at that precarious margin where staying alive is life itself. Disease and famine remain common in many parts of the earth. Where the stomach rules, the mind seldom governs. Acton's dreams of liberty not only seem perverse among many of the emerging nations; they found no echo in the Europe of the dictators. Civilization indeed seemed to be moving tail-first most of the time.

Arnold Toynbee, no determinist, was one who held out a ray of hope. Though the path might appear to lead downward, as Toynbee argued that it eventually had in previous civilizations, perhaps a return to religious ethics would right matters. Few persons endowed with a conscience could regard the tragedies of the modern era without some sense of sin. We must pray for a reprieve,[32] a reprieve not only from our moral transgressions but also

---

[31] Carl Becker, *Everyman His Own Historian: Essays on History and Politics* (Chicago: Quadrangle Books, 1966 [1935]), p. 4; Sherwood Anderson, *A Storyteller's Story: Memoirs of Youth and Middle Age* (New York: Viking Press, 1969 [1924]), p. 214.

[32] Mazlish, *The Riddle of History*, p. 361.

from the spiritual and aesthetic emptiness of materialism. Those to whom modernity seemed more a curse than a blessing would admit the idea of progress. But progress must shed itself of technology. Rather than serving humanity, the machine-god had become its master.

The idea survives, if badly battered. As roses may grow on dunghills, so progress has been resilient enough to survive the worst cataclysms in recorded history. *Is a sense of progress in history necessary?* Without at least a vague notion that the future will be a better place, we might well debate whether modern civilization, impelled by industrialism and consumerism, could continue as we know it. Other civilizations, as we have seen, did not evolve the concept, but neither did they have the science, technology, and economic complexity we live with today, not to mention the escalating population problem. To possess only the past may be to possess futility, a point to which we shall return. Paul Knaplund once asserted flatly that "most of the ills of our age come about because the past is eternally carried on our backs."[33]

No historian, Knaplund included, would argue in turn that progress lacks the need for a past. The orthodox view, one that enrages more radical historians, cautiously covers both front and rear while advancing. Those for whom impatience is set policy deride such ideas as the timid voice of a discredited modern liberalism. Yet, in the words of Arthur Schlesinger, Jr., the center still holds. If history taught him anything at all, avowed his father, it was that a safe advance for society meant to "make haste slowly."[34]

Progress has been an especially important concept to Americans, and not only because of the self-satisfaction inherent in our society's transistor technology and trillion-dollar economy. Historically, the United States has been bullish concerning its future. Countless foreign observers have remarked on the acquisitiveness, boosterism, and eternal optimism of *genus Americanus*. (Mencken had a pseudo-Latin vulgarity for the type: *homo boobus*.) The very newness, the freshness of the American experience—native Americans were not considered—made progress a continually vibrant watchword. Forward, that has been our historic direction. Auto pioneer Charles F. Kettering supposedly dismissed the past

[33] Paul Knaplund, *Moorings Old and New: Entries in an Immigrant's Log* (Madison: State Historical Society of Wisconsin, 1963), p. 237.
[34] Schlesinger, *In Retrospect: The History of a Historian*, p. 41.

by insisting no one made progress while looking in the rear-view mirror.[35]

There is a catch, however, one that perhaps is of importance only to historians, but worth pondering nevertheless. America began with a creed of perfectionism, as John Winthrop's *City on a Hill*, an example and inspiration for all. By the revolutionary period, the French immigrant St. John de Crèvecoeur still could confidently claim that "we are the most perfect society now existing in the world," a boast few Americans would even think of challenging during the next century. The situation is ironic. As Richard Hofstadter has noted, the United States, alone among the nations of the world, "began with perfection and aspired to progress."[36] Logically inelegant, perhaps, but people defy logic as much as they tend to confirm it.

We are left with doubts about the various forms of process. Upon reflection, and not necessarily skeptical reflection, process may sway opinion but not convince. Organicism, cyclism, and progressivism somehow seem vague, ideal, too weak in themselves to bear the weight of historical explanation. True, as concepts they are all readily understandable and debatable. But the stuff of history, humans and human events, appears in them only as an excuse for theory. Process at this level provides food for effective thought, but only as an appetizer. For the main course, we must direct our attention to the men and women of the past—to their energies, their capabilities, their follies. We need not agree with the philosopher Kant that history is the realization of a hidden plan of nature to develop the fullest capacities of the human race.[37] But people are always the central issue, and it is to their intrinsic role in historical process that we now turn.

[35] John B. Rae, *The American Automobile: A Brief History* (Chicago: University of Chicago Press, 1965), p. 242.

[36] Crèvecoeur quoted in Henry Nash Smith, *Virgin Land: The American West as Symbol and Myth* (New York: Vintage Books, 1950), p. 144; Richard Hofstadter, *The Age of Reform: From Bryan to F. D. R.* (New York: Vintage Books, 1955), pp. 35–36.

[37] Mazlish, *The Riddle of History*, p. 109.

CHAPTER EIGHT

History and the Individual

The world pulses with variety; just as well, since sameness bores us as often as it reassures. To the historian, human variety is both curse and blessing. Making sense out of the infinitely diversified parts of human experience is a trying business at best. Square pegs fit into round holes in history as poorly as they do in any other endeavor. Withal, exasperation is a not insignificant by-product of historical labor.

Variety is, however, the sine qua non of the historian's craft. Whether as crude as savage warfare or sophisticated as a minuet among statesmen, variety serves as an index of change and a measure of difference. People—their actions, personalities, accomplishments, failures—in brief, their lives, afford the historian the broadest and most exciting canvas possible. We cannot imagine a past in agreement with itself. In varying degrees people differ, and in their differing they often make history. The need for variety may be as close to an axiom as history ever comes. "Where there is no strain," wrote R. G. Collingwood, "there is no history."[1]

The Indefinite Individual

Eventually historians must come to grips with their subject material in the most generalized way. From personal experience researchers distill what they know about people. Unless made of concrete, scholars have experienced fear, hate, love, and a host of

---

[1] John P. Diggins, *Up from Communism: Conservative Odysseys in American Intellectual History* (New York: Harper and Row, 1977 [1975]), p. 266.

other basic emotions (often in the classroom environment). In short, they have speculated on "human nature," in themselves and in others. They may see people as being essentially nice, or predictably rotten. Humans, to them, may be capable of boundless achievement at either end of the behavioral scale. The individual may be driven—by God, greed, or government. A person may be a free agent, endlessly responsive to possibility or chance. Or, to garble the question even more, the creature may possess no "nature" at all.

The classic statement concerning the reasonable side of humanity is that of John Locke, philosopher and apologist for the Glorious Revolution of 1688. Locke is popular politically as the grandfather of modern democratic liberalism; his views of human nature are the foundation upon which his philosophical edifice is built. Lockean people are equal in a state of nature, unless God's will grants someone sovereignty. But Locke was no apologist for divine right monarchy; he loathed the institution, particularly as he thought he had seen it function under the last Stuart kings of England. Instead, natural equality is the foundation for "mutual love amongst men." This love results in duties owed each by all others. From this point, Locke built his version of a "social contract" that served as a text for the Age of Revolution he did not live to see.[2]

Locke's estimate of human nature was rational. Human self-interest was best recognized in group action, because only in a group could the protection of the rights of all be realized. Many sages of the Enlightenment agreed with the proposition because, they reasoned, each of us is quite capable of anything if left to our own devices. The Scottish Presbyterian minister-historian William Robertson proclaimed that "man is the only living creature whose frame is at once so hardy and so flexible, that he can spread over the whole earth, become the inhabitant of every region, and thrive and multiply under every climate." People were made for industry and action, continued Robertson. Since action uncontrolled was anarchy's chance, human achievement must rest on collective will.[3]

As popular as he became in the newly minted democracies of the West, Locke by no means held the stage alone. An earlier En-

[2] John Locke, *Two Treatises of Civil Government* (New York: Everyman's Library, 1966), pp. 118–19.

[3] Peter Gay and Victor G. Wexler, eds., *Historians at Work*, II: *Valla to Gibbon* (New York: Harper and Row, 1972), pp. 263–64, 278.

glishman, Thomas Hobbes, had also argued that in their secular nature people are equal. But Hobbes, who had the bitter experiences of civil war fresh in his memory as he wrote, believed that such equality rendered people less deserving of respect than contempt. The Hobbesian individual is selfish and greedy, but also fearful; for safety, each person is forced to enter into a contract to obey that government that can provide security to person and possessions. A government so formed must rest in the last analysis on raw power. Collective will does not necessarily aggregate this power, for to Hobbes the human race is a disruptive, disorderly force whether acting en masse or alone.

Historians, like Locke and Hobbes, cannot avoid their own experiences; their intellectual baggage *becomes* their history to a certain extent. It is often difficult to reflect on the mistakes of the past and come up smiling, as John Hicks seemed to do. Hicks is probably in the minority, even given the essential optimism of the America in which he grew to maturity. For Carl Becker, "The selfish propensities of men remain constant. . . . It is only the channels through which these selfish propensities flow that change." Becker stood in a long line of historians who have held bleak opinions of their fellow humans. Giambattista Vico regarded human nature as fixed, and not in a Lockean way. Ferocity, avarice, and ambition are the "three vices which run throughout the human race." And so with Voltaire, who probably rejoiced that humanity in its dreadful constancy afforded such a stationary target for his satiric wit. "All ages resemble one another in respect of the criminal folly of mankind."[4]

On these questions middle ground, of course, exists, but it is treacherous. On some mornings, after getting back a test grade, perhaps, we are sure Hobbes hit the nail on the head. Of an evening, possibly following a great date, we know Locke was right. Obviously the business of "human nature" is as subjective as we ourselves. Yet, within this subjectivism Hobbes and Locke can at times unite to help us see humanity whole, not subdivided into some spiritual Levittown.

Whether we admit the concept of human nature or not, one of the most fascinating aspects of humans is their ability to rational-

[4] Carl Becker, *Everyman His Own Historian: Essays on History and Politics* (Chicago: Quadrangle Books, 1966 [1935]), p. 86; Bruce Mazlish, *The Riddle of History: The Great Speculators from Vico to Freud* (New York: Minerva Press, 1968 [1966]), pp. 40, 65–66; Gay and Wexler, eds., *Historians at Work*, II, 285.

ize, to provide themselves with only the purest of motives. Our evasive estimates of ourselves are continuously remarkable. As James Truslow Adams acidly noted, because making money is our main pursuit, we call it service; each new consumer frippery is puffed as another step toward a higher standard of living; and children become adults in spite of doting parents.[5] A sense of humor is mandatory for the historian, since his subjects usually are as adept in fooling themselves as they are in deceiving posterity.

Human foibles may have purpose. Social philosophers of a century ago were able to convince many people that selfishness was a virtue and plutocracy no vice. A milder tone, but still a stern one, was that adopted by Edmund Burke, who regarded property rights as a positive security against injustice and despotism. Possession was all ten points of the law. Clearly, questions of judgment are involved. The line is fine indeed that the researcher must draw to distinguish acquisitiveness from greed, taste from ostentation, or affection from domination. Only confusion may result. For example, J. T. Adams in one tart sentence accused human nature of two persistent traits: love of distinction and the need to follow leaders. These propositions do not make logically snug bedmates, but their use reflects the exasperation of the analyst.[6]

Many historians conceal their estimates of humanity quite well; others flaunt their opinions from the opening paragraph. Today, very few professional scholars would admit a fixed opinion concerning human nature, because the concept is essentially pre-Freudian and rests on observable character traits rather than an analytical evaluation of conscious or subconscious processes. The researcher who begins with an inflexible notion of other humans is inviting the same sort of cul-de-sac that awaits the determinist—eventually, the evidence will refuse to cooperate. Every so often, saints and sinners will pop up. The most sweeping advice may also be the most sound. The first principle of the spirit of history, said Jacques Barzun, is that humans have no nature. What they *do* have, argued Ortega y Gasset, is history.[7]

[5] James Truslow Adams, *Our Business Civilization: Some Aspects of American Culture* (New York: AMS Press, 1969 [1929]), p. 68.

[6] Edmund Burke, *Reflections on the Revolution in France* (New York: Everyman's Library, 1910), p. 135; Adams, *Our Business Civilization*, p. 14.

[7] Jacques Barzun, *Clio and the Doctors: Psycho-History, Quanto-History, and History* (Chicago: University of Chicago Press, 1974), p. 152; Ortega quoted in Franklin L. Baumer, *Modern European Thought: Continuity and Change in Ideas, 1600–1950* (New York: Macmillan, 1977), p. 437.

If we possess no nature, we still have mind. The revolution in human understanding wrought by Freud and his fellow psychologists was slow to penetrate the historical community, but "psychohistory" has been in vogue for some time and bids fair to become an established part of historical analysis. Studying human psychology in its historical context allows for the somewhat comforting techniques provided by modern science. Real psychotherapy is well beyond the age of jargon.

Psychohistory also fills a basic experiential need felt by many scholars. Human behavior so often seems irrational that only methods designed to analyze the irrational can serve as an explanation. The Romantics of the early nineteenth century were convinced that emotion was the motive force in human behavior, but their credo lay in instinctive action rather than reflective diagnosis. The impact of modern medical science was the prerequisite to empirical attempts to study the mind and its problems.

The historical problem shaped itself around discontent with positivism. Unlike Locke, Hobbes, or Burke, some modern scholars began to discount rational human interest as the sole or even dominant factor in humanity's makeup. Elie Halévy, a French historian who made his reputation scrutinizing his English neighbors, insisted early in the twentieth century that people are governed by beliefs and passions and that inconsistency is a hallmark of human behavior. Others were beginning to agree. "The mere study of documents is insufficient," A. L. Burt asserted in 1919. "The historian of the future must know more of the principles underlying the working of the human mind and human conduct."[8]

American historians in particular were slow to pick up such cues. Scholars naturally were reluctant to concede a place to the nonrational as valid historical material. Not until 1957 did the subject surface bluntly, in William L. Langer's Presidential Address to the American Historical Association, although a few curious spirits had been working with the concepts of symbol, myth, and image for years.[9] Positivist-oriented history, of course, has done far

[8] Peter Gay and Gerald J. Cavanaugh, eds., *Historians at Work*, IV: *Dilthey to Hofstadter* (New York: Harper and Row, 1975), p. 187; Lewis H. Thomas, *The Renaissance of Canadian History: A Biography of A. L. Burt* (Toronto: University of Toronto Press, 1975), p. 46.

[9] John Higham, with Leonard Krieger and Felix Gilbert, *History: The Development of Historical Studies in the United States* (Englewood Cliffs, N.J.: Prentice-Hall, 1965), pp. 229–31; William L. Langer, "The Next Assignment," *American Historical Review* 63, no. 2 (Jan., 1958): 283–304.

more than fight a rear-guard battle. It is rumored that on some campuses the psychohistorians and the computer-stuffers are not on speaking terms.

Undoubtedly, psychohistory is here to stay, but like every mode of historical discourse it brings trouble. For one thing, institutional psychology has the advantage of give-and-take with a live subject. One of the vaunted skills of the psychoanalyst rests in drawing out of the subject information the subject does not want to reveal or does not know he or she possesses. By contrast, the historian generally confronts only somewhat haphazard snippets of a mind once alive. Further, the tendency to build a psychological profile from sparse evidence is strong. (Napoleon was short. He overcompensated for his felt inferiority by conquering Europe.) As a corollary, by no means can all human motivation be explained in psychological terms, and not all human action results from a psychological shove. We need not discount psychology for what, as a science and an art, it was never designed to do—even though his critics charge that Freud wrote awful history.

Finally, psychohistory has a tendency to be *reductionist* in operation; that is, it reduces complex human action to elemental drives couched in psychological terminology. Occasional attempts, blessedly few of them by professional historians, to extend individual psychology to large groups illustrate the tendency. Concepts such as "mass mind" reduce even reductionism. At its best, psychohistory may tell a researcher a great deal about a discrete individual. Given the evidence, connections may even be made between a psychological profile and individual action.

Beyond the individual, however, float the perils of an inductive fog that no psychohistorian has penetrated very successfully. Jacques Barzun was a bit too testy, perhaps, when he wrote that psychohistory fundamentally altered the historical craft, and in a bad way. "Events and agents lose their individuality and become illustrations of certain automatisms." [10] It would be premature to argue from this point that psychology cannot be used eventually for historical group analysis. But for the time being, "psycho-" means individual humans, those beings who unavoidably stand at the center of history.

[10] Barzun, *Clio and the Doctors*, p. 23. The reader is encouraged to examine two notable psycho-biographies by the neo-Freudian Erik Erikson: *Young Man Luther* (New York: W. W. Norton, 1958) and *Gandhi's Truth: On the Origins of Militant Nonviolence* (New York: W. W. Norton, 1969).

The Individual: The Center

Since humanity is a perpetual study to itself, the history of individuals is far older than the craft. Early historians, though conscious of the need to recall the past, lacked many of the pigeon-holes into which we fit individual action today. Herodotus, Tacitus, and Ssŭ-ma Ch'ien knew nothing of nation-states, technocratic societies, or the lock-step of the Hegelian dialectic. But they were nevertheless true to their infant craft, for their work is illuminated by their experiences in the world of people.

Our first consideration must be the possibility that the individual is his or her own best historian. Each of us has unique elements in our personal history. These elements may vary from the trivial to the sublime, but no one else has quite our store of information about ourselves, or quite our perspective on our surroundings. Merely to possess such information, however, is not in itself to think about history. For this to happen, the information needs to be organized and conceptualized, usually in written form.

Without some form of conceptualization, our written fragments are akin to diaries or occasional notes to ourselves, but overall order and plan are lacking. With these, we have autobiography. Autobiographical writings usually are valued as primary history, because they organize as well as recall from the point of view of the involved person. The claims made for·autobiography sometimes have been sweeping. Wilhelm Dilthey saw the literary art of reflecting on one's own life "the root of all historical comprehension." Autobiography alone made possible the achievement of historical insight, and the historian who would be great must examine his or her own life to possess "the foundation of historical vision." [11]

Autobiographical writing is intrinsically interesting not only for the opportunity it gives its subject-object author at self-portrayal but also for the qualities of storytelling that inhere to it. A human life is the fundamental story of history, although autobiography necessarily leaves this story without an end. The parallel with fiction writing is very close, since almost all autobiographers in their recall create their past interaction with people and

[11] Wilhelm Dilthey, *Pattern and Meaning in History: Thoughts on History and Society*, ed. H. P. Rickman (New York: Harper and Row, 1962 [1961]), pp. 86–87.

events, even as they strive to tell their story. As one recent biographer bluntly puts it, "One should not expect autobiographers to be exact in fact, or to recapture the mood and thinking of the past." Mark Sullivan, who left an autobiography, was confident that the best autobiographical writing was that which was closest to fiction.[12]

Many autobiographies should never have been written. A purist might claim there is no such thing as an unnecessary autobiography, but we are not arguing the worth of an individual's life, only the quality and pertinence brought to a life's story. The urbane English historian Sir Charles Petrie gently chided his fellow autobiographers for their tendency to make one's life the excuse for (1) a series of vicious attacks on close associates, and (2) a scrupulously detailed and boring account of important people with whom the subject has broken bread. Sir Charles, in his own story, was always too polite for (1) but proceeded to accumulate several model examples of (2).[13]

Some autobiographies are excellent examples of the subject's self-knowledge; a rare few reveal a tortured, corrupt, or humane soul behind the words. The autobiographer, however, generally is not concerned with rigid rules of historical evidence but instead offers his (informed, uninformed, misinformed) opinion, take it for what it is worth. More than a few autobiographers are convinced their opinions come engraved from Sinai, which may make them very interesting or supremely tedious, as the case may be.

Autobiography is one of history's building blocks, but individuals not infrequently are their own worst witnesses, liable to overstress their influence on events, or not to realize it at all. The autobiographer may eliminate, not regard as important, or cover up information the historian would like to have. Eyewitnesses to events are as important to the historian as to the detective, and the immediacy of a life certainly is historically valuable. But the autobiographer many times is too close (figuratively) to the subject. The flea on the end of one's own nose looks like an elephant.

Lack of perspective in the autobiography generally is resolved in the biography, in which one person's life is retold by another

[12] Allen F. Davis, *American Heroine: The Life and Legend of Jane Addams* (New York: Oxford University Press, 1975 [1973]), pp. 157–58, 168; Mark Sullivan, *The Education of an American* (New York: Doubleday, Doran, 1938), p. 311.
[13] Sir Charles Petrie, *A Historian Looks at His World* (London: Sidgwick and Jackson, 1972), p. ix et passim.

individual. Almost all narrative history is at least in part biography, and arguments that artificially contrive biography as a branch of literature somehow apart from history are irrelevant. Unlike the autobiographer, the biographer, except the spurious part of the breed claiming to be able to write a biography of a still-living subject, has a complete story with which to deal—an entire human life. Again, too much may be claimed for biography. Ralph Waldo Emerson went to extremes in assuming that there was no such thing as history per se, only biography.[14]

Despite its natural narrative qualities, biography has its detractors. A single individual cannot be taken to be representative of great numbers of people, particularly if that person's historical importance clearly differentiates him or her from the mass. An isolated life may be studied for its intrinsic value, but historically the individual's influence or typicality, with few exceptions, is beyond the possibility of completely truthful recapture.

Biographers often tend to divide into defenders or enemies of their subject, either adulators or muckrakers, and historical analysis often gets lost through the gaps thus formed. Samuel Clark, a widely read English biographer of the seventeenth century, frankly posited that biographers must eye their subjects for imitation. The biographers must "look upon the best, and the best in the best," not observe weaknesses or discover shame—"this is a poysonous disposition."[15] Clark's attitude has filtered down to our time and accounts for demonstrated weaknesses in much biographical writing. Nevertheless, the primal quality of the biographical story continues to engage readers of professional and popular historians alike.

Biographers, said an excellent practitioner of the craft, must avoid competing with their subjects for the reader's attention. With the subject in the foreground, even a written life riddled with factual errors might attain a "sort of truth beyond the facts." Yet the biographer should never take liberties with the facts and thus concedes to the novelist a major advantage in the art of storytelling. As certainly, the writing of biography should be an exercise in humility. Human motivations are complex, as we know from our own experience. As remote as knowledge of these complexities

---

[14]Ralph Waldo Emerson, *Essays: First Series* (Boston: Phillips, Sampson, 1855), p. 9.
[15]Peter Gay, *A Loss of Mastery: Puritan Historians in Colonial America* (New York: Vintage Books, 1968 [1966]), p. 62.

may seem in the dim perspective of history, it is "important to try to understand."[16]

The essential and substantial qualities of biography have been accepted for centuries, but acceptance begs the question of whose lives are to be memorialized, and whose to be left out. Clearly no biography this side of complete fiction can be written without the evidence, which polishes off the possibility of most of the lives to date ever being recovered. The remainder, those relatively few people we know something about as individuals, are potential biographical subjects.

The individual is always the point of reference in a biography, Dilthey argued. Simultaneously, this human center must be relevant to a surrounding "dynamic and meaningful system." Biographies could be no more than partially successful in establishing this relevance. As works of art, they can be applied only to "historical personalities," for only they have the power to become relevant as a center to the "system" around them.[17]

The Alexanders, Caesars, and Napoleons of history easily may be categorized as relevant historical personalities. But Dilthey's conceptualization did not permit the inclusion of a "representative biography," a life of a person devoid of real historical influence but indicative of the trends in the world in which that person lived. Dilthey also made the hoary "life and times" approach to biography balance on the knife edge of the unattainable. We might not despair so much of integrating a person with historical surroundings if we reflect that it is impossible for everyone to influence events to the same degree. Full-blown historical personalities like Adolf Hitler will receive biographers for as long as the hand moves the pen, yet part of the debate surrounding them will concern their individual importance, whether they counted more than the forces in the world around them or were merely agents for forces over which they had little or no control.

We are even less certain of what the criteria of an "important" life should be. Napoleon was short, aggressive, a conqueror, a lover, a reformer, an empire-builder, a dreamer, a liar, and more; what are the ingredients of his importance? The Chinese, among all the peoples of the earth, most thoroughly bureaucratized their approach to biography through the rules set down for their official

[16] Marquis James, *Andrew Jackson: Portrait of a President* (New York: Grosset and Dunlap, 1937), pp. 581–83; Davis, *American Heroine*, p. x.
[17] Dilthey, *Pattern and Meaning in History*, pp. 91–92.

court scribes. Chinese historians were not attempting to provide a complete picture of their age through the portrayal of an individual life. Instead, they were trained to winnow from a life those instances that would provide models of behavior for future generations of bureaucrats trained in the Confucian tradition. History had a didactic purpose.

Unlike post-antique western societies, when the individual with attendant rights and obligations was perceived as the elemental unit of the social order, the Chinese saw the solitary human as intimately interconnected with various social groups. Several relationships—with ancestors, family, emperor, bureaucracy, and so forth—involved each person in a sense of collective responsibility. Thus the Chinese saw biography as a record of performance of duty and obligation within these relationships. Where the West has sought the "whole person" biographically, the Chinese tradition (which is the oldest) saw the meaning of an individual's life in some special function.[18]

The modern study of individuals, leavened with the new psychohistory, usually provides a richer and more fully rounded portrait than the narrowly purposeful Chinese approach. But recovering lives as completely as possible is only the most rudimentary of biographical tasks. The importance of the subject relative to the time must be weighed in evidence. To this end, Louis Gottschalk has distinguished mere conspicuousness from actual influence.[19] Frequently, the two qualities are virtually identical in a subject. Napoleon I, Emperor of France, was both conspicuous and influential. More often, though, these qualities vary widely. To her contemporaries, Napoleon's Empress Josephine was most conspicuous; for us, she lacks the historical influence of her husband. Absence of influence does not make a subject less interesting, merely less important historically. Today's rock music idols are nothing if not conspicuous; their ability to influence historical action, rather than merely to reflect cultural trends, is debatable.

Adding to the difficulty are the numerous instances where the historical importance of human action is not recognized by contemporaries, and primary evidence is scarce. Everyone kept tabs on Napoleon's expedition to Egypt. At about the same time several

[18] D. C. Twitchett, "Chinese Biographical Writing," in W. G. Beasley and E. G. Pulleyblank, eds., *Historians of China and Japan* (London: Oxford University Press, 1961), pp. 101, 109–10.

[19] Louis Gottschalk, *Understanding History: A Primer of Historical Method*, 2nd ed. (New York: Alfred A. Knopf, 1969), pp. 247–48.

experimenters in Europe and America were fiddling with the problem of electricity. Napoleon shook the earth in his own lifetime, but who is to say if the achievements of Volta, Oersted, Ampère, and Henry were not in the long run the more important? Fame delayed, for those long dead, is fame no more, but then the broadcasting of individual renown is not the historian's task.

Students beginning to think about history often confuse fame or notoriety with historical influence. When Josephine ascends to Napoleon's side, the barriers to historical judgment rise also. Buzz words like "famous" or "great" often obscure those human flaws that punctuate any study of character. The tiresome quality of these words and the frequency of their occurrence in our age of word inflation has made them useless clichés—which is too bad, since one of the more pressing questions dealing with the relationship of the individual to historical process is whether one man or woman can shape history. At the most elementary level, the question means, do we really count? *Can individuals, of and by themselves, condition historical events?* The debate commonly has centered on the role of the hero in history, on that singular person's possibilities, achievements, and limitations.

Historical Greatness and the Individual

In almost all cultural myths, giants once ruled. Their attributes and flaws alike were gargantuan, and their puny descendants could only retell the fables to gain perspective on their own lives or to condition their young. Human heroes in the western world descended from Olympus well before the time of Christ. In the historical sense, the classical ages of Greece and Rome produced the initial hero-models, men like Leonidas and Caesar. The Chinese had their sage-kings; the Teutonic tribes, their warrior-leaders.

The hero in history has been largely a creature of necessity, called forth by the need of societies for leadership. Whether mythical or having some basis in reality, the attributes of the hero were used in educating young people, inculcating religious precepts, developing loyalty to the state, fostering ethical principles, or perpetuating whatever the hero's strong suit was taken to be. Sometimes heroes appear as saviors, rescuers of ideals or social patterns in danger of extinction. They also may appear as heralds, the harbingers or prophets of a new world and a new social order. Lincoln has been cast in the first mold, Lenin in the second.

Leaders need followers. People may become part of an individual's following for any number of reasons. They may see in the leader the personal or psychological security they lack. The leader may promise material or spiritual rewards. Social analysts speculate that modern leaders may invite a "flight from responsibility" on the part of their followers, which is reflected in a search for simple solutions to complex social problems.[20] The social phenomenon of the leader-hero is extremely intricate in terms of historical analysis.

The classic statement concerning the importance of the hero belongs to Thomas Carlyle, the English historian remembered today both for his resonant history of the French Revolution and his insistence on the significance of Great Men in history. Carlyle occasionally indulged in the shock art of overstatement, but even so his dictum that "the history of the world is but the biography of great men"[21] is true to form. The word "great," as noted, is hackneyed today, but the historian must distinguish among degrees of influence. A common error among biographers, particularly those seeking perfection in the lives of saints (*hagiographers*), is to take "greatness" as a blanket measure of human action. Beyond question, Napoleon was a great general, perhaps the finest military mind in history. Does this mantle of greatness in turn envelop his statesmanship, his regard for humanity, or his skills in the boudoir?

We might reflect that Napoleon did not change the world from his bedroom but from the battlefield, and here is where his greatness lies. If so, then part of the historian's problem is to determine how a subject's life directly influenced human action. People in key positions, such as monarchs, generals, and diplomats, clearly may play a role in making things happen and in shaping the course of events. In Sidney Hook's phrase, they are "eventful men" who were directly responsible for historical change. In the perspective of the historian, though, Hook argued they are not properly heroic, since "accidents of position" rather than intrinsic qualities of intelligence, will, or character gave them their opportunities. In contrast, "event-making men" (Hook's heroic figures) create history, not through position but through their own extraordinary

[20] Sidney Hook, *The Hero in History: A Study in Limitation and Possibility* (Boston: Beacon Press, 1955 [1943]), pp. 3–26. See also Dixon Wecter, *The Hero in America: A Chronicle of Hero-Worship* (New York: Charles Scribner's Sons, 1941), pp. 1–16.

[21] Thomas Carlyle, *On Heroes, Hero-Worship and the Heroic in History*, ed. Carl Neimeyer (Lincoln: University of Nebraska Press, 1966 [1841]), pp. 29, 1.

qualities: Caesar's inner will, Luther's stubborn conviction, Napoleon's flashes of tactical intuition.[22]

Occasionally, the single individual does make the difference. In the fourteenth century Stephen Dushan ("the Mighty") came to the Serbian throne. A great military strategist, he, like Napoleon, also won fame as a lawgiver. Under Dushan, Serbian church architecture flourished; monasteries quickened the pulse of learning; and Serbian nationalism was heightened by the development of an authentic Serbian literature. But the leader became too ambitious. After conquering Albania, Macedonia, Thessaly, and Epirus, Dushan in 1355 marched on the seat of middle eastern power, Constantinople, but died on the way. With him his empire perished as well, crumbling into the disparate elements that had been made temporarily whole through his drive and will.

The same thing happened in the tenth century to the Arabs, who under the leadership of a fierce warrior-statesman named al-Mansur were sweeping the Christians from the Iberian Peninsula. Fortresses and monasteries beyond counting fell to his followers, but in 1002, so ill he had to be carried into battle on a litter, al-Mansur died. "The man who disappeared had carried on his strong shoulders the burden of empire," wrote one authority. After his death the great Arab tide receded. It took an intensifying Spanish nationalism five hundred years to eradicate Arab power from the peninsula, but al-Mansur had come the closest to making Spain Moslem.[23] Can we imagine a Moslem rather than a Catholic age of Spanish exploration?

Obviously most leaders fall far short of the stature of a Dushan or an al-Mansur; only a handful of names rank as true empire-builders. Yet given the right opportunities, the individual may still make a difference—in arenas of lesser scale, perhaps, but still of critical historical importance. A student of World War I has assigned such a key role to the French Marshal Joseph Joffre. "The war was very nearly lost with him, but . . . would almost certainly have been lost without him."[24] Historians constantly must assess the *context* of the leader's achievement. Through an effort of supposition, analysts imagine a situation without the leader's qualities

[22] Hook, *The Hero in History*, pp. 151–83.
[23] L. S. Stavrianos, *The Balkans Since 1453* (Hinsdale, Ill.: Dryden Press, 1958), p. 28; Henri Focillon, *The Year 1000* (New York: Frederick Ungar, 1969), p. 108.
[24] Alistair Horne, *The Price of Glory: Verdun, 1916* (New York: St. Martin's Press, 1963), p. 24.

and then render a verdict on whether that person's action made a crucial difference.

Mythic heroes usually were set apart from their followers by venturing into a supernatural realm where their great deeds involved overcoming superhuman forces. Their decisive victories were followed by the reward of power, which was transmitted to their followers upon their return. Historical heroes are rooted in reality; they operate in a specific context of time and place. Their heroic opportunities are conditioned not only by themselves but by other human action, natural conditions, chance—a variety of mundane factors that a Hercules could blithely ignore.

The thoughtful Swiss historian Jacob Burkhardt, pondering questions of historical greatness, concluded that heroes executed a collective will that went beyond individual desires. For Hegel, these were individuals "whose vocations it was to be the agents of the World-Spirit." The hero is not only irreplaceable; he also has the capacity to simplify programs and issues for his followers and to fasten his will on large numbers of people beyond an immediate following. The hero challenges the status quo; his promise is possibility. In part, these heroic attributes reflect not only heroic merit but also the freedom of the hero to act, to control circumstances.[25] Measured this way, without the proscriptive force of moral judgment, even a Hitler may be called great.

Ultimately, even the greatest are only human. Carlyle's "great man theory" of history, particularly when applied to the tangled interrelationships of modern societies, explains too much with too little. Fleet Admiral William F. Halsey, one of the leaders of the American naval drive on Japan during World War II, is supposed to have said that there were no great men, only great challenges, which men meet the best they can. Freud argued that great discoverers were not necessarily great men. Speaking of Columbus, the Viennese psychoanalyst asserted that "one may find great things without its [sic] meaning that one is really great."[26]

In support of these contentions, consider the possibility of much of history as a dice game. Any number of events may deny the hero opportunity, or, conversely, grant it. Napoleon's is a clas-

---

[25] Joachim C. Fest, *Hitler*, trans. Richard Winston and Clara Winston (New York: Vintage Books, 1975 [1973]), pp. 4–5, 8; Georg Wilhelm Friedrich Hegel, *The Philosophy of History*, trans. J. Sibree (New York: Dover Publications, 1956 [1831]), pp. 30–31.

[26] Paul Roazen, *Freud and His Followers* (New York: Meridian Books, 1976), p. 201.

sic case. As the French expedition sailed to Egypt, it passed during the nighttime within hailing distance of Nelson's fleet, so close the French sentries could hear the muffled booms of the English signal cannons. Given his later record, we might assume the future Lord Nelson would have blown the French out of the water, but for the vagaries of chance. And then, probably—no First Consulship, no Empire, no Russian campaign, no Napoleonic legend.

Might-have-beens are crucial to thinking about history, because thinking about events that never were forces us to consider options. By examining how an individual made a certain decision, what alternatives were available, what alternatives that person *thought* were available, and how well or ill the individual decided, the researcher has some basis on which to assess human influence on events. Imagination and critical judgment are complementary weapons in the arsenal of any historian.

Influence alone is of course too little for greatness, but some, like Admiral Halsey, deny the concept of greatness itself. Leo Tolstoy loathed the *poseur*, the pretender to special knowledge, and above all he hated the "experts" who claimed the skills to manage or explain human affairs. In Napoleon, Tolstoy saw a charlatan who claimed to foresee the correct options and to possess the unerring ability to select the right one, thus controlling events through his superior intellect. Tolstoy was appalled at such hubris; the greater the claim of prescience, the greater the fraud.[27]

The rejection of the idea of the great as the sole makers of history does not erase the uncounted historical moments when the leader has made a difference. Those who are led, however, are the ones about whom the historian would like to know much more. The leader usually leaves records (unless defeated, in which case a leader's history usually gets written by the conquerors), but the followers almost always remain inarticulate. Large groups began to speak, historically, only with the development of printing, and their influence on the historian has continued to increase to the present day. Groups may speak with many voices, or one, or even none. Researchers must ponder which of these is the truest claimant to historical reality.

Despite the increasing voice of the masses, the need for social leadership still exists. As simplistic as it seems, the "great man theory" has not lacked for takers even in the twentieth century. Con-

[27] Isaiah Berlin, *The Hedgehog and the Fox: An Essay on Tolstoy's View of History* (New York: Simon and Schuster, 1970), pp. 18–19.

trol over large numbers of people has been simplified in many ways by modern technology and communication. The irrepressible Mencken insisted that the masses virtually invited their own manipulation by their leaders. He wrote to Upton Sinclair, that great dreamer of impossibilities, that the longer he (Mencken) lived, the more he was convinced that "the common people are doomed to be diddled forever."[28]

We are entitled to hope Mencken wrong, while noting the essential truth of his words in the historical sense. Great or not, leaders have more often than not misled or oppressed their followers or those under their control. The occasional prince nicknamed "Good" or "Pious" shines like a beacon light among the "Terribles," "Assassins," and "Impalers." The individual, unfortunately, usually seems to influence history at some cost in lives or destruction. Historically, and again without moral overtones, this statement is at least partially as true of Christ and Gandhi as it is of Caesar and Hitler.

For those who believe in human free will, the individual's relationship to history must always remain potentially dominant. Institutions and forces beyond the control of the single person also have an historical role to play, however. The question of whether we make events or vice versa should always be debated contextually, but the power of events in influencing history is beyond denial. Historical process rests, then, not only on the individual but on the changing patterns of a person's surroundings as well.

[28]Leon Harris, *Upton Sinclair: American Rebel* (New York: Thomas Y. Crowell, 1975), p. 180.

CHAPTER NINE

Historical Forces

At times we all feel events moving beyond our control. We act because we have to, or are forced to, not because we find the action especially desirable. The student dragging himself to an early morning class has surrendered control of sleep for larger goals: grades, graduation, perhaps even a little education. In the historical sense, these larger goals may not even exist. But the forces outside ourselves are still there. Since we do not live alone but depend in differing degrees on others for the staples and enjoyments of life, so obviously do our lives intertwine with the varied groups of which we are a part.

Each of us, as group members, may be described in many ways. For example, the same person may be a son, student, voter, consumer, subscriber to *Playboy*, and Catholic. Such roles urge behavior patterns on us, and much of the time we respond positively: as a loving son, an "A" student, a liberal democrat, and so on. These pressures from outside ourselves probably have little historical effect when only the individual is considered, but they may have considerably more significance in group action. Some of these historical forces are institutionalized—in the family, the school system, the political party. Some are not. Historians study institutions and forces because people in groups often are impelled to act by influences beyond their individual control.

The Individual and Society

A modern commonplace saying is that more people have lived in the twentieth century than the total number that have ever lived

before. Whether true or not, the saying reflects both the population explosion of recent years and the increasing complexity of
human arrangements in an age where specialists have become necessary. In fact, historical study of the individual has tended to diminish of late, while the search for social structure and historical
forces has escalated. Biography and the examination of elites do
not have the popularity they once enjoyed as explanation-forms in
the nineteenth century. Now classes and causes attract propor-
tionally more professional attention.[1]

The supposition that there is something more to history than
biography is of course not new to our age. The great historian of
Rome, Titus Livius (Livy), admitted that Alexander was a brilliant
general but that he was only an individual. The Macedonian's victories paled beside the "exploits of a nation waging wars now eight
hundred years." Livy's patriotism as a Roman citizen was above
reproach, obviously coloring his insistence that Roman institutions outlasted the efforts of mere men. Yet his estimation of the
importance of society as a whole found echoes. By the time Giambattista Vico wrote in the eighteenth century, claims on behalf of
society as the key to historical understanding were not uncom-
mon. Vico's intellectual disciple Jules Michelet sought in his *History of France* (1833–44) to present a broad-based examination of
his people. "I shut the books, and placed myself among the people
to the best of my power, the lonely writer plunged amongst the
crowd, listened to their noise, noted their words."[2]

Social forces, such as those Michelet sensed in his crowds,
have been highlighted in the past century by the developing social
sciences: anthropology, sociology, political science, even psychology and economics. One authority, Carl Gustavson, has listed six
different types of social forces, i.e., economic, religious, institutional (mainly political), technological, ideological, and military.
Gustavson calls these forces "human energies which, originating
in individual motivations, coalesce into a collective manifestation
of power."[3] As a definition, this is as suitable as any, but we must

[1] Fritz Stern, *Gold and Iron: Bismarck, Bleichröder, and the Building of the
German Empire* (New York: Alfred A. Knopf, 1977), p. xx.
[2] Peter Gay and Gerald J. Cavanaugh, eds., *Historians at Work*, I: *Herodotus
to Froissart* (New York: Harper and Row, 1972), p. 174; Peter Gay and Victor G.
Wexler, eds., *Historians at Work*, III: *Niebuhr to Maitland* (New York: Harper
and Row, 1975), pp. 67–69.
[3] Carl G. Gustavson, *A Preface to History* (New York: McGraw-Hill, 1955),
p. 28.

note that social forces are complex, often contradictory, and tend many times to overlap.

Our present point is simply that there are historical alternatives to studying individuals. Even collective biography, the life stories of groups of people, provides only partial answers. Bismarck, who certainly was in a position to form an opinion, once asserted that "events are stronger than the plans of men." The architect of modern Germany has been described many times as having had a master plan for German unification, to which he adhered with stubborn tenacity. But the man himself conceded that people could not create events; they could only try to control them.[4]

Studying social forces moves the historian away from elitist materials and into a realm where indirect evidence and inference predominate. The human components of these forces ("masses," "mob," "crowd") are not recoverable as individuals, except in special circumstances. Most of the time they naturally are sympathetic figures, for they tend to be the underdogs of history. Voltaire's concern for the fate of the French laborer was typical. Work was the lot of man, he observed, and the majority of people in all countries of the world (in his preindustrial age) must exist by manual toil. "The greater numbers of such men are bound to be poor," wrote the Sage of Ferney, "but they need not be wretched."[5]

The problems of examining society are those common to examining individuals, with one important addition. The "common man" usually is inarticulate. Such a person speaks to the historian only when immersed in social action, and sometimes not even then. Anonymity may be pierced occasionally. We catch fleeting glimpses of plain folks in wills, court records, newspaper reports, the comments of articulate observers. More often the individual in the crowd speaks as a component of the crowd— in censuses, voting polls, army musters, riots. Yet historically the crowd has significance and must be assessed.

Historians recently have been doing excellent work in recovering areas of human experience long thought beyond recovery or insignificant. Studies in the history of the family, and of women and children, have become increasingly common. So have examinations of educational patterns and of the histories of racial and ethnic groups. Even sexuality, the most private and therefore the most elusive of subjects, is beginning to find its scholars. What has

[4] A. J. P. Taylor, *Bismarck: The Man and the Statesman* (New York: Vintage Books, 1967 [1955]), pp. 60, 70.
[5] Peter Gay and Victor G. Wexler, eds., *Historians at Work*, II: *Valla to Gibbon* (New York: Harper and Row, 1972), p. 325.

emerged is a more balanced picture of our past. People have been far more than mere political animals or circumstantial cannon fodder, yet most history down to the twentieth century, when it departed from basic biography, concerned itself either with political institutions or with political institutions and philosophies in opposition (wars). To a significant degree, the newer forms of historical writing regard human behavior in repose—in the interaction of the family unit, the endless debate over the young, or the timeless interweaving of the sexes.

How may the historian analyze human beings in the mass? Suppose we were to write the sentence "The wars of Louis XIV bled France white." The meaning of the phrase is clear—lots of people got killed fighting under the Bourbon flag and many more felt the economic pinch of war. But not everyone in France fought, and not every soldier was killed. Our generalization clearly does not fit every citizen of France, yet it is a reasonable one from the evidence. The obvious corollary is, alas, a false one. We might suppose that simply by analyzing a majority, we might then make a reasonable historical statement. We would argue that since a majority of the people in the France of Louis XIV were directly and negatively affected by his wars, then our statement is permissible. But any historian can point to numerous instances where historical events, in terms of cause and effect, did not directly influence the action of a social majority. The histories of many revolutions, at least in their early stages, afford our most pertinent examples.

Individuals, then, are difficult to isolate from the crowd. Indeed, when examining social forces the historian directs attention to *aggregates*: political parties, armies, consumers, intellectuals. The commonalities of these aggregates afford the evidence. In these cases, it is the generality, not the particularity, that has historical weight.

The most prevalent example of an historical aggregate is the nation-state. Although some scholars, like the masterful Belgian historian Henri Pirenne, have felt that nationalism was of little help in interpreting historical fact, the nation-state has dominated the organization of much modern historical writing. There is a tendency to regard the state and the society it represents as "two aspects of a single reality." As one authority has noted, however, "the state is simply the normal government of an areal society."[6]

[6] Peter Gay and Gerald J. Cavanaugh, eds., *Historians at Work*, IV: *Dilthey to Hofstadter* (New York: Harper and Row, 1975), pp. 82–86; Edward Whiting Fox, *History in Geographic Perspective: The Other France* (New York: W. W. Norton and Company, 1971), pp. 38–39.

The society itself may overlap political or geographic boundaries; it often may function virtually independently from borders drawn on maps.

Until recently the writing of national histories tended to assume the unique qualities of the nation-state. It is in the interests of the state to create its own official histories, thus cementing its claims to power. The Syrian government, for example, proclaimed in 1947 that the purpose of history was "to strengthen the nationalist and patriotic sentiments in the hearts of the people . . . because the knowledge of the nation's past is one of the most important incentives to patriotic behavior."[7] History becomes positive patriotism, proving that the citizens have a special and important past.

Likewise, some of this writing led indirectly to the promotion of "national" attributes that verged on the stereotypical: the efficiency of the Germans, the phlegmatic Englishman, the inscrutable Chinese. To analyze social forces effectively is to work with commonalities, not nationalities—else the researcher starts with the proof, which is hardly critical thinking. The analysis of social forces begins with social order, with how societies organize themselves for maintenance and for collective action.

History and Politics

Human communities are necessary and unavoidable, but unavoidable too is the conflict generated within these communities. The resolution of these conflicts at the community level, so as to make community life tolerable to its members, is the task of politics. Sometimes politics succeeds, sometimes it fails; but always, political behavior is part of the social order.

Thucydides has a fair claim to being the father of political history. For him, the true meaning of humanity was contained in politics. Human behavior could be examined most readily through political events and what social or military consequences these events produced. Thucydides believed political events conditioned the cyclic movement of history; we recall that Polybius thought likewise. Polybius regarded the study of history as training for political life. His cycles were much more rigid and inexorable than those of

---

[7] Bernard Lewis, *History: Remembered, Recovered, Invented* (Princeton: Princeton University Press, 1976), p. 65.

Thucydides.[8] Both men saw political behavior as a basic component of human existence, and both assumed that history should be written to reflect this fact.

Historians almost always come to their task with formed political opinions of their own. The difficulty in doing political history is to avoid taking sides beyond what the evidence allows. Unfortunately, politics begins with a soapbox, and the urge to join the speech-making is tempting for the historian. Roy Nichols, in an early attempt to get at the core of historical study, created a logic chain: "To know history is to know the psychology of peoples, to know the psychology of peoples we must know the psychology of individuals, those individuals in history that are most articulate are the politicians." So far, this is a statement concerning a basis for historical thought. But Nichols in later life followed with the assertion that the chief responsibility of the historian is to supply knowledge of the long evolution of self-government.[9]

Some thinkers have advocated historical research as a vehicle for political education. Theodor Mommsen, who made his reputation as an historian of ancient Rome, nevertheless maintained a modern and didactic position on the question. "Whoever writes history, but especially contemporary political history," he wrote, "has the duty to be a political teacher."[10] The temptation for the researcher to become an advocate, not just an educator, often overrides such scholarly impulses.

The problem is an endlessly perplexing one, both because researchers are political animals and because political practice has varied widely through time. Traditionally, history and politics have been so closely allied that it is impossible to tell where one begins and the other leaves off. Discerning men of action, like Sir Walter Raleigh, tended to believe that historical materials served to quicken political judgment and help adjust social institutions to historical change.[11] But just as there may be several differing assessments of the historical evidence, so people may differ over political solutions based on history. The classic debate in this regard concerns the political relationship between freedom and restraint. When does freedom become license and restraint a violation of hu-

[8] Gay and Cavanaugh, eds., *Historians at Work*, I, 56, 108–109, 111.
[9] Roy F. Nichols, *A Historian's Progress* (New York: Alfred A. Knopf, 1968), pp. 37–38, 238–39.
[10] Gay and Cavanaugh, eds., *Historians at Work*, IV, 67.
[11] Gordon Connell-Smith and Howell A. Lloyd, *The Relevance of History* (London: Heinemann Educational Books, 1972), pp. 15–16.

man rights? The parameters of the question change through time, and the historian must be aware not only of personal biases but also of the political attitudes of the time under examination.

Political history reached its apogee in combination with the development and persistence of the nation-state, a process that continues today. Pirenne, who strove to be as precise as possible, once avowed that national independence was inseparable from independence of mind.[12] This proposition is highly debatable (which would have delighted Pirenne), but at least it suggests a convenient framework for historical analysis. The nation-state has been the most frequently used, and abused, historical concept for the past two hundred years. As concept it is more common in Europe, East Asia, and the Americas. In India and the Middle East it must still make room for cultural patterns such as Hinduism and Islam, or even smaller groups such as the tribe or the village.

The abuse lies in the direction of assuming that history and politics, within the context of the nation-state, are one and the same. The role of national institutions in modern history has been so dominating that the assumption is understandable, if regrettable. The national model often has been claimed as a surrogate for history itself. Hegel, caught in the euphoria of an age of waxing nationalism, contended that historians should examine the growth of freedom in conjunction with the rise of the nation-state. Political history afforded all that was important in history. Hegel imagined a "universal spirit" unfolding through time; he argued that in every epoch of world history there was a "nation of world historical consequence" that bore the spirit in its current stage. Unlike his fellow Germans Fichte and Schiller, Hegel did not regard Germany as the predestined carrier of this torch ad infinitum. The dominant nation of the world would be that nation of world historical consequence. Today, perhaps, Germany; tomorrow, another political grouping.[13]

Apart from the raw power implicit in national organization, historians traditionally have examined the intermixture of national wills in two major forms: diplomacy and war. No one has ever argued that nations have behaved toward each other with a bow in the direction of the Golden Rule. Most historians view statecraft with the jaundiced eye of the realist Machiavelli, who

[12] Gay and Cavanaugh, eds., *Historians at Work*, IV, 95.
[13] Haskell Fain, *Between Philosophy and History: The Resurrection of Speculative Philosophy of History within the Analytic Tradition* (Princeton: Princeton University Press, 1970), p. 213; Gay and Cavanaugh, eds., *Historians at Work*, IV, 39.

saw in Renaissance Florence and the other Italian city-states a lesson for survival. Machiavelli's prince operates beyond the moral boundaries of most individuals; he must, because the survival of his state depends on his estimates of the best interests of the institution. So, too, do historians attempt to judge the actions of the nation-state, trying objectively to measure diplomacy in the demanding arena of international power.

When diplomacy fails, and sometimes even when it seems to succeed, war results. Here again the objectivity of historians is hard-taxed, since they may subscribe to the national ideals of one of the belligerents. Because war so often has been of decisive importance historically, it has been probably the most studied of all historical topics. Romance, glory, heroism, tragedy—all may be found in abundance on the battlefield, as seen by the scholar. Psychologists may speculate as to humans' aggressive instincts, and anthropologists derive concepts like "territorial imperative" from nature; for the historian, the complexion of the past is endlessly pocked by war, and he is forced to come to grips with its issues and results.

A pessimist would conclude that wars are inevitable, the most "natural" aspect of history. "Politics and warfare seem unhappily to be the two most natural professions to man," concluded Voltaire. "He must always be either bargaining or fighting." Voltaire observed, with his customary wit, that those most fortunate at either game we call the greatest, and the luckiest we style the most meritorious.[14] To study war is to deal with winners and losers. Alongside the resounding triumphs of Napoleon on the battlefield must be balanced innumerable results, possibilities, probabilities. The shape of Europe without the Napoleonic Wars must be imagined; otherwise, the impact of Napoleon's armies cannot be judged with any clarity.

The historical effects of war, moreover, are akin to the widening ripples formed by a stone cast in a pool. Where the Grand Army marched, political institutions changed. French, and even European, society was altered to a certain degree as well. Men and women who never would have seen the inside of a palace in Bourbon France rode the Napoleonic coattails to positions of subordinate but very real power. Social opportunity broadened to some extent—"a marshal's baton in every knapsack." Everywhere pulses quickened to the tramp of the French legions; Napoleon was liberator as well as oppressor. The historical forces he symbolized were

---

[14] Gay and Wexler, eds., *Historians at Work*, II, 296.

not only of himself but of his time. War was his element, and much of his fame rests therein. But the results of his wars are historical in other areas as well and cannot be ignored.

Napoleon's story, which is unique in himself (Corsican outcast to emperor to exile), is also a story of the increasing hegemony of France in Europe, followed by the decline of French power under the combined blows of an international alliance. The social energies Napoleon unleashed may have found outlets anyway; we can only speculate. The debate continues as to whether Napoleon was simply an agent for these forces, or whether he shaped them to his will, or whether a combination of both possibilities is closest to historical truth. We misuse our example, though, if we insist that our understanding of the Napoleonic achievement be confined to the political arena.

The older type of historical writing, which thought of politics and history as two sides of the same coin, could not see beyond its own artificially imposed blinders. The tendency was strong to take the chance and accident out of politics and to see statesmen and politicians as consistent masters of their situations. We should recall the judgment of John Morley, the English statesman: "Politics are [*sic*] a field where action is one long second-best, and where the choice lies constantly between two blunders." [15]

Politics is a great game; the stakes are high and the historical results usually important. But it is not the only game in town. A recent critical appraisal of the Kennedy administration has censured the Kennedy family for making politics coextensive with life itself.[16] Regardless of the merit of the criticism, the wider point is that many human problems are incapable of political resolution. As important as it is, the narrow conceptualization of history either as politics or as extensions of politics cannot fully illuminate the past. Beyond politics, beyond the powerful political engine of the nation-state, there are other historical forces at work.

History and Economics

Histories of economic life also have habitually used the nation-state as a framework. Any measure of national wealth includes the

[15] Allan Nevins, *Hamilton Fish: The Inner History of the Grant Administration* II (New York: Frederick Ungar, 1936), p. 887.

[16] Henry Fairlie, *The Kennedy Promise: The Politics of Expectation* (New York: Dell, 1974), p. 289.

resources of a nation—people, national endowments, amount of goods. Every society chooses how to allocate its finite resources. Thus, economic history is to some extent the study of scarcities. Generally, two models of resource allocation have been tried within the context of the nation-state. A free-enterprise economy depends on price systems and production to divide wealth. A centrally controlled economy artificially assigns prices and allocates production priorities by design rather than demand. There are, of course, many variations between these two poles.

The study of economic forces attempts to explain institutional changes occurring as the process of making a living changes. In Napoleon's day there were no electricians, just as there is no great call today for musket manufacturers. Different ways of making a living produce great changes in a society and fundamentally alter the perspective of people on themselves and their surroundings. We are living in the second century of a period of economic growth unparalleled in history. Historians also study this growth process in its varying facets. The rise of capitalism, the creation of modern technology, the evolution of business and commercial practices, all are grist for the mill.

Because economics is itself a theoretical science much given to models as explanation-forms, historians occasionally attempt to test theoretical propositions in their historical context. Given the data, questions such as inflation or unemployment may be examined historically. Economic cycles are common in history, and a narrow view would assert this cyclical motion of economic life as true for all humanity. The best students of economic history, though, are well aware that economics, like politics, cannot be separated from the social whole of which it is a part.[17]

The ingredients of economic history are diverse. They include the study of agriculture, labor, capital, commerce, industry, finance, banking, transportation, and communication. Historians do not simply regard these aspects in a vacuum. They must consider interrelationships in the marketplace and interlocking social nature through the process of government. A jumble of theories clamor for attention, from Adam Smith's ideas concerning the classic market economy to Marx's sermons on class struggle.

As with politics, economics has had its champions for supremacy in the examination of history. The most famous of these was Marx, who went to the extreme of claiming that all human con-

[17] Ross M. Robertson, *History of the American Economy*, 2nd ed. (New York: Harcourt, Brace and World, 1964), pp. 1–16.

sciousness was wrapped up in the material conditions of life. The Marxist man is a paradox: on the one hand, he is moved by the inexorable forces of materialism. These forces have created the capitalist and laboring classes, the social groupings that impel the doctrine of class struggle. Yet Marx believed that man eventually could control materialism, in a rational and scientific way.[18] Without downplaying the obvious effects of conscious materialism in modern societies, we note that human greed antedated the assembly line, and that status symbols did not begin with the Stutz Bearcat.

Economic motivations in human life are strong, enduring, and often of crucial historical importance. People may act on questions of material status before they even think of questions concerning ideals or honor. Much political activity is conditioned directly by economic questions, all the way from simple bread-and-butter issues to the most convoluted riddles of high finance. Economic causes increasingly have been used to explain diplomatic activity and to account in large measure for modern war. For example, William Appleman Williams has argued that American leaders in the 1890s believed that political and social objectives could be achieved only through economic means. From this premise he indicted American imperialist diplomacy as a failure in its attempts to advance the domestic economy by establishing markets overseas.

Williams has called the question of whether economics makes foreign policy or vice versa a "pseudo-problem." In his historical case, the growth of American imperialism, there perhaps was a consensus among political and economic leaders as to the fundamental truth that economic actions produced all general welfare.[19] But there exists no assurance that every historical case may be so considered. Wars may have a wide variety of causes, and often the immediate cause is the most historically trivial. The War of Jenkins' Ear, ostensibly begun when an unsavory trader produced his severed aural organ in the House of Commons and claimed the damned Dons had cut it off, was actually the result of the long-standing embroilment of England and Spain in commercial rivalries.

Likewise, in the 1920s and 1930s it was common to explain

[18] Bruce Mazlish, *The Riddle of History: The Great Speculators from Vico to Freud* (New York: Minerva Press, 1968 [1966]), pp. 292–93.
[19] William Appleman Williams, *The Tragedy of American Diplomacy* (New York: Delta Books, 1962), pp. 30, 71–72n.

World War I and its causes in economic terms. Depending upon whom one read, the whole thing was caused by international commercial rivalries, the manipulations of money-mad financiers, speculation orgies by munitions manufacturers, or status considerations involving decadent European monarchies. Simplistic analyses like these, few of them from the pens of professional historians, are scapegoating history. Since economics is at least crudely related to the study of human need and greed, economic analyses have a tendency to become reductionist. Human motivation becomes oversimplified, and so too does the historical view. Not every economic historian can write as powerfully and as pertinently as Marx, nor does an economic analysis rooted in one place and time necessarily translate elsewhere.

We are all entrenched in a certain economic order. We have an income (or lack of it); we have reasonably fixed ideas on what we wish to use that income for; we surround ourselves with the tangible and not-so-tangible results of the income; we expect others to see in these results at least part of what we are. If the results are unsatisfactory to us, we are likely to get upset. If enough of us get upset, social and political change may follow, and our personal sense of economic well-being may be translated into action of historical importance. Of course, the historian has no great scroll upon which to read these relationships. Were he to make the statement "The desire of Parisian housewives for bread eventually brought Napoleon to power," he would not be received kindly by his peers. Since Marx, the economic component of our existence has been elevated to high favor, perhaps too high, in terms of historical analysis.

The shifting balances of economic order obscure the point that human beings are more than a bundle of materialistic impulses. Although we are all too obviously avaricious, we are on occasion prone to idealism and altruism. Economic analysis is not the final word on historical forces; no narrow focus is. As Robert Heilbroner has noted, at the heart of economics is the search for order and meaning in social history.[20] In other words, economic life is basic to understanding the past, but it is not the entire past. Nor do politics and economics together form a whole.

[20] Robert L. Heilbroner, *The Worldly Philosophers: The Lives, Times and Ideas of the Great Economic Thinkers*, 4th ed. (New York: Simon and Schuster, 1972), p. 14.

Thought and Action

The force of ideas has at least as much power as the more worldly actions of political and economic life. Indeed, politics and economics depend on ideas to influence human action, just as ideas must rely on politics, economics, and other avenues of transmission to reach the public. Ideas generally are not created in an instant, leaping full-blown into the brain of some intellectual Hotspur. Rather, they are the products of many minds over many years, their shapes changing with the historical patterns by which they are formed and influenced. The idea of liberty was seen differently by the Greek citizen of the fourth century before Christ, by Renaissance courtiers, by the English gentry of one hundred years ago, and by the rebellious youth of the 1960s.

The strongest advocates of the role of ideas in history view the human mind as central to historical understanding. Perry Miller, a well-known analyst of Puritan America, announced early in his career that he was naive enough to believe that thought influenced action. Miller reasoned that history was part of the life of the mind; he insisted that mind was the basic factor in history. From this perspective, the mind leaves permanent imprints through time. Creative thought is history; the rest, mere transience. "The details and devices of politics sink into oblivion," observed Voltaire, "but sound laws, institutions, and achievements in the sciences and the arts remain forever."[21]

Thought that does not influence human action is thought unfulfilled. Yet the problems the historian faces in relating thought to action and vice versa are most difficult. Ideas abhor a vacuum; they are neither born independent of their human environment nor can they flourish apart from it. A trite observation, perhaps, but necessary, considering the persistence of the notion that ideas somehow have a life of their own, moving from generation to generation without effect. *Can an idea without historical effect be of historical importance?* Contextually, it depends, the cautious observer would reply. A few Greeks knew the secret of steam propulsion well before the time of Christ, yet the idea of steam power was not realized with historical effect until a century or more after Luther and Calvin.

Ideas have the power to animate marching armies. They may

[21] Gay and Cavanaugh, eds., *Historians at Work*, IV, 355; Gay and Wexler, eds., *Historians at Work*, II, 345.

raise humans to the rarest heights of noble purpose and debase them beyond recall. Embedded in tradition, ideas may act as a powerful governor on the pace of change, to a point where a traditional society may be shattered by its inability to respond to outside ideas. Ideas derive their essential force from interacting with society, but their development may be studied—from embryo to maturity, as it were. If researchers chose to be picky enough, they could trace the idea of the automobile to the first wheel, or even the first footpath trampled by nomads as they followed the game and the seasons. Tracking down the origins and intricacies of ideas through time is challenging research, but ideas meshing with historical action provide the most testing analytical game of all.

Living in the wake of two centuries of evolving democratic institutions, we might get the "idea" that thought has served as a one-way ticket to individual freedom. But ideas hold no belief, political or otherwise. By themselves, they are neutral and colorless, taking their meaning only from their interaction with the human community that produced them. To Marx, ideas were a vehicle of oppression, the merest excuse for control by a ruling class. James Truslow Adams, with forty more years of history to chew on, admitted that the dominant ideas of an age must be those of the dominant classes. Where Marx saw only oppression, however, Adams saw a business ethic that was uncivilized but open, exploitative but relatively unoppressive.[22] Both men regarded as unquestionable the assertion that each age has its "ruling ideas."

The question of whether cultures may inherit or produce ruling ideas is historically moot. Many historians, we should note, proceed along the lines of this unstated assumption. Carl Becker thought the best way to express history was to study the few articulate people who helped determine the ruling ideas or dominant thought of an age.[23] Obviously, ideas do not occur to large numbers of people through mass flashes of intuitive insight. Most ideas of historical importance need time to percolate, to do their spadework, much as the patient labor of winter storms is needed to produce the road potholes we fruitlessly attempt to avoid each spring. Historians are interested not only in the people initiating

[22] Mazlish, *The Riddle of History*, p. 297; James Truslow Adams, *Our Business Civilization: Some Aspects of American Culture* (New York: AMS Press, 1969 [1929]), pp. 30–31.

[23] Charlotte Watkins Smith, *Carl Becker: On History and the Climate of Opinion* (Carbondale: Southern Illinois University Press, 1973 [1956]), p. 196.

or changing important ideas but in the social effect that these ideas have.

To be effective historically, an idea must do historical work. It must *influence* people in a demonstrable way. How many people? Here the problem attains the complexity of the Gordian knot. Unlike Alexander's famous sword stroke, which quickly resolved that problem, the unraveling of ideas into a chain of cause and effect does not lend itself to simple solutions. Earth-shaking ideas, like those concerning individual liberties, have had to reach large numbers of people to become historically effective. "Ideas may arise from the minds of isolated geniuses or madmen," Eugene Genovese has written, "but their transformation into world views implies their acceptance by substantial numbers."[24]

Not all ideas can claim such blanket significance. Some thought is a way-station to larger issues; other thinking provides interesting sidelights on prevalent idea patterns. For example, the religious community of Shakers by itself was of no world-historical importance. When its religious practices are examined, though (one way of researching thought in action), the Shakers are found to provide an interesting illustration of the by-paths taken by modern religion.

The influence of ideas is difficult to assess. Thought may lie dormant for years and then pop up unexpectedly and effectively. Political reform, impelled by ideas, tends to work in this way—an explosive, intensive burst of activity, a dwindling of action once short-range goals are reached, a period of quiescence. But the unfulfilled ideas are still there (unless crushed out of existence, like the Albigensian Heresy), working away like the ice under those roadbeds.

This hide-and-seek quality of ideas, added to the question of numerical influence, makes the history of thought an exercise in exasperation. Ideas are supposed to be explosive, fumed J. T. Adams in the 1920s—a period not known for a frenetic pace of reform. Yet in America, he concluded, ideas were as harmless as "duds."[25] In his frustration, Adams made the dangerous error of assuming that the life of an idea is fixed and finite; that if it fails to do historical work at one particular time, its opportunity has passed forever. No one familiar with the vicissitudes of thought

<hr>

[24] Eugene D. Genovese, *The World the Slaveholders Made: Two Essays in Interpretation* (New York: Vintage Books, 1971 [1969]), p. 123.
[25] Adams, *Our Business Civilization*, p. 84.

over thousands of years would subscribe to this view for a minute. Today monarchists, flat-earthers, and subscribers to *bushido* are in the distinct minority. Who would care to predict their day will not come again?

The most tangible level at which ideas have historical effect is in the areas of science and technology. From better mousetraps to Poseidon missiles, modern technology has influenced our lives almost beyond estimation, sometimes in unintended ways. Through technology we have compressed our human universe even as we have expanded it; the red dust of Mars appears in our living room. We assume ourselves masterful because we annihilate space and time. The assumption is an idea, as is the scientific thought that made the assumption possible. Here is an example of "idea linkage" that makes the study of the history of thought difficult, but necessary.

"Ineffectual history" is one critic's name for the linkage of ideas. We stress again that these ideas are only parameters in the historian's mind, "concepts" if you will. Napoleon might think himself a benevolent dispenser of liberalism to the continent of Europe; a modern scholar might rank him as a precursor of modern totalitarianism. Liberalism and totalitarianism, as concepts, are not the same, but they may appear as part of the same historical truth, i.e., an examination of Napoleon.

Concepts become unglued for the historian precisely at that point where they begin to stick to themselves. That is, historians in relating idea-concepts have a tendency to interrelate them exclusive of surrounding societies. One idea produces another, independently of humanity and its environment.[26] An idea, like a flame, cannot exist in a vacuum. The historian must either strive to show it doing work in the world or be left with the meaningless perfection of a "system."

Ideas whose time has come work with powerful, if imprecise, historical force. Other thoughts, perhaps equally noble or profane, sputter and die; their historical moment passes, perhaps never to come again. Historians must be cognizant of the ideas undeveloped. They must try to recapture the partial success, or retrieve the lost thought. It is a vexing task, but a rewarding one, for ideas knit together the worlds of social, political, and economic life into thematic wholes that make the past comprehensible if not

[26] Fain, *Between Philosophy and History*, pp. 173, 266.

understandable. With ideas as a binding force, the historian may confront the combined potential and problem of universal history.

Debating Universal History

We live in an age of specialization. Brought up in a world where everyone must "do" something, we are trained to believe no one can "do" everything. Modern life is too complex, we are told. A lifetime of training will not suffice to acquaint the individual with even a small facet of the environment.

So, too, for the past century, the historical craft increasingly has given itself over to specialization. There even exists a clumsy verb for the extreme tendency—to "namierize." "Namierization" (not to be found in any dictionary) derives from the research and analytical methods of Lewis Namier, a scholar born in Russian Poland, but a man whose life and historical studies focused on Great Britain. Namier cultivated a thread-by-thread examination of the tapestry of history. He examined minutely the biographical and social characteristics of institutionally defined groups, the most celebrated case being the English Parliament in the age of George III.[27] "Microhistory," history seen through a microscope, is advanced as a means of establishing patterns of change and of opening up the hidden underlayers of historical process through examinations of institutions like families or political factions.

The basic assumption of Namier and his followers was that history may be understood as a coherent whole only after understanding its varied parts. Thus microhistory centers on the year, the month, the day. The larger picture is cast aside, at least temporarily, in favor of complete immersion in a specific time and place, thus ostensibly bringing one closer to historical "reality." Beyond this type of research, which produced original and evocative analyses, perhaps an inductive picture of the sweep of history could be formed.

Namier's approach would not do for historians like Arnold Toynbee. To Toynbee, history was *necessarily* whole; it must be perceived whole, because any partial consideration warps its true meaning. Thus Toynbee exemplified "macrohistory," the study of

---

[27] Gay and Cavanaugh, eds., *Historians at Work*, IV, 272; Lewis Namier, *The Structure of Politics at the Accession of George III*, 2nd ed. (New York: St. Martin's Press, 1968).

univcrsals in history. Macrohistory may cover centuries in a paragraph, searching for unifying themes that explain human development in all its forms. Where microhistory attempts surgically to dissect institutions at one precise moment of time, macrohistory plays with giant issues involving civilizations, religions, cultures. As Karl Löwith has noted, however, merely to examine X number of civilizations does not make history "universal"—merely general.[28] Unifying themes are necessary.

Logically, in any debate between the Namierites and Toynbee (there are no "Toynbeeites"), the Namierites hold all the trumps. As one critic of Toynbee queried, "How can we say anything at all about the whole until *after* we have looked at its parts?"[29] But logic is not in itself history; if it were, the past would be mathematics, and so would be the future. Perversely enough, the illogical aspects of history are Toynbee's strongest defense. Even should all the parts of history be examined componentially, what then? What is history's atomic particle chronologically—the year, the day, the hour? Institutionally—the parliament, the faction, the individual? To examine such parts to form some kind of total whole would take forever and beyond. Namier's approach always must be incomplete. Logically, then, the opportunity for universal history would be lost forever.

We might reply, however, that in history the sum of the parts is not always the whole. Suppose an infinitely numerous team of graduate school monkeys *did* examine every part of history. Then perhaps the head monkey, or dissertation director, would add up the parts and produce the whole, which in turn would be a meaningless hash without theme or coherence. Knowing the impossibility of ever completing a reconstruction of historical parts, daring and inquisitive minds will not rule out the possibility of universal history. Only universal history, remarked Ranke, concerns the past life of the human race in all its totality. Only here does history attend to all the sources of life.[30]

Problems abound in the practice of universal history. In the age of the specialist everyone mines one lode, becomes "expert in his field." The larger the compass of research, the more glaring the

[28] Karl Löwith, *Meaning in History* (Chicago: University of Chicago Press, 1949), p. 111.
[29] Mazlish, *The Riddle of History*, p. 364 (emphasis in original).
[30] Leonard Krieger, *Ranke: The Meaning of History* (Chicago: University of Chicago Press, 1977), p. 140.

errors. As popular as Toynbee was with his amateur audience, to most professionals his reach so far exceeded his (or anyone's) grasp as to be ludicrous. And if a Toynbee, with his colossal learning and erudition, could not pull it off, who could?

All history should begin by admitting the possibility of error. Universalism, in practice, should go one step further and frankly confess the probability of error. Once conceded, error diminishes as a blocking factor, and the analytical skills of the historian may extend to their broadest scope. Universal history is not universal in theme. There is no "key," no single explanation. But universal history is a compound of major themes changing through time. With the universal historian we might debate the life and death of entire civilizations; see cultures flourish dynamically; follow the ebb and flow of humanity in the great population movements of the past. Unifying themes that transcend time and place afford the measure of analytical success or failure. These include politics, statecraft, finance, family life, religious practice. Indeed, they include virtually every aspect of ourselves that is human and not simply we as individuals.

Universal history has diminished in favor not only because of the rise of the specialist but also because some major unifying themes of the past have decayed or vanished. Christianity was one such theme, but thinkers like Voltaire undercut the Bible as the ultimate historical authority. Secularization and specialization have seemed to fragment modern history, and the fragments have been hardened in the press of nationalism. No professional can ever be as convinced of the righteousness of history as was Bishop Bossuet. So modern attempts at universalism are risky ventures. Toynbee has been criticized for his "heroic though misguided attempt";[31] he has even been considered a bit of a fraud for confusing metaphysics with a philosophy of history.

There is an imperative, however, in universal history. Microhistory and macrohistory are complementary, not antagonistic. Each serves as a check on the excesses of the other. Today we have a greater command of our past than ever before. There are, to be sure, enormous gaps in our knowledge that may never be filled. Yet common sense requires the establishment of interrelationships, a synthesis and comparison of the widely varied areas of our understanding. To be effective, such syntheses cannot be simplistic. Con-

[31] Gay and Wexler, eds., *Historians at Work*, II, 281; Mazlish, *The Riddle of History*, p. 375.

sider the following: "From every past civilization the only things which remain of value to humanity are the creative works of those who were not business men." [32] This is a sweeping generalization, precisely the sort of thing that tends to cripple universal history.

All historical writing generalizes, as we have noted. There is no rule as to when generalities become vacuities and specifics become nit-picking bores. Modern history has concentrated on the specific and, in the last analysis, larger generalities must rest on lesser ones. Such a statement lacks the pristine logic of a wholes/parts axiom, but historians do not promise a rose garden of mathematical inevitability. [33] In sum, we find our history in the most minute by-ways of our past, but we find it also in the broad sweep of centuries.

Historical process thus admits the possibilities of both approaches. As Benedetto Croce cautioned, "To negate universal history does not mean to negate the universal in history." [34] We are all special, and we are all parts of a greater, human whole. We are both agents of process and process itself. And thinking about the many natures of historical process—there is both the puzzle and the challenge.

[32] John Higham, *Writing American History: Essays on Modern Scholarship* (Bloomington: Indiana University Press, 1972 [1970]), p. 173; Adams, *Our Business Civilization*, p. 25.

[33] For an interesting discussion of whether a generalization may be true even when its parts are not, in this case examining Jacob Burkhardt's conception of "Renaissance Man," see Ernst Cassirer, *The Logic of the Humanities*, trans. Lawrence Smith Howe (New Haven: Yale University Press, 1961), pp. 137–40.

[34] Benedetto Croce, *History: Its Theory and Practice*, trans. Douglas Ainslie (New York: Russell and Russell, 1920), p. 59.

III. Meaning

CHAPTER TEN

History and Morality

We cannot understand or care about historical discourse unless it contains some sort of relevance for us. Without meaning, the past must be forever unsatisfactory in the present. One of the main tasks of historical research is to provide meaning. Stripped of significance and purpose, history would truly be Shakespeare's "tale told by an idiot."

The elements of historical meaning are far from fixed. But certainly history may take part of its tone from moral judgments delivered by researchers of the past. Morality is not confined to any one nation, or race, or sect, although such claims constantly are made by the self-anointed. Most of us make distinctions between the moral and the immoral; we usually find it difficult to understand or even tolerate amorality of any kind.

We beg the question of how moral patterns are created, while noting that quite a bit of "human nature" usually gets tangled in the issue. Henry Adams, who made a fetish of pessimism, was convinced that selfish interests decided morals—it was the one law that ruled all others. To him, morality was a "private and costly luxury."[1] Even so, it is the one luxury everyone can afford. Historians certainly can as individuals; the question is whether they should exercise moral judgment in their profession.

The Demand for Moral Judgment

Like Fustel de Coulanges, the advocate of the historian as the mere conduit by which the past speaks to the present, some histo-

---

[1] Henry Adams, *The Education of Henry Adams: An Autobiography* (Boston: Houghton Mifflin, 1946 [1918]), p. 335.

rians have insisted on moral impartiality. A compiler of the Chinese Ming history cautioned that official history was different from private writing. One's personal views could be aired in the latter type, but as to the history compiled by imperial order, "One should not trust his own opinion and indulge in criticism." August Hennings, an eighteenth-century Danish historian, went even further. "The true historian does not praise nor [*sic*] criticize when he is fully informed," Hennings grandiloquently proclaimed. "He just narrates, and history is his sentences and his proofs."[2]

Yet these have been minority views. For thousands of years historians in most cultures assumed that simply recording the past was not enough. Although the dry bones of chronicle at times sufficed, most discriminating readers of history wanted to see the historian as well as the history on the page. The record had to be evaluated, weighed in the context of the historian's own value system. Regarding the Chinese Spring and Autumn Annals, which cover the period 722–481 B.C., one commentator remarked that in the Annals a word of praise was like the gift of a princely robe, while a word of blame was as severe as capital punishment. Of course, the reasons for "praise and blame" may differ, not only from culture to culture but from individual to individual. The point is that the bestowal of praise and blame was conceived to be not only part of the historical record; the apportionment of these qualities was deemed a significant aspect of the task of the historian.[3]

Determining praise and blame assumes a relatively fixed ethical system, and this the Chinese certainly had. Almost all Chinese historians regarded this determination as essential to the writing of history. To them, history reflected political ethics, which in turn could be judged according to Confucian standards.[4] Praise would go to those who most rigorously reaffirmed Confucianism in their conduct of affairs. Blame would be the lot of people seen to depart from the basic system.

[2] Lien-sheng Yang, "The Organization of Chinese Official Historiography: Principles and Methods of the Standard Histories From the T'ang Through the Ming Dynasty," in W. G. Beasley and E. G. Pulleyblank, eds., *Historians of China and Japan* (London: Oxford University Press, 1961), p. 53; K. Glamann, "Danish Historical Writing on Colonial Activities in Asia, 1616–1845," in C. H. Philips, ed., *Historians of India, Pakistan and Ceylon* (London: Oxford University Press, 1961), p. 213.

[3] Lien-sheng Yang, "Organization of Chinese Official Historiography," in Beasley and Pulleyblank, eds., *Historians of China and Japan*, p. 52.

[4] Herbert Frank, "Some Aspects of Chinese Private Historiography in the Thirteenth and Fourteenth Centuries," in ibid., p. 120.

Recall that the underlying premise the Chinese shared with many other cultures was that the central function of history is *didactic*—to pass on the accomplishments and mistakes of the past. Arai Hakuseki, a statesman-scholar of Tokugawa Japan and a contemporary of Locke, reflected this assumption when he wrote that history "is to narrate events in accordance with the facts and show men the lessons thereof."[5] To Hakuseki and countless other historians, both East and West, history is a vehicle for both individual and collective improvement. One should learn from the past. Otherwise, the study of history has no purpose.

Patterns of learning dovetail with patterns of behavior. To behave well in the present, one should pay attention to the guideposts provided by previous generations. The record has to be matched with some sort of ethical system, which is not that difficult to do. Not every culture possesses the deeply ingrained Confucianism of the Chinese, but every culture claims to adhere to certain codes or principles of conduct. Such principles are a basic force helping to bind the culture together.

Right conduct further implies a system that defines patterns of good and evil. For Livy, what was particularly nice about the study of history was that the past displays every variety of conduct. From this rich mosaic the individual can select appropriate models for imitation, at the same time avoiding what is "shameful in the undertaking and shameful in the result."[6] The basis of such judgments might shift, of course. One person's morality is another's sin, one person's vice a complete bore to someone else. Livy based his judgment on the type of behavior he believed would advance the fortunes of the Roman state.

The Christian era presented the West with another code, one that was rooted in individual behavior but that looked to the promise of salvation as the goal of human affairs. The dichotomous valuations of good and evil are important to every devout Christian, just as they are to subscribers to any of the world's great religions. The medieval monk William of Malmesbury was typical in his belief that history through example should encourage people to pursue good and avoid evil. Although the basis of value judgments advanced by Christians like William is not independent of

[5] W. G. Beasley and Carmen Blacker, "Japanese Historical Writing in the Tokugawa Period (1603–1868)," in ibid., p. 258.
[6] Peter Gay and Gerald J. Cavanaugh, eds., *Historians at Work*, I: *Herodotus to Froissart* (New York: Harper and Row, 1972), p. 161.

religious infrastructures, the question of good and evil, right and wrong, certainly is. Historians as far back as Tacitus have insisted that the task of the researcher is synonymous with that of the moralist. "This I regard as history's highest function," Tacitus wrote, "to let no worthy action be uncommemorated, and to hold out the reprobation of posterity as a terror to evil words and deeds."[7]

With the advance of rationalism, skeptics generally took a more tolerant view of moral questions, allowing more shadings of meaning between those absolutes of good and evil that had been the theoretical pole-stars of the universal church. But the relevance of morality remained undiminished. To men like the Scottish thinker David Hume, history is no less than the "great mistress of wisdom." Every moral precept is on display, for those who will look hard enough.[8] History, as a mirror of morality, has the capacity to show the human from every angle, warts and all. An increasing number of scholars were beginning to shade their historical judgments in the knowledge that bits of heaven and hell dwell in all of us. Angels and devils should no longer be allowed to cut cards for the mortal soul.

Increasing tolerance did not imply a diminution on the scale of individual morality. Good thoughts and actions continued to be held in the highest esteem. It was no accident that the Enlightenment placed great store in the classic ages of Greece and Rome. Even today one finds occasional declarations of value in this vein: "A man's moral fibre and his actions when confronted with difficulties are more important than his failure, or his success, in overcoming these difficulties."[9] Individual morality writ large would be the measure of civilizations, and "praise and blame" would winnow out the chaff there as well.

Moral judgment, then, was regarded almost everywhere as a fundamental aspect of history as the nineteenth century dawned. Historical materials in their raw form were the building blocks of individual behavior in the present, if only people were willing to model themselves on what they read. Most historians did not shirk the task of arranging these blocks to illuminate the desired point: the virtues of Rome, the purity of the Christian church, the innate authority of monarchy. But a powerful opponent to these

[7] Ibid., pp. 347, 205.
[8] Peter Gay and Victor G. Wexler, eds., *Historians at Work*, II: *Valla to Gibbon* (New York: Harper and Row, 1972), p. 249.
[9] Christopher McKee, *Edward Preble: A Naval Biography, 1761–1807* (Annapolis: Naval Institute Press, 1972), p. vii.

ancient assumptions was gathering strength. Over a century ago scientific objectivism began a war with historical moralism that has yet to end.

The Historian as Moralist

The haze over the battleground between objectivism and moralism lifted very slowly. History and morality seemed as permanently attached as Barnum's celebrated "Siamese Twins," Chang and Eng. From 1760 to 1892, for example, the chair of history at the Collège de France, which was occupied by Jules Michelet from 1838 to 1851, was called "chaire d'histoire et de morale."[10] History still was seen by most people primarily as a moral drama. War's havoc still tended to be explained in moral terms. The occasional revolution, particularly after 1789, most often registered as a moral (or immoral) crusade. Although the latter half of the nineteenth century saw greater credence given to "objective" forces in history, the canons of Marxism and other forms of objectivism were slow to be applied. Everyone feared the drabness of chronicle. The scene was dominated by those who were not reluctant to wield a moral broadsword, men with sweeping pens like Macaulay and Carlyle.

Those committed to moral judgments in history met the advancing tide of science without flinching. The trick was to erect a set of moral *absolutes*, in much the same way a scientist designing a thermometer might arrange for a freezing and boiling point in terms of numbers. Lord Acton thought the great moralist historians of his day, such as his countrymen Macaulay and Carlyle, steeped in error. Great leaders, the lives of whom particularly invited Carlyle's loving discourse, were almost always in error, Acton argued. The moralists, in elevating these heroes to a moral pinnacle, demeaned ethical principles by making these principles flexible. The authority, dignity, and utility of history were to be found, rather, in an inflexible moral code. Enough of shifting standards, of bending the knee to the powerful and the influential. "Suffer no man and no cause to escape the undying penalty which history has the power to inflict on wrong."[11] In this way history

[10] P. Demiéville, "Chang Hsüeh-ch'eng and His Historiography," in Beasley and Pulleyblank, eds., *Historians of China and Japan*, p. 183, n. 70.
[11] Gertrude Himmelfarb, *Lord Acton: A Study in Conscience and Politics* (Chicago: University of Chicago Press, 1962 [1952]), pp. 161, 198.

would become, Acton hoped, a science with ingrained axioms of judgment.

Either way, by bestowing bouquets upon the mighty or by erecting a rigid and unforgiving code of morals, history and morality continued as allies. Charles Francis Adams, father of Henry and biographer of his own grandfather John, was one of thousands of thinking people on both sides of the Atlantic who sincerely believed in the moral function of history. The purpose of studying the past was to praise excellence in fullest measure, in order to pass these examples on to posterity. Here was a formula as old as European civilization, one well suited to an Adams. Charles Francis was also typical in his moderation, which would allow no filiopietistic eulogy of the second president, yet suffused the entire work with moral pronouncements.[12]

The problem exemplified by men like Acton and Adams, whether or not they sensed its dimensions, is related to the essential subjectivism of historical research and writing. Because no one writing history is truly amoral and in fact probably is inclined in the opposite direction, some scholars have argued that historians should bluntly recognize their own moral biases. Since historians cannot avoid a philosophy or an ethical code, introspection is the first step along the path of historical judgment. All very well; but one person's code will not in all likelihood agree with another's, especially concerning specific points in history. Acton's inflexible morality was anchored firmly in the classical liberalism of nineteenth-century England. He was of his time, as each of us is of ours.

Acton's ideas of moral constancy in historical writing have gone unrealized, but the possibility of general agreement on some principles of morality obviously exist. To deny moral constants is no invitation to complete moral relativism. Most cultures place taboos on murder, incest, and various other social transgressions. Beyond such basics, however, judgment becomes much more flexible. Consider the possibility that three hypothetical scholars— one French, one Egyptian, and one Russian—are working independently on Napoleon's Egyptian Expedition of 1798. They may even agree on all the facts, but what do the data mean? The French scholar might conclude that the affair was a legitimate exercise of French power, with substantial scientific and geopolitical reper

[12] Martin Duberman, *Charles Francis Adams, 1807–1886* (Stanford: Stanford University Press, 1968 [1961]), p. 206.

cussions. The Egyptian might regret the trampling of Egyptian armed forces while sadly admitting the benefits of western technology and bureaucratic organization ushered in during the following century. The Russian might regard the episode as a classic example of a colonial power exploiting a less advanced culture. These hypothetical judgments may *all* have some basis in historical reality.

What criteria should the historian use in making moral judgments? Self-knowledge, as noted, is the first step. Introspection is not enough, however, since most of us are indifferent students of ourselves at best. Next, a firm foundation in the moral codes operative at the time under study is imperative. Otherwise, analysts run the risk of transposing their moral codes into societies and cultures whose standards differ significantly from their own. Finally, moral issues must be decided on a case basis. Even the "truthful" historical statements need qualification in this regard. For example, we may write two statements, both with relatively high truth value:

Napoleon was responsible for the deaths of many people.
Hitler was responsible for the deaths of many people.

Yet historians will assign differing moral values to these statements, given supporting evidence in each case.

Paradoxically, moral judgments are at their weakest when they are the most sweeping, at their most ineffectual when most narrowly construed. "We do not draw the moral lessons we might from history," moaned Edmund Burke. Most of history, he sourly concluded, was composed of the rotten fruits of pride, ambition, avarice, revenge, lust, and "all the train of disorderly appetites." Believing this, we may equally believe Acton's pronouncement that "no priest accustomed to the Confessional, and a fortiori, no historian, thinks well of human nature."[13] The past is but a sewer, the stench of which permeates the present.

History by misanthropy is tempting, of course. The past is plentiful with error; every vice known to humanity *is* on display, and the pessimistic always will enjoy a rich harvest. "War may be an armed angel with a mission," wrote a witness to the American

[13] Edmund Burke, *Reflections on the Revolution in France* (London: Everyman's Library, 1910), p. 137; Gertrude Himmelfarb, *Victorian Minds: A Study of Intellectuals in Crisis and of Ideologies in Transition* (New York: Harper and Row, 1970 [1952]), p. 183.

Civil War, "but she has the personal habits of the slums."[14] Yet every statement that sweeps all of humanity into some sort of moral dustbin is so manifestly false as to impugn its author on at least two counts: an imbalanced view of the past and an unduly pessimistic sense of self.

In fact, the sweeping statement tells us much more about the value structure of its author than it does about the subject of the author's analysis. The trenchant moralists are thus the special delight of historiographers. When Burke writes that a perfect democracy is the most shameless thing in the world, he does little to enlighten us on the course of the French Revolution.[15] But he does tell us quite a bit about his own value system as a placeman in a government of oligarchy and faction. We do not mean by this that moral categorizations are *wrong* in historical writing; logically, this would be a claim as sweeping as those made by our examples. But it takes a very good writer, basing his thoughts on often wearisome research, to make the big judgment stick. Intuition may still score occasionally, but usually for the wrong reasons. In its absence, and without the evidence, history will metamorphose into literature. The change will not necessarily be a negative one, but the result will no longer be history.

Moralism and Objectivity

We have slighted thus far the possibility that moral judgments in history should not be made. If we consider the issue philosophically, we arrive at the outlines of another dilemma. If an objective historical reality is denied, the historian cannot be expected to discover objective moral criteria. Since moral certainty seems impossible under these circumstances (Lord Acton notwithstanding), some thinkers argue that moral judgments are not only outmoded history but that their use creates subjectivist fiction in the guise of history. The shape of the dilemma became clarified as the claims of scientific objectivism grew more forceful.

Not that the purely scientific approach ever held the field alone. Hegel, for one, regarded moral certainty as not only possible but necessary. Moral criteria, he argued, are imperative, else

[14] Daniel Aaron, *The Unwritten War: American Writers and the Civil War* (New York: Oxford University Press, 1973), p. 41.
[15] Burke, *Reflections on the Revolution in France*, p. 90.

taste dictates morality and judgment descends to whim. History is on the side of moral absolutes, because moral criteria could be seen evolving dialectically through time. These absolutes are discernible in the legal framework of the nation-state. The laws of humanity provide objective criteria with which to judge.[16] Though these criteria change, they hold consistent for their epoch.

The possibility of moral certainty often was debated inside the framework of moral evolution. In particular, admirers of the ancients were given to pondering if the world had improved at all since the times of Herodotus and Tacitus. The Frenchman Fontenelle perhaps illustrated the question best, when he created an imaginary dialogue between his countryman Montaigne and Socrates. Montaigne believes the modern world outstrips the ancients in foolishness and corruption; Socrates answers by observing that his times were pretty bad, also. The heart of humanity is constant, the Greek goes on. "Nature always acts with great regularity, but let us not judge how she acts."[17]

Fontenelle, obviously, was doubtful that moral progress was possible. And even if such progress were to occur, how would it be measured? Some thinkers recoiled from the idea of a legal system as a moral arbiter. Hegelian worship of the nation-state never took root in the United States. Taking their key for moral certitude from religion, ethics, or intuition, many American abolitionists, for example, found laws and constitutions that tolerated and even promoted slavery to be repugnant. Americans tended to extol ethics outside of system or national institutions. The abolitionist Theodore Parker, saturated with transcendentalism, believed that in telling what has been, historians also should tell "what ought to be." In this way history would truly be philosophy teaching by experience. The present would receive the warning signals from the past and create a better future.[18]

If Hegel's statism is unsatisfactory, Parker's assumption that historians should determine the "ought" of history is at least equally so. We live in a world of moral pluralism, of differing moral patterns. Christian and Moslem, monarchist and democrat,

[16] Haskell Fain, *Between Philosophy and History: The Resurrection of Speculative Philosophy of History within the Analytic Tradition* (Princeton: Princeton University Press, 1970), pp. 212–13.

[17] Franklin L. Baumer, *Modern European Thought: Continuity and Change in Ideas, 1600–1950* (New York: Macmillan, 1977), p. 135.

[18] Henry Steele Commager, *Theodore Parker: Yankee Crusader*, 2nd ed. (Boston: Beacon Press, 1960 [1947]), p. 143.

master and slave, all have differed historically unto death. When moral certitude means life itself, human worth becomes morality. A witness to the trial and execution of the fiery abolitionist zealot John Brown was forced to admit that "one's faith in anything is terribly shaken by anybody who is ready to go to the gallows condemning and denouncing it."[19]

Historians cognizant of differing moral patterns throughout the past thus were reluctant to pronounce judgment with the assurance of Hegel or Parker. Instead, the search for certitude began to center in historical reality. Rationalism, it was hoped, would create through assimilated evidence the hard facts of reality. The facts themselves would judge the case; the more thorough their nature, the more sound the judgment. Wilhelm Dilthey recoiled against the "introspective brooding" that supposedly was to teach us self-knowledge. Here was the great "Nietzschean disorder" that made a warped subjectivism into a falsely triumphant moralism. Historical reality, created by humanity itself, was the only sure path to an equitable assessment of good and evil.[20]

Dilthey's position was not new, although it represented a spirited attempt to mate scientific empiricism with the requirement for value judgments in history. As early as the seventeenth century, the Benedictine monk Jean Mabillon had noted that historical study could not develop unless falsehood and error somehow could be separated from truth. Mabillon advanced a doctrine of patient analysis. Only a long, constant observation of the coincidences and circumstances composing the past would lead to the truth, which in turn then could be couched in terms of moral certitude.[21] Even though they were two centuries apart in historical perspective, Mabillon and Dilthey might have agreed that truth based on evidence is the only possible measure of historical morality.

Not so Lord Acton. Confident in his claim for moral absolutes, Acton envisioned an ultimate history. In this history, certainty was to be final and the last word really would be written. He trusted the claims of positivism, believing that eventually (and why not now, bathed in the radiant glow of nineteenth-century English global supremacy?) historical science would account for both his-

[19] Aaron, *The Unwritten War*, p. 24.

[20] Peter Gay and Gerald J. Cavanaugh, eds., *Historians at Work*, IV: *Dilthey to Hofstadter* (New York: Harper and Row, 1975), p. 7.

[21] Gay and Wexler, eds., *Historians at Work*, II, 170.

torical morality and historical meaning. History must be first and foremost moralistic; only then could it be genuinely objective.[22]

The relationship of these classic arguments, whether historical fact should condition moral judgment or vice versa, is not quite so simple. The equally classic relationship of means and ends intrudes. Moral idealism tends toward purification; the ends often get scooped up along with the means in the analyst's net. If politicians play the game underhandedly, yet some sort of political reform of ultimate social benefit results, historians cut from Acton's cloth might throw out the clean baby (result) with the bath water (dirty tactics). But moral assessment need not depend upon outcome alone,[23] any more than it need depend solely on the various steps taken in reaching the outcome. Historians should be sensitive to the stages in historical causation as well as to the final result. A melding of means and ends, rather than the confusion of parts and wholes in one grand morality play, is the wiser analytical goal.

The necessity for some moral judgment is practically inescapable in all save the most pedestrian forms of historical writing. Not that the moralist always wields the more dynamic pen—many a good snooze has been precipitated by a surfeit of moralism. Yet the art of rendering moral judgments is certainly a delicate business, or should be. It involves self-analysis, a continuous striving for objectivity, and a commanding sense of the values of the time and place under examination.

The urge to inflict one's own moral codes on the past is endlessly tempting. At times the apple is simply too delicious not to be tasted, and the urge expands into a great, overwhelming showcase for classifying historical events in an exclusively moral order. David Hackett Fischer, who never could be accused of lacking opinions on the subject, has called this tendency the most hateful form of the "genetic fallacy," the conversion of historical cause and effect into an all-encompassing ethical system.[24] Though Fischer (and others) have delivered hammer blows to the heads of historicists for committing this primal sin, the historicists are not

[22] Himmelfarb, *Victorian Minds*, pp. 173–74.

[23] For reasoned comment on the problem, see John Higham, "Beyond Consensus: The Historian as Moral Critic," *American Historical Review* 67 (April, 1962): 618–22.

[24] David Hackett Fischer, *Historians' Fallacies: Toward a Logic of Historical Thought* (New York: Harper and Row, 1970), pp. 155–56.

alone. Every researcher carries a personal minisystem of ethics when confronting material. If the researcher dominates the evidence, rather than merging with it, the result has the potential of system.

One last problem: even though almost all of us operate under some ethical scheme, no matter how ramshackle, the possibility exists that historical action is itself amoral. Once this perspective is admitted, moral judgments become irrelevant, since amoral action cannot be understood without an amoral ethical system. Since such a system is a contradiction in terms, perhaps the best stance for the moralist, some argue, would be "hands off."

Certainly most of us in our darker moments are convinced that wars and other results of human greed, indifference, and lust for power outstrip individual ethics. Many commentators have remarked on the behavioral differences between people as individuals and people in the mass. *Should states, cultures, and civilizations be judged by the same ethical standards one applies to individuals?*

Perhaps human aggregates operate on a plan apart from ethics. Such at least was the case to Frederic Howe. Like the Canadian historian A. L. Burt, Howe viewed the Versailles Conference in 1919 with dismay. "Facts were of little value," wrote Howe, a Progressive reformer who had trusted in facts to spearhead social change. "Morality did not guide men." [25] For the disillusioned Howe, plunder was the central object of combined human action, and plunder meant the use of force. Once force was applied, no ethical code could govern—indeed, could not be permitted to govern.

Every researcher must come to grips with the moral issues of a chosen topic. At times, naturally, these issues will be almost nonexistent. But since history is about people, and since most people advocate certain codes of behavior, the requirements for a moral statement form a continuous backdrop to research. The history that examines important aspects of the past and ignores moral issues is not going its job properly, any more than is the history that oozes moral didacticism from every page. No one enjoys the self-satisfied moralist. As Garrett Mattingly once wrote to his friend and fellow historian Bernard DeVoto, there comes a point

[25] Frederic C. Howe, *The Confessions of a Reformer* (Chicago: Quadrangle Books, 1967 [1925]), p. 318.

in historical writing "where a conscience is just a God damned nuisance."[26]

For each part of the past, there is room for praise and blame, although not always in equal measure. Justice may be blindfolded as she holds her scales; the historian cannot afford to be. Moral issues are a great testing point, for in examining morality in history, the researcher is also examining self. The researcher, if dutifully honest and introspective, will know whether the product is itself praiseworthy. In this sense, perhaps the Jansenist mystic Pascal was right when he proclaimed that thinking well was the only morality.

[26] Wallace Stegner, *The Uneasy Chair: A Biography of Bernard DeVoto* (Garden City, N.Y.: Doubleday, 1974), p. 330.

CHAPTER ELEVEN

Past, Present, Future

Historical meaning encompasses more than moral issues, even though religion usually is loathe to admit the possibility. If the span were not broadened, history and ethics would be undifferentiated and the past would be a school for behavior only. Putting the matter a bit too rigidly, meaning in history, seen apart from human behavior, is most often provided by how we perceive the historical continuum.

Some historians insist the past should be studied for its own sake. The past is coherent in and of itself, and we should examine it for the same reason people climb mountains: "because it's there." A more common view in modern times has seen the vital function of history as one of enabling a better life in the present. The past from this perspective must influence current time to be effective. The oldest mode of perceiving the past regards history as primarily a guide to the future. A few adventurous souls have even been willing to utilize history as a crystal ball.

We arbitrarily label these various persuasions purist, didactic, and prophetic history. In each case, elements of historical meaning are shaped by our consciousness of how history is being *used*. If we require the "truth" about the past, purist history will do its level-headed best. Should we seek the ingredients of a better life today, the libraries are full of the sins of our fathers. In case we are curious about the shape of things to come, history may be used to supply the mold. Historical study is most certainly not the utility infielder of the humanities, endlessly serviceable wherever needed. But different people have had different uses for history, and as usage changes, so, too, does our historical perspective change.[1]

[1] For a chatty introduction to history as utilitarian, see A. L. Rowse, *The Use of History*, rev. ed. (New York: Collier Books, 1963).

The Limits of the Past

"It's a poor sort of memory that only works backwards," said the White Queen to Alice.[2] Our purist would disagree, arguing that memory works backward by definition. For such an historian, the past is all there is. The future is vague, hazy, its form ill defined and its path unpredictable. Purist history holds that the business of the historian is with the past, and only with the past. Thus, the meaning of the past is in its reconstruction.

Not that purists ignore the future. They simply tend to see it in terms other than historical. Seemingly, a flight of imagination is necessary to think otherwise. In 1886, two years before he published his famous utopian novel *Looking Backward*, Edward Bellamy wrote a short story called "The Blindman's World." In it an earthling confronts a Martian and—such being the nature of the fiction of the day—they fall into philosophic discourse. The Martian reveals that his memory looks forward rather than backward. Does it not seem rational, he says, that mental vision should illuminate the path of the future, rather than disclosing "the course you have already trodden, and therefore you have no more concern with?"[3] Every age has its seers, prophets, and prognosticators, but the possessor of future memory has not yet been found. Pending his discovery, we must ponder other perspectives.

No one, not even the most dedicated antiquarian, is totally immersed in the past. Like it or not, we live in the present. Whether "that's all there is" is up to us. Most people live with the future as well. If you *plan*, for example, you are thinking about the future, basing your plans on the past. The concern with posterity is also rife among us. We tend to think of our immediate family in this regard, but posterity is a crucial issue with cultural elites who believe they are important enough to warrant a look from historians of the future. One thinks of the numerous felons involved in the Watergate scandals scurrying to tell their side of the story, or of the regrettable habit of creating "presidential libraries" in celebration of individuals of decidedly differing talents. In a basic sense, most people share some concern for posterity. Franklin put it bluntly, in one of his almanacs:

If you would not be forgotten
As soon as you are dead and rotten,

[2] Lewis Carroll, *Alice's Adventures in Wonderland and through the Looking Glass* (London: Allan Wingate, 1954), p. 188.
[3] H. Bruce Franklin, *Future Perfect: American Science Fiction of the Nineteenth Century* (New York: Oxford University Press, 1968 [1966]), p. 309.

Either write things worth reading
Or do things worth the writing.[4]

Just as none of us faces totally backward, so no one of sound mind is without a sense of the past, even if that past is narrowly bounded by personal experience. Historians as a group have a special inclination to value the past, but we all possess the tendency. Modern humanity, until the rude shocks of the twentieth century, has gingerly assumed that knowledge of the past may help smooth the way into the future. "People will not look forward to posterity," asserted Edmund Burke, "who never look backward to their ancestors." His claim is sturdy intellectual conservatism, but it becomes less solid with an increasing leaven of determinism. The more deterministic the history, the more iron-clad the future. Bishop Bossuet, rooted deeply in Catholicism and with the Sun King for a patron in an age when France dominated Europe, could claim confidently that "what is past assures us of what is to come."[5] Bossuet's future was Christian and monarchist, without question, yet we know that secular forms of determinism exist as well.

The great historical engine of Marx is the classic example of the past steamrolling inexorably into the future. The powerful Marxist formula for the unfolding of history was only the strongest reflection of a general optimism regarding the potential of the past. The French poet Lamartine, who died in 1869, did not live to see Marxism come a cropper in the Paris Commune. Lamartine nevertheless was convinced that history could teach anything, including the future.[6] There is a subtle distinction to be made here. Deterministic forms of historical logic are highly suspect, as we have noted. But if we back off a step and argue that history provides a foundation, not for divining the future but for *dealing* with the future, we certainly have firmer footing.

[4] Emily Morison Beck, ed., *Sailor Historian: The Best of Samuel Eliot Morison* (Boston: Houghton Mifflin, 1977), p. 287. One yearns for the candor of Ulises Heureaux, the mulatto dictator of the Dominican Republic from 1882 to 1889 and no benevolent despot. When he was reproached with the possibility that history might not favor his regime, he replied he cared not since he would not be around to read it. See Dexter Perkins, *Yield of the Years: An Autobiography* (Boston: Little, Brown, 1969), p. 130.

[5] Edmund Burke, *Reflections on the Revolution in France* (New York: Everyman's Library, 1910), p. 31; Peter Gay and Victor G. Wexler, eds., *Historians at Work*, II: *Valla to Gibbon* (New York: Harper and Row, 1972), p. 218.

[6] Jacques Barzun and Henry F. Graff, *The Modern Researcher*, 3rd ed. (New York: Harcourt, Brace and Jovanovich, 1977), p. 43.

The past is limited with itself. We interject that these limits are not concerned with either process or order. Process presupposes a future not completely divorced from the past, and in many ways built upon the past. Order is also flexible and may extend into the future in the form of planning. Even the order of the past is convention. Imagine learning history backward, taking a course that begins at today and moves backward in time to point x, say 1789. Though unusual, the procedure violates no grave canons of historical logic. We are still dealing with the past, and moving backward rather than forward might even help to clarify historical cause and effect. Order is necessary, but never preordained.

When we move through the present into the future, though, we enter *terra* which, if not quite *incognita*, is nonetheless without historical evidence to help us understand it. Bellamy's Martian may have somehow divined his evidence in advance, but this we cannot do. Since we have no evidence concerning the future, we are left with past and present in the historical sense.

We do not mean that history should have nothing to do with the future. The English historian Macaulay, one of the grandest of the literary historians of the nineteenth century, believed that no past event had any intrinsic importance. He argued that knowledge of the past was valuable only insofar as it leads us to calculate the future more finely.[7] The purists part company here. For them, the past has nothing to do with the future, but exists for its own sake. The importance of the event is in the event itself and in the past events connected with it. *Should the past be studied for itself alone?*

Some cultures, we should interject, have denied the utilitarian idea of the past. Traditionally, Islam borrowed freely from other cultures in what it considered usable sciences, such as medicine, mathematics, and philosophy. But there was, with only minor exceptions, no usable heathen past from the Muslim point of view, and thus Islam tended to neglect history outside its own.[8] The usable sciences could help people in this life and condition the soul for afterlife. In other words, the present was of immediate importance.

Socially conscious historians in the early twentieth century,

[7]Gordon Connell-Smith and Howell A. Lloyd, *The Relevance of History* (London: Heinemann Educational Books, 1972), p. 19.

[8]Bernard Lewis, *History: Remembered, Recovered, Invented* (Princeton: Princeton University Press, 1976), p. 31.

such as the American Progressives, emphasized the argument that history must function in the present to perform its proper task. The past hundred years have seen a renewed concern with utilitarian history that serves primarily to instruct the present.

The Past in the Present

Narrowly construed, the present is never and always. It is here and gone with the tick of the clock, then here again. Historians do not paddle well in this sort of philosophical deep water, and such questions are best left to those who wish to addle their minds considering them. The more reasonable historical dimension of the present usually is that of the hour, day, month, or year. However we may conceive the present, it is full of the future even as it reflects and perpetuates the past.

The present's perspective on the future is an ancient one, probably older than history itself, but it is one not necessarily shared by all cultures. The concern with the secular future reached its strongest pitch in the West, most prominently in the Age of Industrialization. Indeed, the defamation of cultures that placed no great store in the future, seeming to live from day to day, was once common. William Robertson, Burke's contemporary, believed that civilization itself is defined by a concern for futurity. Not to plan for tomorrow is to concede that life is ruled by ignorance and produced only sloth.[9] Thus the future became conceptually embodied in the notion of progress, and there it has remained almost to the present day.

Unsurprisingly, historians who support ideals of progress have shown strong concern for what lies ahead. This concern is not only the natural one of being human and trying the best one can to shape an individual future. There is an intellectual side to be considered as well. Walter Prescott Webb remembered that Lindley Miller Keasbey, one of his teachers at the University of Texas, told him that the easiest questions were When, Where, and How. Why and Wherefore were somewhat harder, said Keasbey, but the hardest of all were Whence and Whither.[10]

In the attempt to get a handle on Whence and Whither, some

[9] Gay and Wexler, eds., *Historians at Work*, II, 279.
[10] Necah Stewart Furman, *Walter Prescott Webb: His Life and Impact* (Albuquerque: University of New Mexico Press, 1976), p. 42.

students of the past have occasionally manipulated their evidence to conform, not to any past scenario, but to the shape of things to come. If the things to come are already past (i.e., writing today about Napoleon in 1798 and foreseeing his role as European conqueror), we have a particularly tricky form of historical writing that may make good literature but little else.

If, however, the future is ahead of us as we read, the historian will be manipulating not only the evidence but us as well, if we are not careful. The manipulation is somewhat akin to fitting pieces of a puzzle together. The first piece determines the limits of the next pieces to be used, and so on. The procedure makes history a mechanism, and a flawed one at that, when we consider its truth value. The *truth* of history is unavoidably in the past; part of the *meaning* of history may lie in the future.

No manipulation is necessary to claim that the future will be enhanced by the truthful discovery of the past. Bernard Sternsher has cautiously argued that "the most objective knowledge of the past that is attainable would appear to be one means of bringing about a better future." But Sternsher's assertion, modest as it is, begs the question of what our objective knowledge of the past discovers. Suppose objectivity brings forth pessimism or even nihilism? Certainly the potential of the abyss has left historians of progressive mien undeterred. Charles Beard, whose idea of progress went well beyond economic determinism, did not see the concept as a way to explain the past but as a "heroic attempt to control the future."[11]

The present seems to be in the dilemma of the passenger on a railway siding who wants a local, but only the expresses whiz by, none stopping to pick him up. Indeed, some ways of thinking pay as little attention to the present as the express engineer pays to the forlorn passenger. The Jewish faith finds the immediate present virtually nonexistent. The Jewish past is rich and varied, and the future is to be the age in which Judaism will have its basic character restored. But the present, particularly in this age of Auschwitz, seems only a hollow mockery.[12] Thus both past and future are

[11] Bernard Sternsher, *Consensus, Conflict, and American Historians* (Bloomington: Indiana University Press, 1975), p. 293; Cushing Strout, *The Pragmatic Revolt in American History: Carl Becker and Charles Beard* (Ithaca, N.Y.: Cornell University Press, 1966 [1958]), p. 110.

[12] Günther Bornkamm, *Jesus of Nazareth*, 3rd ed., trans. Irene and Fraser McLuskey with James M. Robinson (New York: Harper and Row, 1975 [1959]), p. 55.

"alive," whereas the present presents for many a crushing burden.

Historians have shown a tendency to come closer and closer to the present in their work, Jewish experience notwithstanding. The present is, after all, a sort of capstone to the past, produced by the past and in turn helping to produce the future. Judging the recent past, though increasingly common, remains a sticky business for many scholars. Centuries ago Sir Walter Raleigh warned "that who-so-ever in writing a modern Historie, shall follow truth too neere the heeles, it may happily strike out his teeth." [13] Source material, the hard data of history, usually reveals itself with exasperating slowness. Evidence often takes years to enter the public domain. Further, the historian's view of the material might be discolored by participation in the topic. The soldier who came home disillusioned and maimed from war might write of it differently than the person who received awards, promotions, and publicity for his part.

Yet the writing of recent history (or "contemporary history") continues to increase, not only because of the potentially wider popular audience, but also because this type of history has its advantages. Participants in events may still be around to be interviewed, which is a bonus for researchers long frustrated by their inability to indulge in a give-and-take dialogue with the dead. Many historians, both of antiquity and of modern times, including Tacitus and Voltaire, have used interviews to enhance their writing.

The purist will not admit the validity of the interview technique. It smacks of journalism, which means it is fraught with distortion and downright lies. Purists tend to hold history at arm's length, a position insisted upon by most of the newly emerging positivist professionals of the nineteenth century. When Charles Petrie was "up at Oxford" during World War I, his modern history course ended with the Treaty of Berlin in 1878. Petrie was rash enough to question his teacher about an event that had occurred in 1881; the horrified pedagogue replied that he was there to teach history, not to talk politics. The attitude was general and extended into the ranks of the famed gentlemen amateurs. William Hickling Prescott, who normally worked with sixteenth-century material, once said he would "rather not meddle with heroes who have not been under ground—two centuries—at least." [14]

[13] Peter Gay, *A Loss of Mastery: Puritan Historians in Colonial America* (New York: Vintage Books, 1968 [1966]), p. 43.

[14] Sir Charles Petrie, *A Historian Looks at His World* (London: Sidgwick

Against the conception that history needs time to settle itself before it may be rediscovered adequately, didactic historians are conscious of the need for history to instruct. The argument of lack of evidence is no deterrent, since most of these scholars are pragmatic and flexible to a certain degree. They tend to regard history as a discipline in a natural state of flux, with even evidence hundreds of years old being reshaped constantly. Contemporary history holds no horrors for them; in fact, its study is taken to be of considerable use. A secondary reason for lack of concern is that contemporary history will get written anyway. Why not by professional researchers as well as the omnipresent hacks?

Even more rigidly confined to the present is the assertion that the only effective history is that written by those literally involved in their topic. The noted essayist Montaigne once said that the only good histories were those written by people who commanded or participated in the affairs whereof they wrote. The premise is a bit tough for the practicing historian. Where, for example, would one go to get Custer's side of the Little Big Horn fight? If we back off a bit from this extreme position, we still have contemporary history in two useful guises. First, it is history informed by immediate experience, which may make the subject more vivid and expressive, as well as meaningful. Second, it is potential evidence for later historians who must work at arm's length and beyond. No less a personage than the doughty Samuel Eliot Morison, a "conservative" historian if ever there was one, admitted that he always relied on contemporary evidence unless it was demonstrably false.[15]

Contemporary history is not without its perils, but these it shares (only to a greater degree) with historical research at further remove. Apparently the nature of things is for the present constantly to attempt to monitor the past, as if continually taking its own pulse. Understandably, that part of the past of most frequent interest to the nonprofessionals is the recent past. In that reading they can often match their own experiences against the printed

---

and Jackson, 1972), p. 80; C. Harvey Gardiner, *William Hickling Prescott: A Biography* (Austin: University of Texas Press, 1969), p. 279. For a modern argument that it is impossible to write history about contemporary culture, see Roland M. Stromberg, *After Everything: Western Intellectual History since 1945* (New York: St. Martin's Press, 1975), p. 105.

[15] Donald M. Frame, trans., *The Complete Essays of Montaigne* (Stanford: Stanford University Press, 1948), p. 304; Samuel Eliot Morison, *Admiral of the Ocean Sea: A Life of Christopher Columbus* (Boston: Little, Brown, 1942), pp. 48–49.

page, which is certainly one aspect of thinking about history. The very recent past is highly susceptible to severe distortion. But since historical interpretations are not engraved on stone but written on paper, they are malleable and perishable. Also, the mere survival of historical evidence is not in itself validation of that material. In this sense all history is made only to be remade, a never-ending succession of presents contemplating pasts. Like time itself, history is both changeable and changeless.

The present continuously anticipates the future as well. Our desire to "know" the past is at least equaled by our need to shape the future. In Ibsen's drama *Hedda Gabler*, Hedda's husband and her lover compete for a prestigious chair of history. The lover has finished a book, he tells the husband, but finds it unsatisfactory since it carries history only up to the present. His new book, the lover proclaims, will be a continuation. The husband is naturally amazed. In reply to his question of how such a thing can be, the lover says the new material concerns the future. No one knows anything about what is to come, interjects the husband. Perhaps, comes the response—but there are some things that can be said about it anyway.[16]

We often think, in our purist moods, that since history draws its sustenance from the past, historians have no relevance to the future. A more utilitarian view would hold that historians have everything to say about the future, and have as much or more right to say it than anyone else. Either way, the question will not vanish. The future is potential in us all, and besides, there are some things that can be said about it anyway.

The Problems of Prediction

History may illuminate the future in at least two ways. First, much of the past seems to occur in trendlike fashion: a period of anarchy, growing industrialization, an increasing sense of social responsibility. Many of these trends take centuries to develop fully, and many of them may be traced into the present. A reasonable assumption, given the weight of custom, tradition, and downright inertia in most societies, is that certain trends will continue into

[16] Haskell Fain, *Between Philosophy and History: The Resurrection of Speculative Philosophy of History within the Analytic Tradition* (Princeton: Princeton University Press, 1970), pp. 224–25.

the future, barring some sort of cataclysm. Automobiles will not disappear tomorrow. We will continue to be able to travel faster and faster (to what purpose, no one has yet foreseen). We will continue to live longer. These are trends for which historical study can supply reasons. History does not predict precisely the course trends will take, but knowing a considerable bit about their nature narrows the guesswork remarkably.

Second, the past may serve both present and future by analogy. Analogous reasoning is useful at times, and historians occasionally wish that statesmen and other decision makers paid more regard to the past when considering the future. Obviously, no event is an exact duplication of the past. Analogous history gets shakier the more we are convinced "it is happening all over again." We nevertheless may make educated guesses on the basis of analogy. Hitler had Napoleon's disastrous experience in invading Russia in 1812 before him as he planned Operation Barbarossa in the winter of 1940–41. The German dictator ignored the "lesson" and pressed on to his own disaster with the invasion of the Soviet Union. The historical researcher with a firm grip on possible analogies is much more able to reason appropriately concerning the possibilities, probabilities, and impossibilities of his topic.[17] The use of analogy sometimes assists in evaluating the paths not taken, serving as a further aid to historical judgment.

Even many of the paths taken in the past are obscure, perceived from any vantage point devoid of hindsight. No wonder, then, that what lies ahead seems murky at best. "The future is a land of which there are no maps," A. J. P. Taylor has noted.[18] Our question must be, in this uncharted situation, are historians the best guides? *Should part of the province of history be the attempt to forecast and evaluate the future?*

There is a world of difference between prediction and reasoned opinion. The philosopher W. H. Walsh has argued that although modern historians may not be prophets (there are a few who might like to think of themselves in this guise), they are often

---

[17] Louis Gottschalk, *Understanding History: A Primer of Historical Method*, 2nd ed. (New York: Alfred A. Knopf, 1969), pp. 276–77. For an excellent discussion of the pitfalls of historical analogy, in this case dealing with the making of American foreign policy during the previous forty years, see Ernest R. May, *"Lessons" of the Past: The Use and Misuse of History in American Foreign Policy* (New York: Oxford University Press, 1973).

[18] A. J. P. Taylor, *Bismarck: The Man and the Statesman* (New York: Vintage Books, 1967 [1955]), p. 70.

in a position to prophesy.[19] This position is achieved by a command of the past. Command does not imply control or even mastery, but it certainly suggests knowledge surpassing that possessed by most of the rest of society. Given a somewhat hesitant axiom, that the past gives birth to the future, the temptation to utilize this knowledge to wax prophetic is fairly strong, at least among those not steeped in the purist tradition.

The urge to prophesy is common to most cultures, particularly in times of secular or spiritual crisis. We must not assume, however, that prophecies are maps to the future. Many prophecies are annoyingly vague, intentionally including virtually every possibility. Even in cultures displaying rudimentary states of technology and living close to nature, where we might expect prophecy to flourish, predictions can be extraordinarily casual. Geronimo, one of the Apache leaders in the Indian Wars, remembered in later life that "as to the future state, the teachings of our tribe were not specific, that is, we had no definite idea of our relations and surroundings in after life. We believed that there is a life after this one, but no one ever told me as to what part of man lived after death."[20]

The Apache concern for the future was spiritual. Time seemed to the Apaches to be in a sense changeless, since life on earth is defined by the seasons and the ageless rhythm of the human cycle. The spiritual future with which Geronimo was familiar deals largely with afterlife, whereas a second future, the secular, occurs in human time.

Each of these futures has its place in prophecy, and each of them is based on a strong interpretative sense of the past. Dream of an afterlife in heaven or dream of a heaven on earth, the future is the dream either way. Christian thought about the future has been concerned mostly with chiliasm and the great chance of human ascendance to the side of the angels. Most varieties of these beliefs rest on faith rather than social action, although many zealous movements have acted as though God needs an earthly push now and then.

On earth, perfectionist futures have varied widely. The strongest tendency in secular perfectionism for about eight hundred years has centered on egalitarianism. In the High Middle Ages

---

[19] W. H. Walsh, *Philosophy of History: An Introduction*, rev. ed. (New York: Harper and Row, 1967), p. 41.

[20] S. M. Barrett and Frederick W. Turner III, eds., *Geronimo: His Own Story* (New York: Ballantine Books, 1971 [1906]), p. 178.

many people believed that a society in which all were equal in wealth, status, and opportunity had vanished in the distant past. In a very brief period of time (one scholar dates the change from 1380) a new view began to gain credence, one that pictured a new Golden Age in the immediate future.[21] From the fourteenth century to the present, secular prophets have come and gone, most of them armed with predictions of secular perfection based on some sort of religious idealism.

So strong has been the influence of Christianity that its power has muddled as well as clarified the future. Whether heaven is to be established on earth or earth is to ascend to heaven remains unclear. So does the issue, largely emphasized by Christian belief, over whether history has an end, which means that the future would be finite. Are we living an endless story, or are we proceeding to a point at which the past will be all there is? Christian believers live in a state of tension between present and future, secure in their faith and trusting their hope.[22] The situation cannot be comprehended on logical grounds. The historians usually bail out of the debate at this point, feeling there is nothing more they can contribute.

The past, strictly speaking, can prove nothing about teleology, because we know history has continued, in spite of many lacunae, to our time. We may *infer* from the past that historical trends point to some kind of end. The discovery and unleashing of the enormous power of the atom make cataclysmic predictions more plausible, but who can say the ultimate blast will be triggered by divine will or human error?

Dreamers such as the philosopher Kant might make a providential explanation out of a teleology of nature, wedding sacred and profane in one cosmic purpose. Kant believed the future to be a developing of God-ordained order. The Creation, or beginning, is never complete. The divine plan continuously unfolds without end.[23] Historians cannot see the path so clearly. Bellamy's Martian, alas, exists only in fiction.

[21] Norman Cohn, *The Pursuit of the Millennium*, rev. ed. (New York: Oxford University Press, 1970), p. 198.

[22] Karl Löwith, *Meaning in History* (Chicago: University of Chicago Press, 1949), p. 188.

[23] Bruce Mazlish, *The Riddle of History: The Great Speculators from Vico to Freud* (New York: Minerva Press, 1968 [1966]), p. 122; Stephen Toulmin and June Goodfield, *The Discovery of Time* (Chicago: University of Chicago Press, 1977 [1965]), p. 130.

The perfect future is not the only future. A straw poll might well indicate that past imperfect decrees future imperfect. The future, perceived in this way, simply seems to be more of the same, just "one damned thing after another." Even Vico, whose historical cycles spiraled in an upward direction of sorts, was no optimist. He could see no future where reason reigned and peace prevailed. People would remain the same, their greed, viciousness, and cruelty unaltered by the passage of time. No utopia could be built from such unfinished brick; the future would invariably follow in the footsteps of the past.[24]

Utopia, the idea of a perfectible future for humanity, remains a potent ideal. For some, the dream may be everything, and this absorbing interest carries the impetus for change with it. Visionaries often are crucial elements in history. Never mind that utopia, in the words of one historian, may be "the debtor's prison of historians who declare history bankrupt."[25] As long as dreams influence people, so long will dreams make history, even though the dream itself may not have the slightest chance of realization. In such a way does the sense of the future become an important component of historical logic.

Among professional historians today, the idea of a utopia would find few takers. The life of experience has a way of sapping belief and making skeptics of us all. There are a few septuagenarian optimists around, but most of them seem to receive newspaper comment as oddities rather than cultural spokesmen. "It seems hopeless to look forward to better times in the future," Karl Löwith has written. "There is hardly a future which, when it has become present, does not disappoint." He adds that humanity's hopes are deceptive and illusory, yet necessary.[26] Hope seems mandatory but unfulfilling, an endless dissatisfaction and an endless need.

Even so, the future holds hope for historians as for other people, and for some scholars it holds even more—the chance for vindication. No one delving into the past will get the chance to second-guess historically minded successors. The historian puts all the cards on the table for the current generation and for those who follow. Though it is one thing to concede jauntily that history is rewritten every generation, it still is hard to imagine one's lifework torn to bits by the wolves of posterity. For a man like Charles Beard, faith in humanity was an operating principle. History was

---

[24] Mazlish, *The Riddle of History*, p. 41.
[25] Strout, *Pragmatic Revolt*, p. 161.
[26] Löwith, *Meaning in History*, p. 204.

moving in a certain direction (Beard believed toward a "collec-
tivist democracy"), and he asked for an "act of faith" that this was
so. Beard flatly asserted that "the verdict of history yet to come"
would judge today's historical accuracy. The researcher must in
part play to the future, just as the seasoned ham actor will play to
the back of the house.

Beard had no pat formula for his peers to follow. He did say
the future could be realized only by "prophetic discernment." The
historian vindicated by posterity would be a success; the historian
not so vindicated. . . . Beard's scholarly face was set in a forward
direction. For him, the past existed to serve the present *and* the
future. His contemporary, Arthur Schlesinger, also was proud of
what he regarded as the predicting function of history. Schlesinger,
unlike Beard, did not insist on vindication by the future. But he
was pleased with the identification of what he described as the cyclical operation of American politics, and he clearly regarded the
future as important. In a preface to an historical series he coedited,
Schlesinger described part of the historian's task as divining the
verdict of the future through imagination.[27]

Beard, and Schlesinger to a lesser degree, were representative
of scholars with a strong and confident sense of the future. In
Beard's case in particular, the absorption with the future emerged
as a perplexing problem. Historians do not share the predictive
function of science. If a ball rolls off a table and falls to the floor
ninety-nine times, and the experimental conditions are unchanged,
we expect it to fall to the floor the next time as well. Science sup-
ports predictions such as this with various "laws" that hold "true"
on earth with a great deal of credibility. In history, past facts never
submit with such cooperation. And apart from Bellamy's Martian,
no one can tell us what the future facts may be. In appealing to the
future, Beard was appealing from the known to the unknown. He
dreamed of that impossibility in history, omniscience, even as he
recognized that history is not prophecy, and cannot be.[28]

True, there are some analysts who—through chance, insight,
perverse logic, or other means—do occasionally come up with rea-

---

[27] Strout, *Pragmatic Revolt*, p. 55; Arthur M. Schlesinger, *In Retrospect: The
History of a Historian* (New York: Harcourt, Brace and World, 1963), pp. 144,
127; Arthur M. Schlesinger and Dixon Ryan Fox, eds., *A History of American
Life*, XII: *The Great Crusade and After, 1914–1928*, by Preston W. Slosson (Chicago: Quadrangle Paperbacks, 1971 [1930]), p. xi. It is worth noting that the
diplomatic historian Dexter Perkins, following Schlesinger, discerned a "kind of
rhythm" in American foreign policy as well. Perkins, *Yield of the Years*, p. 139.
[28] Strout, *Pragmatic Revolt*, pp. 58–59.

sonably correct answers about the future. Consider this paragraph, penned in 1790 by Burke and based directly on the English historical experience with Cromwell:

> In the weakness of one kind of authority, and in the fluctuation of all, the officers of an army will remain for some time mutinous and full of faction, until some popular general, who understands the art of conciliating the soldiery, and who possesses the true spirit of command, shall draw the eyes of all men upon himself. Armies will obey him on his personal account. There is no other way of securing military obedience in this state of things. But the moment in which the event shall happen, the person who really commands the army is your master; the master (that is little) of your king, the master of your assembly, the master of your whole republic.[29]

Here is Napoleon, years before the fact. Burke, using loose historical analogy, was remarkably accurate concerning the future course of the French Revolution. He was no seer, but he was an informed politician with a decided prejudice against the "mob" and with no reluctance whatsoever to use past examples to illuminate both present and future.

Burke's case rested on custom and tradition. His prediction was informed, if prejudiced, and we should not be surprised when even a reckless prophecy hits the nail on the head. By this process the soothsayer does not become an historian, nor vice versa. There are limits to historical logic. Burkean predictions certainly are superior to those divinations that begin, "On the ninth of July next year the following events. . . ." or to the perpetual junk dished out by astrologers and cultists of all kinds. The future is not history, even if it is conditioned historically.

Caution might suggest that the past is opaque enough, without worrying about the future. While purist ideals are commendable, in neglecting the present and future as proper areas of historical concern these ideals fail to satisfy basic human instincts for self-realization. Perhaps the best way of appreciating the problem is to see history as a delicate set of balances, tripartite if you will, in which past, present, and future speak to each other through the researcher.

Under these conditions, a finely tuned mind is necessary to comprehend the various meanings history may provide. Marc Bloch, a very brave French historian who was executed by the

[29] Burke, *Reflections on the Revolution in France*, p. 216.

Nazis in 1944, once wrote that history was a "science of change." No two events are exactly alike; what happened yesterday will not necessarily happen tomorrow. The past will not continuously reproduce itself. If this sounds like prediction, it is only history by analogy, the result of a lifetime of immersion in the past. We know, said Bloch, that yesterday differed from the day before. We are reasonably assured that tomorrow will differ from yesterday.[30] Historical meaning is unclear as future becomes past, not for lack of theories or solutions, but because human beings cannot be more precise.

[30] Marc Bloch, *Strange Defeat: A Statement of Evidence Written in 1940* (New York: W. W. Norton, 1968), pp. 117–18.

CHAPTER TWELVE

A Question of Purpose

The unavoidable imprecision of concepts of historical meaning leads not only to indecisiveness but also to denial. People ignore meaning in history for a variety of reasons, extending from finely honed logic through cultivated ignorance to plain cussedness. Since history divested of meaning makes no sense, ignoring meaning tends to foreclose thought. The best part of the past is lost.

On the other side of the coin, history and meaning may be interlocked so closely that one is the other, each incomplete without the other, like the Chinese concepts of *yin* and *yang*. The relationship is most obvious when history is considered to be *purposeful*, or goal-oriented. History with purpose axiomatically is replete with meaning, since the meaning is in the purpose and, depending on one's angle of approach, may be the purpose itself. With or without purpose, meaning takes its life from the past. A poor sense of the past results in an equally poor sense of historical meaning. We have reached a point in our discussion where no "schools of thought" can offer much help. It is time to speculate.

The Denial of Inherent Meaning

A person who does not think about history might rest content with the assertion that historical fact and historical meaning are the same. In the event lies the meaning; every historical act makes its relevance manifest in and of itself. Yet people continue to search for meanings behind historical events, as they have done for thousands of years. If meaning was inherent in the event, the quest would be unnecessary; but for the inquisitive types who abound in every generation, the absence of meaning leads to the search.[1]

The virtually endless seeking for meaning is our best proof that history is far more than mere rote memorization. We cannot agree with the historian of Mughal India who blissfully observed that "it is one of the graces of God that He made it easy to learn (history) although the science is extremely beneficial and useful; and He did not make it difficult to learn as is the case with other sciences. And that (science) can be learnt only if one cares to learn it by memorizing all occurrences. When one learns the facts and events about the people who lived in the past and devotes his time to remember them he, undoubtedly, attains his purpose."[2] It is no accident that India, among all the areas of the earth, has one of the weakest historical traditions.

Rote memorization cannot even address the great questions of history, much less attempt to answer them. What set of facts do we use to analyze historical forces and trends? How do we judge, on events alone, what weight to give Marx, Vico, and the rest? How do we discern the place in history of the individual, of the crowd, of classes? How do we "know" what we know about history (*epistemology*)? Meaning has many handles for the thinker to grasp. The key is in the thinking, not necessarily in the production of any fixed results. A vague definition, such as "man's developing historical consciousness," will not do, since it mistakes a process for basic meaning itself.[3]

Several arguments have been used to deny meaning to history. Few of these are as shallow as that of our Indian historian, who, like television's Joe Friday, wants only the facts. These arguments are all alive today, even flourishing in consumer-oriented popular cultures that grow more ahistorical by the year. A constant cari-

---

[1] Karl Löwith, *Meaning in History* (Chicago: University of Chicago Press, 1949), p. 4. Philosophically, my position is that meaning *in* history cannot be distinguished from the meaning we take *from* history. Leonard Krieger, *Ranke: The Meaning of History* (Chicago: University of Chicago Press, 1977), p. 345, argues that the German historian was the first to weld objective and personal meaning into an indissoluble whole.

[2] Abdur Rashid, "The Treatment of History by Muslim Historians in Mughal Official and Biographical Works," in C. H. Philips, ed., *Historians of India, Pakistan, and Ceylon* (London: Oxford University Press, 1961), p. 151.

[3] The phrase is from Bruce Mazlish, *The Riddle of History: The Great Speculators from Vico to Freud* (New York: Minerva Press, 1968 [1966]), pp. 8–9. For a concise and handy series of major questions involving meaning in history, see pp. 6–8, n. 1.

cature we all recognize is that of the ostrich-historian, a hopeless creature with his mind forever in the past and thus forever irrelevant to the present. Lacking a precise utilitarian function, such an historian is not "now" and is thus devoid of meaning. Some very bright people have tended to reject the past, as we have seen, on grounds of its presumed uselessness. One of Marx's famous lines holds that "the tradition of all the dead generations weighs like a nightmare on the brain of the living."[4]

We should not press Marx too hard, since like most renowned thinkers he studied history intensely, only to cudgel the past relentlessly into his personal vision. Yet the aura of ahistorical thought still hovers around those who suspect that history is essentially useless to the present. The philosopher-mathematician René Descartes, standing at the dawn of the Age of Science, was typical in giving short shrift to the past. "When one is too curious about things which were practiced in past centuries," he wrote, "one is usually very ignorant about those which are practiced in our own time." Descartes lived in his mind's eye, but his attitude was shared by many public men as well. France in Descartes' day was run to a great degree by the practical Cardinal Richelieu, a master of political realism. "In politics," the adroit cardinal stated flatly, "the past cannot apply to the present."[5] Of course, Descartes and Richelieu, like Marx, used the past even as they continued to reject it.

A second point advanced against meaning in history places historical research in the balance with pure science and finds history a pathetic lightweight. Historical study does not seem to "advance" with the seven-league boots of science. In the past fifty years the study of physics has been revolutionized, while biochemistry, petrochemistry, and a host of other applied sciences continue to make rapid strides. As one authority has remarked, this has marked a revolution in our *ontology*—in the way we per-

---

[4] Haskell Fain, *Between Philosophy and History: The Resurrection of Speculative Philosophy of History within the Analytic Tradition* (Princeton: Princeton University Press, 1970), p. 122; Peter Gay and Victor G. Wexler, eds., *Historians at Work*, III: Niebuhr to Maitland (New York: Harper and Row, 1975), p. 123.

[5] Descartes quoted in Gordon Connell-Smith and Howell A. Lloyd, *The Relevance of History* (London: Heinemann Educational Books, 1972), p. 16; Richelieu quoted in Ernest John Knapton, *France: An Interpretive History* (New York: Charles Scribner's Sons, 1971), p. 156.

ceive reality.⁶ Historians, lackluster plodders that they are, can offer no such dynamism.

As a poor second best to the sciences, history has been described as incapable of raising intellectual problems worthy of special attention. A philosophical position called "logical positivism"
has held that history must be a science or it is nothing. Things are
bad enough as it is, with history as the "softest of the soft sciences," just a hair's breadth away from the total disgrace of sociology. Most positivists saw history as a kind of sociology with
documents, undeserving of the respect to be accorded the physical
sciences.⁷ Because its "truth value" was so low, any meaning to be
derived from history would be metaphysical, subjective, and un-
empirical—in a word—useless. To look to history for the answers
to the big questions was to build a skyscraper in a swamp.

The ostrich-historian caricature and the Charles Atlas metaphor of the sciences that continually kick sand in Clio's eye at least
presuppose enough interest in history to reject it for alternatives.
We must be aware, however, that many people literally do not give
a damn about the past, taking their value structures almost en-
tirely from the present. In southern California, a part of the world
that always seems a step ahead in careless hedonism, one observer
has claimed that people's fantasies necessarily dominate. There is
no history to be experienced meaningfully, only the synthetic
pabulum dished out by Disneyland or Knotts' Berry Farm.⁸ To
avoid a sense of nullity, Californians must fantasize; they will have
their sun, surf, and smog because they do not have their past. History is denied, to a considerable degree, by those who have never
troubled to think about it in the first place.

Historical meaning may be rejected ultimately because of its
multiplicity. Science offers *answers*, while history seems to restate
constantly the same questions. Such uncertainty easily registers as
a consummate bore. Living with uncertainty and its arcane companion, mystery, is no easy task, and acceptance of the impossibility of total historical veracity is equally difficult. Yet even
Ranke admitted that "for the muse of history, if I understand it
aright, there are things that can be allowed to rest undisturbed."

⁶Murray G. Murphey, *Our Knowledge of the Historical Past* (Indianapolis:
Bobbs-Merrill, 1973), p. 52.
⁷Fain, *Between Philosophy and History*, pp. 4–5.
⁸William Irwin Thompson, *At the Edge of History: Speculations on the
Transformation of Culture* (New York: Harper and Row, 1972 [1971]), p. 11.

His countryman Goethe had once remarked that the highest happiness of man as a thinker was to probe the knowable and quietly to revere the unknowable.[9]

It would be so much easier if historical study offered a sense of the concrete, the ultimate, and the final. History does not serve up meaning on a platter. In this sense, the past has no outcome. *Is there a "problem" of history, one that may be "solved" in terms of meaning?* Only experience and mind can answer, and never in the human aggregate.

A pessimist would argue that the problem of meaning can never be solved because "man's historical experience is one of steady failure."[10] The difficulties of staying alive are timeless, regardless of how we cushion the shocks of living. People constantly require food, warmth, shelter, and a certain sense of psychological stabilization. The world has never been able to insure these, and thus the age-old problems continue. Since the human race cannot master its situation, says the pessimist, it is no surprise that it cannot extract meaning from its own past.

We may ignore the possibility of meaning in history by denying it, but denial is not proof. The rote memorizers and the empiricists, the indifferent ones and the pessimists, all are entitled to reject meaning on whatever grounds they please. Yet for every rejection, an affirmation exists that history *does* have meaning, deep-seated purposes that involve us all.

History with Purpose

Traditionally, history has had two practical purposes, extending back to the days of Herodotus. Educated people consistently have held that the study of history was an aid in tackling contemporary problems. Beyond its use in problem solving, history was also perceived as an exemplary model of instruction. Purposeful history did not fare well under the new professionalism of the nineteenth century, when the common dictum became that the past was to be studied for its own sake.[11] But notions of prac-

[9] Leonard Krieger, *Ranke: The Meaning of History* (Chicago: University of Chicago Press, 1977), p. 318; Franklin L. Baumer, *Modern European Thought: Continuity and Change in Ideas, 1600–1950* (New York: Macmillan, 1977), p. 271.
[10] Löwith, *Meaning in History*, p. 191.
[11] Connell-Smith and Lloyd, *The Relevance of History*, pp. 7–8.

ticality survived, and interest in purposeful history has been re-kindled in a century painfully aware that science, far from holding all the answers, contributes significantly to many of the problems.

Purpose in history is not to be confused with the purpose of self-serving ambition. Historical writing has a "patron tradition" thousands of years old, whereby hirelings would be paid to float their employer's reputation right-side up down the river of time. This sort of "purpose" was common in court histories commis-sioned by royal dynasties. Writers interested in where their next meal was coming from were not likely to scruple over the finer points of historical evidence. During the Golden Age of the Ot-toman Empire, for example, the Ottoman sultans sponsored a number of historical works that were directed toward one primary goal: promoting the claim of the Ottoman family to rule over the various peoples of the Empire.[12] The histories subsequently writ-ten were of course not completely devoid of worth, but their di-rected purpose made them "winner's histories."

Histories written by the victors and their paid pens combine purpose and meaning. They are written as eulogies, hagiographies, or instruments of social control. Their meaning is embedded in the reasons for which they were written. Other historical works have sought to *discover* purpose rather than advertise it. These are more pertinent examples of thinking about history, because al-though they never depart radically from the two traditional prac-tical purposes of historical research and writing, they are imbued with a sense of search and discovery lacking in the more self-serving variety.

Most obvious in the large numbers of histories directed to-ward meaning are those that proceed from the assumption of in-finite human potential, or perfectibility. Many Buddhist histories proceeded from the principle that the main historical purpose of humanity was to perform meritorious deeds. In so doing, we might be born to a better condition in life, or attain heaven, or even reach the blessed state of *Nirvāna*. Because of the emphasis on deeds, these attitudes were not fatalistic, and far from being superficial, they underlay an entire culture.[13]

[12] Stanford J. Shaw, *History of the Ottoman Empire and Modern Turkey*, I: *Empire of the Gazis: The Rise and Decline of the Ottoman Empire, 1280–1808* (Cambridge: Cambridge University Press, 1976), p. 145.
[13] L. S. Perera, "The Pali Chronicle of Ceylon," in Philips, ed., *Historians of India, Pakistan, and Ceylon*, pp. 34–35.

Many histories do not regard the past as a failure *per se*, but as a great overture to the future. Such writers see the central purpose in history, and hence its meaning, as being "ordained" in some way. The heavenly city of Augustine is a classic example. The heavenly city recognizes the great variety of human manners, laws, and institutions on earth but also sees that in spite of this heterogeneity, all tend to the same end of earthly peace. For Augustine, "The supreme good of the city of God is perfect and eternal peace," which he defines as the peace of freedom from all evil. Future life is blessed, the more so when we compare it with the wretchedness of contemporary existence.[14]

The teleological ideal identifies meaning and purpose in one grand cosmic scheme. The past serves as prelude for a future that is everything. Many ancient cultures saw history as finite; that is, they believed the future had an end. The followers of Iranian Mazdaism supposed a shroud of winter and night would blanket the earth at the end of eleven thousand years, to be lifted only with the return of the resurrected dead. Similar beliefs were common in certain Islamic communities and in German mythology. The most popular form of the resurrection belief has been Christian millenarianism. Here historical meaning takes its cue from Christ's return to earth to rule for a thousand years. While millenarianism is a continuation of Judaic tradition, it is also authentically "Christian" in its meaning: the return of Christ, the Last Judgment, and the establishment of the Glorious Kingdom on earth.

Millenarianism, in short, envisages an end only as a beginning, a door opening to perfection everlasting. It might be called an optimistic apocalypse. The Apocalypse, however, is usually perceived as bleak and foreboding. As one scholar has observed, "Every time mankind is shaken to its depths by a political, military, or moral cataclysm, it will evoke the Apocalypse." Apocalyptic thought breaks the nice round numbers implicit in millenarianism. With the Apocalypse the end is, for the majority, more punishment than promise.[15] Historical meaning sours, and the sins of humanity become an unbearable burden.

Either way, historical meaning is teleological, taking its impress from a sense of impending history. The purpose and the

[14] Peter Gay and Gerald J. Cavanaugh, eds., *Historians at Work*, I: *Herodotus to Froissart* (New York: Harper and Row, 1972), pp. 308–10.
[15] Henri Focillon, *The Year 1000* (New York: Frederick Ungar, 1969), pp. 41, 50.

meaning are one. The implication is that history has a final goal that transcends its own evidence. Regardless of the patterns of earthly activity, there is a definite end toward which all is tending.

There exist other possible ways of conceiving meaning beyond regarding meaning and purpose as identical. Several cultures have admitted concepts of meaning to history while denying the existence of an historical goal. The Greeks regarded historical events as filled with import, just as they did individual destinies. But Greek thinkers possessed no sense of finality in history.[16] There was no ultimate end, perhaps because the gods never tired of playing games with vainglorious mortals.

Much later, some thinkers of the eighteenth-century Enlightenment perceived history as a kind of process that tended always toward a goal without ever reaching it. The process itself was achievement enough. The reward came in taking part, in consciously advancing the human situation. Many of the *philosophes* reasoned that human perfectibility was history's unswerving destination. The road to this pinnacle would be smoothed by the triumph of rationality, the steady and inexorable accumulation of humanity's sum of knowledge.

Does history tend toward an end? Nonthinkers may shrug and say "who knows?" or even "who cares?" Certainly historical beginnings are varied: perhaps lost in the expanse of Darwinian time, or concurrent with our first attempts to record ourselves, or maybe commencing with the birth of a religious figure—Buddha, Christ, Muhammad. How, though, can we "know" the ending? The point is, we do not have to know, only to believe, for in the belief lies the meaning.

Sometimes meaning may occur in a much more muted sense. Fatalists and optimists alike may take solace in the wake of shattering events, trusting in the future to set things right. After surrendering his forces at Appomattox, Robert E. Lee wrote to a friend that he did not yet despair of the future. Lee's name was defamed throughout much of the North, and he was under threat of indictment for treason. Men are easily discouraged, he said, because individual efforts seem so unavailing. There was, however, one solace; "It is history that teaches us to hope."[17]

As comforting as they might be to the individual, hope and

[16] Löwith, *Meaning in History*, p. 6.
[17] Clifford Dowdey, *Lee* (New York: Bonanza Books, 1965), p. 605.

optimism are weak pegs on which to hang a theory of historical meaning. Most of the famous systematizers, and other theorists as well, have rooted historical meaning deep within their systems or philosophies. Vico with his spirals, Hegel and his world spirit, even Lord Acton with his concepts of liberty, all tried to unify history with a declaration of meaning.

Hegel and Acton, though far from being historical pen-pals, provide useful examples of this tendency. Hegel argued that "the History of the World was nothing but the development of the Idea of Freedom," which in turn was the work of God. For him, meaning was implicit in God's governance. Though he by no means created a giant system on the scale of a Hegel, Acton was adamant in insisting that liberty was "the unity, the only unity, of the history of the world, and the one principle of a philosophy of history." Neither man was a democrat, as we understand the term today; Acton in particular cultivated a distaste for democracy and admired his own aristocratic caste. But Acton nevertheless believed that in spite of liberty's uneven history, the idea was imperishable—the greatest dream and hence the most profound meaning of the human experience.[18] Both men sought meaning in basic "historical" principles but arrived at their results through totally different routes.

Acton's thinking is proof that meaning in history need not be systematized, in either a religious or a secular sense, to be effective. Meaning may be treated in a didactic fashion as well, not as some rigorous and full-blown body of belief meshed with fact, but as a useful and pertinent pattern of instruction. We may puzzle over whether history has one or several big meanings, or many little meanings, or no meaning at all. At least as early as Polybius, thinkers pondered the relationship of parts of history to the entirety of the past. Did the part or the whole encompass historical meaning best? The answer of Polybius, that examining a part of history may give some idea of the whole, was incomplete, as Polybius himself realized. "Episodical history," for him, offered but little comfort to those trying to grasp the presumed verities of universal history. Only by weighing the separate parts of the whole could the Grand Design be discerned.[19]

[18] Georg Wilhelm Friedrich Hegel, *The Philosophy of History*, trans. J. Sibree (New York: Dover Publications, 1956), pp. 456–57, 36; Gertrude Himmelfarb, *Lord Acton: A Study in Conscience and Politics* (Chicago: University of Chicago Press, 1962 [1952]), pp. 132, 142–43.
[19] Gay and Cavanaugh, eds., *Historians at Work*, I, 113.

Debating parts and wholes is far from a chicken-and-egg question insofar as the argument involves historical meaning, for upon its resolution depends the possibility of taking historical meaning, in its entirety, from one's own experience. The relationship between historical parts, by way of cause and effect, is yet another way we may appreciate meaning. History may be seen, not as a series of discrete events, but as a series of interrelated causes. This conception sees history as dynamic rather than static. The implication is that meaning exists in historical *movement*. Possibly such meaning is best comprehended by our own experience. One scholar has argued that the significance of any historical event is not in its "terminal consequences." Rather, the "near" causes and effects of a given event are the more relevant,[20] precisely because we can scale them to our own passage through life. Napoleon's Egyptian Expedition is virtually unknown to today's public; in 1798 it was the talk of Europe.

Of course, historical meaning may reside in the future, as we have observed. We must not imagine, however, that historical meaning is an objective quality that, once discerned, holds true for any and all analytical situations. Russel Nye has written that "history has a kind of built-in early warning system for those who know how to listen to it."[21] Presumably, historians and people who "understand" history are the ones who "know how to listen to it." This is foggy thinking. No one knows the frequency of the "built-in early warning system." If we did, history would be less a grand cavalcade of mistakes and disasters and more of what optimists have always dreamed it should be.

Yet the study of history can teach—not in a fixed, rote way but in a multiplicity of directions that are contingent only upon the individual's will to think. Jean Bodin, who possessed a legalistic and ordered mind, was confident that historical books could incite some people to virtue and frighten others away from vice.[22] But there is at least equal truth in the assertion that virtue is jolliest for someone else and that vice can be lots of fun. Clio is a muse who would seem to have no single function, no grand purpose, yet thinkers for thousands of years have imagined it must be so.—And perhaps it is.

[20] Murphey, *Our Knowledge of the Historical Past*, pp. 121–22.

[21] Russel B. Nye, Foreword to Donald V. Gawronski, *History: Meaning and Method*, 3rd ed. (Glenview, Ill.: Scott, Foresman, 1975), p. ii.

[22] Peter Gay and Victor G. Wexler, eds., *Historians at Work*, II: *Valla to Gibbon* (New York: Harper and Row, 1972), p. 66.

The Limits of Meaning

At the root of meaning is the *credibility* of history, whether or not we believe what is being served up. In a sense, history predates the merchant; *caveat emptor* might well be the rallying cry of the serious historical thinker. "For myself," proclaimed Herodotus, "my duty is to report all that is said, but I am not obliged to believe it all alike—a remark which may be understood to apply to my whole history."[23]

Although simple explanations sometimes suffice quite nicely, and although many books have been launched so overfreighted with different analyses as to sink of their own accord, there is a difference between the simple and the simplistic. A story concerning Alexander the Great and his court historian, Aristobulus, illustrates the point. It seems that the youthful conqueror and the elderly servant were sailing down the river Jhelum, in India, Aristobulus reading aloud from his history of the expedition to the princely Macedonian. Aristobulus thought to please Alexander by embellishing the tale with fictitious heroics, but Alexander threw the book into the river, exclaiming: "And the same, Aristobulus, is what you deserve, fighting those duels on my behalf and spearing all those elephants with a single javelin."[24]

A simple explanation spears one elephant with a single javelin; the simplistic one spears many. Historical meaning often will disintegrate when a simplistic weight is pressed against it. "Whig" history, which filters the past through the present to a considerable degree, partakes of this tendency. When Lincoln Steffens saw Jesus as the first muckraker, or the advertising man Bruce Barton saw Him as a super salesman,[25] they were perceiving Christ totally in twentieth-century perspective. Their visions were without historical meaning, since their evidence matched their present against a past that was dreamed rather than reclaimed.

To be credible, history must enlist less than dreams and more than facts. It must supply the questing mind with an imaginative integration of the past. The ancients sensed this requirement and

[23] Herodotus, *The Persian Wars* (New York: Modern Library, 1942), pp. 556–57.
[24] Robin Lane Fox, *Alexander the Great: A Biography* (New York: Dial Press, 1974), p. 194.
[25] See Lincoln Steffens, *The Autobiography of Lincoln Steffens* II (New York: Harcourt, Brace and World, 1958 [1931]), pp. 525–26; Bruce Barton, *The Man Nobody Knows* (New York: Review of Reviews, 1925).

acted upon it. Polybius, for one, knew that if the special province of history was ascertaining the facts, history was incomplete unless a statement of cause was made. Otherwise, history might be interesting, but it would remain uninstructive.[26]

Further, historical study must be cognizant of its limits, for by claiming too much historians diminish their power in the present. If everything has purpose, lack of interest may soon result, as the American Puritans learned to their chagrin. Not all knowledge of the past is historical. There are past frames in which the human past is not in the picture, i.e., geological strata. Beyond this limitation, there is no single *method* of studying the past, and thus there is no single way of eliciting historical meaning. To assume that there is one road to the past, and only one, is to court the belief that what happened in the past was simply "in the nature of things," in Carl Degler's words. Comparative history highlights the point when it examines in different cultures similar historical conditions that lead to different consequences.[27] Historical meaning, in other words, is not necessarily implicit in the historical situation.

Can historical meaning be definite and lasting regardless of time? Another way of asking the question is to consider whether meaning is independent of culture. Once European-centered thinkers believed it so, but current historians insist on flexibility. Roy F. Nichols was typical of modern scholarship when he argued that every generation has to discover and restate meaning "in terms of current behavior." Thus meaning, in this perspective, will always be incomplete and undefined. The present is a perpetually fogged set of goggles through which we glimpse the past. Benedetto Croce, who went further in this regard than most thinkers, even claimed that "only an interest in the life of the present can move one to investigate past fact." It followed, then, that "every true history is contemporary history,"[28] and that in a nonrigorous sense, an interest in the present determined the quality of meaning in the past.

To Croce, our real desire is to recreate the past in the imagina-

---

[26] Gay and Cavanaugh, eds., *Historians at Work*, I, 127.

[27] W. B. Gallie, *Philosophy and the Historical Understanding*, 2nd ed. (New York: Schocken Books, 1968), p. 52; Carl N. Degler, *Neither Black nor White: Slavery and Race Relations in Brazil and the United States* (New York: Macmillan, 1971), pp. x–xi.

[28] Roy F. Nichols, *A Historian's Progress* (New York: Alfred A. Knopf, 1968), p. 292; Benedetto Croce, *History: Its Theory and Practice*, trans. Douglas Ainslie (New York: Russell and Russell, 1920), p. 12.

tion of the present. No one, he argued, wants to leave the present and "fall back into the dead past." Only vapid romantics could even consider such a proposition, and then only as an illusion. Indeed, the present is recognized today as an inescapable sounding-board for the historian. Most historians frankly admit they are conditioned by the present and must live in their own time. Recently, historians typed as "social critics" or "social activists" have warred with other members of their profession over the issue of engagement in the problems of contemporary society.[29] We are not concerned with these internecine squabbles except for one point: though values taken from the present are part of every historian's consideration of the past, these values ideally should not totally encapsulate the meaning of the past for the researcher.

In the end, meaning in history must be distilled into terms that the individual not only can understand, but relate to on a personal level. "It is I whom I paint," wrote the wide-ranging Montaigne. "The greatest thing in the world is to know how to belong to oneself." A pertinent point, this, because if you truly belong to yourself you must have a reasonable idea of what you possess. And you possess not only your corporal body. You are the heir, like it or not, of your family, your ancestors, your region, your culture—in short, your past. The study of history is a path to self-knowledge at the most personal level. David Hume was surely right when he observed that "a man acquainted with history may, in some respect, be said to have lived from the beginning of the world, and to have been making continual additions to his stock of knowledge in every century."[30]

As the centuries have piled up, however, the ways of examining the past have changed, and so too have the meanings people have taken from their past. Indeed, it is more correct to say "multiple pasts," since fashions in history (like all fashions) fluctuate through time. Perspective makes a difference; this year's robes are next year's rags. "What [historians] once accepted as gospel, they now denounce as myth; what they once regarded as reasonable generalizations, they now discard altogether or replace with modified versions."[31]

[29] Croce, *History: Its Theory and Practice*, p. 277; Bernard Sternsher, *Consensus, Conflict, and American Historians* (Bloomington: Indiana University Press, 1975), p. 284.

[30] Montaigne quoted in Knapton, *France: An Interpretive History*, p. 122; Hume quoted in Fain, *Between Philosophy and History*, pp. 9–10.

[31] John D. Hicks, *My Life with History: An Autobiography* (Lincoln: University of Nebraska Press, 1968), p. 317.

A fine question thus emerges as to whether meaning in history is as inconstant as the fashions of historical study. Paradoxically, multiple purposes may lead to purposelessness. To be sure, there always exist what Franklin Baumer, and many others, called "the perennial questions."[32] These questions center on the unknown and the unknowable. Humanity usually is a puzzle to itself, both individually and in the mass. We are given to pondering our environment, our gods, and our past. All these concerns are filled with meaning; if they were not, we simply would not be interested in them as questions.

We need not become entangled in considering if thinking about such things makes us "philosophers" rather than "historians." If we could pigeonhole knowledge, pulling out a box filled with "meaning" whenever we required it, all would be well. A common idea holds that historical meaning is something that only comes in a philosophical way, through abstract thought.[33] But the meanings of the past must be highly personal to make sense, and since you are not an abstraction, the ways you relate to the past are to this extent non-abstract as well.

Ultimately, our senses of the past are formed through a bridge of meaning. The historian's true *art* lies in making the past relate to the present, and true *science* lies in making this relationship believable. The historian "creates" meaning,[34] both for self and for audience, although the wisdom of Solomon could not unravel the question of how such meaning is actually born.

We have arrived at certain limits beyond which thinking about history cannot proceed without a convoy of metaphysicians. Doubtless, we have "solved" nothing. While she offers countless puzzles, Clio shields no ultimate secret. "There is no . . . last simple word of history uttering its true sense," Dilthey stated, "any more than there is such a thing to be extracted from nature."[35] We may sense these limits, and still feel the game is worth the candle. The past unceasingly provides ample fuel for the mind on fire.

[32] Baumer, *Modern European Thought*, p. 11.

[33] Norman F. Cantor and Richard I. Schneider, *How to Study History* (Arlington Heights, Ill.: AHM Publishing, 1967), p. 254, argue that studying the philosophy of history too intensely may actually inhibit true historical study. My argument is that abstract thinking about history and concrete historical research should be complementary.

[34] Connell-Smith and Lloyd, *The Relevance of History*, p. 118.

[35] Peter Gay and Gerald J. Cavanaugh, eds., *Historians at Work*, IV: *Dilthey to Hofstadter* (New York: Harper and Row, 1975), p. 4.

EPILOGUE

A Concern for All Seasons

Speaking of the past, the Chinese sage Confucius pronounced judgment: "What is over and done with, one does not discuss. What has already taken its course, one does not criticize; what already belongs to the past, one does not censure."[1] All around us, people who never read Confucius act in agreement. Though we all "possess" a history, and though the past is part of our everyday discourse, we seldom pause to think. It is as if Pierre Bayle, one of the founders of modern historical criticism, was correct when he claimed that history was nothing more than the tale of humanity's crimes and misfortunes.[2] Who wishes to dwell on such dreary fare when there is life to be lived?

We are creatures who have our being in history. We may live without history, indeed we may have a tremendous time without once looking back, but we have not the slightest chance of understanding ourselves without examining our historical dimension. Thoughtful inquiry into this "semi-monstrous subject"[3] has the potential to take us outside ourselves, worlds away. At the same time we can never be wholly detached from history, because the past is human experience.

[1] Arthur Waley, trans. and ed., *The Analects of Confucius* (New York: Vintage Books, 1938), p. 99. Waley notes that this comment is phrased so as to refer to the remote rather than the immediate past. Confucius and his followers were much concerned with distinguishing the moral from the immoral in human affairs.

[2] Walter L. Dorn, *Competition for Empire, 1740–1763* (New York: Harper and Row, 1963 [1940]), p. 216.

[3] Bruce Mazlish, *The Riddle of History: The Great Speculators from Vico to Freud* (New York: Minerva Press, 1968 [1966]), p. 1.

When we think about the past, we make history "legitimate" in our minds. The past becomes part of our experience in meaningful ways. Without legitimacy, the reconstruction of the past is a species of nihilism, echoed in the droning recitals of schoolchildren as they commit their texts to memory. If we cannot make the effort to understand history, to make the past work for us, then we admit a degree of mental bankruptcy that is in itself inhuman.[4]

The mind needs a broad and varied diet to sustain itself. "Closed" minds with which we are all familiar are lazy minds, not especially unproductive, but bloated with the common, the easy, and the trite. A heterogeneous mental fare gives the intellect a change to exercise. Reason and imagination are marvelous conditioning agents, and both are to be found in history in generous proportions. Through exercise, we admit, the mind may never "know" with any certainty. This need not lead to despair. "Reason can forego knowledge, but cannot put up with absurdities."[5] At the very least, we should take from history the inclination not to suffer fools gladly.

As we gain in experience, our ability to think does not necessarily keep pace. Since no one can ever "know it all," our interest in the exercise flags easily; we become compartmented, confined, and yearn for stability above all. Even the patience of a sage may become fatigued. Confucius tells us that at the age of fifteen he set his heart upon learning. At thirty, his feet were planted firmly on the ground. At forty he no longer suffered from the perplexities of life. By fifty he knew the biddings of heaven, and at sixty he "heard them with docile ear." Finally, at seventy, Confucius could follow the dictates of his heart, for what he desired no longer overstepped the boundaries of right. Lest this seem too heavy a dose of fatalism, he added; "He who learns but does not think is lost."[6] The open mind is a mark of aging well.

Thinking about history aids the individual in manifold ways. Through history we realize, even if only with dim understanding, limits concerning ourselves and our surroundings. In a world in

[4] Gertrude Himmelfarb, *Victorian Minds: A Study of Intellectuals in Crisis and of Ideologies in Transition* (New York: Harper and Row, 1970 [1952]), p. 197; Cushing Strout, *The Pragmatic Revolt in American History: Carl Becker and Charles Beard* (Ithaca, N.Y.: Cornell University Press, 1966 [1958]), p. 2.

[5] The phrase is Niebuhr's, in Peter Gay and Victor G. Wexler, eds., *Historians at Work*, III: *Niebuhr to Maitland* (New York: Harper and Row, 1975), p. 12.

[6] Waley, trans. and ed., *The Analects of Confucius*, pp. 88, 91.

which much blather is continually loosed concerning "human potential," limiting perspectives serve as bracing tonics. After all, as Franklin cautioned, a benevolent man should allow a few faults in himself, else he loses friends.[7]

As we think, we learn more about the future as well, not in order to divine what is to come but to cope with a heightened sense of possibilities. Furthermore, the moral and didactic aspects of history are always there, ready for the mind that requires their special powers.[8]

In sum, in thinking about history (as in all thinking) we play games. Imagine a card game in which every player is dealt the same hand, over and over. When we cease thinking about history, the past wears the same vapid aspect. But to think means a continuous reshuffling of the deck of evidence placed before us. Fresh hands are the order of the day, because any game played with the same old cards will go stale sooner or later.

To scrutinize the past in this manner is to operate with an "unbalanced" mind, a mind purposefully kept on edge. Critical thinking is perpetual dissatisfaction with the given. Without the component of criticism, thought too easily slides into "learning." The rewards of history favor the unbalanced minds; the maximum joys belong to the curious, the dissatisfied, the particular, and the perverse.

And why not? What else do we have, in the final analysis, save ourselves? "[History] hath triumphed over time," rhapsodized Sir Walter Raleigh, "which besides it nothing but eternity hath triumphed over." So the historian seeks to enlarge life in the present by reflecting on the past. There is no life so rich with the pleasures of today that it cannot profit by a look at yesterday. The beauty of the backward glimpse is that there is absolutely nothing esoteric about it. Historical perspective, after all, may be in the words of Irving Howe, nothing more than decency of feeling.[9]

The ultimate importance of history, then, must lie in its immediate, personal relationship to the single, questing human mind. In

[7] Benjamin Franklin, *The Autobiography of Benjamin Franklin and Selections from His Other Writings* (New York: Modern Library, 1944), p. 101.

[8] W. B. Gallie, *Philosophy and the Historical Understanding*, 2nd ed. (New York: Schocken Books, 1968 [1964]), pp. 127, 64.

[9] Sir Walter Raleigh, *The History of the World*, ed. C. A. Patrides (London: Macmillan Press, 1971), p. 48; Irving Howe, *World of Our Fathers: The Journey of the East European Jews to America and the Life They Found and Made* (New York: Simon and Schuster, 1976), p. 245.

all the seasons of humanity, history is forever germane. True, Hegel once bluntly stated that we cannot learn from history. But even he admitted that history made us self-conscious. In turn, this self-consciousness—in historical perspective—defined our being.[10] But we do not need to be so highfalutin to make the point; not every bird flies best in rarefied air.

Far closer to home would be the genteel reminiscences of Edward Gibbon, who was given to reflecting on the "sedentary amusement" of reading and meditation. Gibbon speaks powerfully to an age that is moving toward functional illiteracy, and thus toward a diminished ability to think critically, faster than we care to contemplate. When with his library, wrote the historian of Rome's decline and fall, "I might say with truth that I was never less alone than when by myself."[11]

Need we add that immersion in the past need not diminish one's experience in the present by one whit? On the contrary, people who live with Clio's puzzles might well argue that the present is, for them, a more tolerable place precisely because of their interest in the past. Uncertainty, to a seasoned thinker, is a way of life—not especially relaxing, but varied, enjoyable, even necessary. Uncertainty is not an automatic recipe for thought paralysis; F. Scott Fitzgerald once defined a "first-rate intelligence" as "the ability to hold two opposed ideas in the mind, at the same time, and still retain the ability to function."[12] Substitute "several" for "two" and the "first-rate intelligence" becomes a critical thinker.

Critical thinking cannot be taught so much as it comes through experience. Many opportunities to think pass our way; it is a sadness verging on tragedy that we prefer to ignore or file them rather than ponder. After a lifetime of action on a scale almost larger than human, and long after he captured the world's gaze with his expedition to Egypt, Napoleon contemplated history as he withered away on St. Helena. Much of his thought also centered on his son, whom he mistakenly hoped would add further sheen to the Napoleonic luster. And what was the paternal advice, after Egypt, the Consulate, the Empire; after Marengo, Austerlitz, Wagram; after Moscow, Elba, Waterloo? "My son should study much history,

[10]Mazlish, *The Riddle of History*, pp. 139, 140, 181.
[11]Edward Gibbon, *Memoirs of My Life*, ed. Georges Bonnard (New York: Funk and Wagnalls, 1969), pp. 95–96.
[12]John P. Diggins, *Up from Communism: Conservative Odysseys in American Intellectual History* (New York: Harper and Row, 1975 [1971]), p. 262.

and meditate upon it," the dying Emperor said to his comrades-in-exile, "for it is the only true philosophy." [13]

We would take issue with Napoleon's exclusion of other ways of thinking, but his counsel was sound. Notice that his son was advised, not to find the answers, but to meditate. Perhaps Napoleon sensed, at the end of a life lived in the historical arena, that the basis of thinking is not the answer, but the question. And so we conclude with the most pertinent question of all: *What is history?* [14]

[13] Will and Ariel Durant, *The Age of Napoleon: A History of European Civilization from 1789 to 1815*, XI of *The Story of Civilization* (New York: Simon and Schuster, 1975), pp. 253, 774.

[14] This question is cheerfully purloined from Edward Hallett Carr, *What Is History?* (New York: Vintage Books, 1961). It is fair to say that Professor Carr, with considerable pungency, believes he has the answer.

Afterword

Here is the usual place to tuck in a bibliography, but in this instance the reader would be ill served by such an exercise. At best, a bibliography would be a recapitulation of the rather diverse material already cited in the notes; at worst, it would be a grim and tedious recital of the author's favorite books. Instead, with the notion that true interest in history stems from personal inclination, I offer a few suggestions for satisfying historical curiosity and honing critical skills.

At the primary level, genealogical studies have recently flourished. There has always been a genealogical market in the United States, formerly mostly confined to Brahmins and southern aristocrats, but at present the industry is booming. You might become interested in your family tree—it really is amazing how much information may be winkled out of a host of sources, some available in your local library. In itself, genealogy is probably not quite history, but it is certainly a doorway to historical thinking. Suppose you find that Great-great Uncle Charlie moved from Wisconsin to Colorado in the 1880s. Was he unique in his mobility? What forces drove him to leave, attracted him to his new home? Perceived in this way, a genealogical tree has roots in historical action and is an excellent entrée to historical discourse.

Many of us are firmly attached to our localities—urban areas, counties, a patch of countryside linked for generations to our extended family and friends. Local history societies, so often the bane of cruel jokes from professional historians, are in most cases prime repositories of exceptional historical material. Many localities have readily identifiable "personalities" stemming from ethnicity, language, political behavior, economic patterns, and a host of other discriminating factors. To delve into these aspects of your locality is to add depth and meaning to the commonplaces of your everyday life. I might add that in my experience local history specialists, while they can on occasion bore one to tears, seem to be almost uniformly friendly and eager to share their concerns with others.

Do you think of yourself as a westerner? Southerner? New Englander? Our country abounds with regional histories and historical "explanations" as to how these regions interacted over the years, and to what consequence. Again, if your interests run in the direction of regional identification, such studies may be evocative and exasperating, since many regionalists have a way of lauding their particular portion of the American scene and downplaying others. Indeed, until about 1900 much of American history tended to be New England history.

Read the news, watch the news. Is there anything in current events that attracts your attention? What is the PLO, anyway? How is the Soviet Union governed? Why is there *apartheid* in South Africa? All historical inquiry essentially begins with questions, and the individually satisfactory answers are both historical and evolutionary. You might try doing history backward, starting from current events of interest. Remember, if you accept present action as simply "given," you certainly cannot claim to understand it in any meaningful sense.

We all have interests, things or people or happenings that intrigue us and to which we devote a considerable part of our time— call them "topics" if you like. Do you enjoy sex? Like woodworking? Are you involved in PTA? Innumerable subjects are historical in nature. Try to fit an historical perspective on what intrigues you personally in the here and now. You will be pleasantly surprised that (1) historical dimensions exist for your topic, as they almost surely do; and (2) that the study of these dimensions will enrich your enjoyment of your topic in the present.

Perhaps you have a favorite historical personage about whom you would like to know more. I threaded Napoleon throughout this book simply because he is a widely known "name," but the little Corsican is obviously not everyone's cup of tea. Are you interested in women's rights? Democratic politics? National defense? Then try the Grimké sisters, Andrew Jackson, or James Forrestal, all of whose lives give both excitement and coherence to these topics. Biographical writing is never out of style, nor is autobiography, but be on the alert for the ghostwritten hype or the "celebrity biography," both bastardized versions of an outstanding historical and literary format.

Yet another relatively painless way to come to grips with historical thinking is to read historical novels or science fiction, both literary devices that are occasionally embedded with an exceptional amount of historical research. The best historical novelists are painstaking in their attention to historical detail, and science fiction writers often display, through their imaginative creation of other worlds, an intuitive insight into the problems and prospects of their own time.

We are all immersed in the world of mass communication, particularly motion pictures and television. These two media often display an historical dimension, one that is the more tricky because it is so vivid, visual, and immediate. One argument of this book is that visual media are relatively poor conduits for communicating history, compared with the richness of the printed page, yet what is omitted or distorted in pictures may open the mind to inquire or differ. Movies or TV need not be an automatic mental novocaine.

Ultimately, the critical historical thinker is a person who ignores no possible resource, yet who lets no single resource become his or her historical explanation. History comes at us from so many different directions, our lives are filled with so many historical possibilities, that we merely disgrace ourselves when we argue against the relevance of historical study and historical thought. We are a compound of our individual and collective history; what has gone by is omnipresent, immediate, and influential. So why not do some thinking about the past?

Index

Fichte, Johann Gottlieb, 148
Fischer, David Hackett, 175
Fitzgerald, F. Scott, 211
Fontenelle, Bernard le Bouvier de, 173
Franklin, Benjamin, 17, 30, 179–180, 210
French Revolution, 121, 137, 172, 192
Freud, Sigmund, 4–5, 95–96, 99, 121, 129, 139
Friday, Joe, 195
Frost, Robert, 88

Gallie, W. B., 106
Gandhi, Mohandas, 141
Gauss, Karl Friedrich, 37
"genetic fallacy," 175
Genovese, Eugene, 156
geography: history and, 90–95
George III (King of England), 158
Geronimo, 188
Gibbon, Edward, 17, 42, 80, 119, 211
Glorious Revolution of 1688, 126
Goethe, Johann Wolfgang von, 198
Gottschalk, Louis, 135
"great man" theory, 136–141
Guicciardini, Francesco, 79
Gustavson, Carl, 143

hagiography, 137, 199
Hakuseki, Arai, 167
Halévy, Elie, 129
Halsey, Fleet Admiral William F., 139–140
Hedda Gabler (Ibsen), 186
Hedgehog and the Fox, The (Berlin), 53–54
Hegel, Georg W. F., 54, 100, 139, 148, 173–174, 202, 211
Hegelian dialectic, 100, 131
Heilbroner, Robert, 153
Hennings, August, 166
Henry, Joseph, 136
Henty, G. A., 19–20
Herbert, George, 84
Herder, Johann Gottfried von, 91
Herodotus, 131, 173, 198, 204
Hicks, John, 9, 11, 18, 20, 51, 67, 78, 110–111, 127
Hinduism, 148
historian as moralist, 169–172

historical change, 77–88
historical cycles, 46, 112–117
historical evidence, 62–63
historical fact, 13, 23–29, 34–35, 103–104
historical forces, 142–161
historical greatness, 136–141
historical models, 52–53
historical movement, 203
historical nihilism, 28–29, 46
historical order: institutionalization of, 57–73; limits of, 52–56; possibilities of, 46–52
historical positivism, 3
historical prediction, 186–193
historical process, 77–78
historical quantification, 37, 42
historical research, 57–63
historical subjectivism, 35–40
historical synthesis, 7
historical trends, 115–116
historical "watershed," 44–45
historicism, 104–107, 175–176
history: as "act of faith," 47, 49, 190–191; as art, 207; as autobiography, 131–132; as biography, 132–136; and Christianity (see Christianity: and history); and chronology, 48–49; credibility of, 204; and diplomacy, 148–149; and economics, 150–153; and fate, 48; and geography, 48–49; and God, 49–50; and the individual, 125–141; and influence, 156–158; and the irrational, 43, 49–51; and morality, 165–177; and nationalism, 102–103, 145–146; and politics, 146–150; and progress, 47–48, 117–124; and purpose, 194–207; and racism, 102; reading of, 12–22; as repetition, 112–117; and science, 23–29, 207; senses of, 5–6; and teaching, 70–73; and teleology, 96; and thought, 154–158; topical, 48–49; truth value in, 29–35, 85–86, 183, 197; variety of, 3; and war, 149–150; writing of, 6–12
History of France (Michelet), 91, 143
History of Liberty (Acton), 10, 22
Hitler, Adolf, 102, 134, 139, 141, 171, 187

Moses, 47
Motley, John Lothrop, 33
Mozart, Wolfgang Amadeus, 37
Mughal India, 195
Muhammad, 201
"multiple pasts," 206

Namier, Lewis, 158–159
Napoleon I (Emperor of France), 5, 12,
    22, 24, 36, 80–83, 94, 130, 134,
    137–138, 140, 149–150, 153, 157,
    170–171, 183, 187, 192, 211–212;
    and the Egyptian Expedition (1798),
    24–26, 31, 48, 54, 93, 106–107,
    139–140, 170–171, 203, 211
Napoleonic Era, 44
narrative history, 8
Navalia (Pepys), 21–22
Nelson, Horatio Lord, 25, 107, 140
Newton, Isaac, 4, 115
Nichols, Roy F., 17, 63, 106, 147, 205
"Nietzschean disorder," 174
Nirvāna, 199
Nye, Russel, 203

Oersted, Hans, 136
ontology, 196–197
Operation Barbarossa (1941), 187
organicism, 46, 108–112
Orosius, 120
Ortega y Gasset, José, 128
Ottoman Empire, 46, 111, 199
Otto of Freising, 70–71
Outline of History, The (Wells), 66

Pali Chronicle of Ceylon, 34
"parasitic gradients," 94
Paris Commune, 180
Parker, Theodore, 27, 173–174
Parkman, Francis, 33, 90
Pascal, Blaise, 177
past in the present, 182–186
"patron tradition," 199
Patterns of Culture (Benedict), 54
perfectionism, 188–189
Pericles, 30
periodicity, 113
Persia, 21
Petrie, Sir Charles, 132, 184
Phaedrus (Plato), 14

philosophes, 201
Pirenne, Henri, 145, 148
Plato, 14, 53
Plutarch, 30, 83
Polybius, 67, 96, 113–115, 146–147,
    202, 205
prediction: problems of, 186–193
Prescott, William H., 8–10, 16, 33,
    36–37, 184
progress, 117–124
"prophetic discernment," 191
prophetic history, 178, 186–193
psychohistory, 37, 129–130
purist history, 178–179, 184, 192

Raleigh, Sir Walter, 147, 184, 210
Ranke, Leopold von, 26, 50, 71, 84,
    104–105, 159, 197
reactionaries, 81
reductionism, 130
relativism, 28–29, 38–39, 105
revolutionaries, 81–82
Richard III (King of England), 84
Richelieu, Cardinal, 196
Robertson, William, 126, 182
Robinson, James Harvey, 88
Robinson Crusoe (Defoe), 18, 57
Roman Empire, 46, 81
Romanticists, 95–96, 121, 129
Romulus and Remus, 43
Rousseau, Jean Jacques, 62
Ruskin, John, 19
Russell, Bertrand, 27

Schiller, Johann C. Friedrich von, 148
Schlesinger, Arthur, 20, 58, 71, 117,
    191
Schlesinger, Arthur, Jr., 52, 123
Schliemann, Heinrich, 60
Schweitzer, Albert, 11, 63
scientific rationalism, 37
Scott, Sir Walter, 19
Seeger, Pete, 86
Shakers, 156
Shakespeare, William, 17, 53, 84,
    164
"Shaw, Nate," 13, 36
Shotwell, James T., 16–17, 120
Sinclair, Upton, 141
skeptical relativism, 3